Visual Perception
Theory and Practice

by

TERRY CAELLI

The University of Newcastle,
New South Wales, Australia

PERGAMON PRESS

OXFORD · NEW YORK · TORONTO · SYDNEY · PARIS · FRANKFURT

U.K.	Pergamon Press Ltd., Headington Hill Hall, Oxford OX3 OBW, England
U.S.A.	Pergamon Press Inc., Maxwell House, Fairview Park, Elmsford, New York 10523, U.S.A.
CANADA	**Pergamon Press Canada Ltd., Suite 104, 150 Consumers Rd., Willowdale, Ontario M2J 1P9, Canada**
AUSTRALIA	Pergamon Press (Aust.) Pty. Ltd., P.O. Box 544, Potts Point, N.S.W. 2011, Australia
FRANCE	Pergamon Press SARL, 24 rue des Ecoles, 75240 Paris, Cedex 05, France
FEDERAL REPUBLIC OF GERMANY	Pergamon Press GmbH, 6242 Kronberg/Taunus, Hammerweg 6, Federal Republic of Germany

First edition 1981

British Library Cataloguing in Publication Data

Caelli, Terry
    An introduction to modern approaches in visual perception.—(Pergamon international library).
1. Visual perception—Physiological aspects
I. Title
612′.84   QP475   80-40167

ISBN 0 08 024420 3 Hardcover
ISBN 0 08 024419 X Flexicover

Printed and bound in Great Britain by
William Clowes (Beccles) Limited, Beccles and London

To four lovely girls:

    Kate

    Luisa

    Emma

    Lia

Preface

THE aim of this book is to familiarize the reader with recent technologies being used in vision research, and to review current findings and theories of visual information processing which use such technologies. For this reason the book has two parts: Part I—which briefly exposes the technologies as such; and, Part II—a review of more central areas of vision research including spatial vision, motion perception, and colour.

One of the greatest problems with working in a multi-discipline area, as vision research is now, is that of communication—in particular the understanding of various languages which are drawn from one discipline and applied to a common issue. We have all had the experience of wanting to understand a particular process but have just not become familiarized enough with the technology to adequately comprehend the process. In most cases we have so little time that it is not possible to start from our first-year undergraduate days and work upwards. Often, when we nobly decide to do just this, we end up flipping through some esoteric book precisely on the subject—in search of some easy-to-read statement about the specific issue that drove us to such a reference.

This is particularly true in areas where both humanities and science graduates are involved—like vision. In one way the scientist has little introduction to the historical and philosophical traditions behind the subject, while the humanities researcher just does not understand the intricacies and assumptions underlying specific procedures. This latter position generates ritual replications of past paradigms—at best justified by the argument to authority. The former error can generate meaningless technical exercises, which have little to do with solving more central problems in vision.

This book is aimed at overcoming the technical problem. It will not satisfy the dedicated mathematician, engineer, etc., and I hope it is not presuming too much for the not so technically minded.

Acknowledgements

THIS book is the product of research in visual perception over the past 5 years during which time the author has realized just how important objective definition and communality in technological skills are to the unification of research areas. It is simply not sufficient to find colleagues conducting research in an area where one employs a language completely not understood by another. The point is that many excellent ideas and models exist in the literature which are just not understood by many other researchers in the same area. This book is aimed at helping to solve this problem.

    I am greatly indebted to all my fellow researchers in visual perception for helping me in my striving to think better thoughts in this most fascinating subject and, simply, for their creative contribution to vision research. In particular I thank Peter Dodwell, Bela Julesz, and William Hoffman for sharing their various thoughts with me over the years, and John Keats and David Finlay for that academic company most essential for all.

Contents

1. *Introduction: Languages, Processes, and Perception*   1
   References   5

Part I. Technology Relevant to Visual Perception   7

2. *Light and Introductory Optics*   9
   2.1. On the nature of light   9
   2.2. Common light sources in vision research   17
   2.3. Introductory optics   21
   2.4. Some optical systems   30
   2.5. Conclusions   33
   References   34

3. *Convolutions and Fourier Methods*   35
   3.1. Introduction   35
   3.2. Fourier series and Fourier transform   35
   3.3. The discrete Fourier transform   44
   3.4. Linear systems, modulation transfer functions, and filtering   46
   3.5. Digital image processing and the Fourier transform   48
   3.6. Convolutions, autocorrelations, and other transforms   50
   3.7. Fourier transform routines   55
   3.8. Summary and conclusions   56
   References   56

4. *Network Theory and Systems*   57
   4.1. Introduction to networks   57
   4.2. Networks in vision   60
   4.3. Statistical and probability analyses of systems   67
   4.4. Summary   70
   References   70

5. *Introduction to Geometric Structures*   71
   5.1. Introduction   71
   5.2. Projective and affine geometries   73
   5.3. Vector analysis and metrics   81
   5.4. Some properties of curves   83

5.5. Properties of surfaces   87
5.6. Transformations of curves and surfaces   93
5.7. Special topics   97
5.8. Conclusions   100
References   100

Part II. Applications and Current Approaches to Visual Perception   101

6. *Spatial Vision*   103
6.1. Introduction   103
6.2. Contrast and intensity perception   103
6.3. Texture perception   115
6.4. Contours and illusions (mechanisms)   125
6.5. Spatial equivalences and perceptual invariants   137
References   144

7. *The Perception of Motion*   147
7.1. Introduction   147
7.2. Psychophysics of real motion perception—relativistic perspective   148
7.3. Transformations and analysis in motion perception—depth effects   157
7.4. Apparent motion   163
7.5. Conclusions   169
References   169

8. *Specific Issues in Vision*   172
8.1. Colour vision   172
8.2. Stereopsis   186
8.3. Conclusion   188
References   189

9. *Conclusion*   190
References   191

Index   193

CHAPTER 1

Introduction: Languages, Processes, and Perception

IF WE consult any one of a variety of journals specializing in vision research we shall find that the area is most diverse covering issues from retinal biochemistry to visual memory and our perceptions of depth. In addition, we should find on closer examination that there are many different approaches to precisely the same problem—particularly in visual perception. Although the development of microelectrode recordings has revolutionized some aspects of vision research over the past 20 years, even such "objective" measures of cortical encoding of visual images have not unified vast areas of visual perception research.

Perhaps one of the greatest gaps in communication in the area of visual perception lies between those who use engineering/mathematical languages to describe events and processes—and those who do not. Those who do not use such technologies argue that the visual system could not enact such processes and that qualitative descriptions are more realistic. Those who use these methodologies argue that descriptions, which are not quantitative or explanations which do not involve an algorithm, are simply not useful or testable.

These issues raise the more fundamental problem as to the role of analogy in explanation and the criteria for metalanguages in a given system. I use "metalanguage" not in the sense of a predicate calculus but rather in the sense that many different explanations or models in visual perception make assumptions about things like the description of the stimulus, processing, and response relations, which all involve specific languages. For example, to describe a stimulus in terms of its amplitude and phase spectra generates different "explanations" than describing it (simply) geometrically. Some argue that this problem is not solvable but, rather, that a language is as powerful as the hypotheses and models or explanations it can generate. We shall see a clear example of this issue in Chapter 6 when dealing with current approaches to textures, contour extraction, and visual illusions.

It is also clear that our criteria for explanation are changing—possibly due to the influx of scientists from other disciplines. I remember speaking to a colleague concerning an experiment where the absolute threshold was found to increase over time for a particular visual stimulus. He confidently responded that the *explanation* for this was "adaptation". On further questioning I discovered that adaptation was defined in two ways: (a) by an increase in threshold, and (b) some vague notion of nerve cells getting "fatigued". Such "explanations" are becoming less popular.

There have been attempts to define generative languages to represent perceptual events—in accord with reasonable principles of neurophysiological function. The early "perceptrons" language of Minsky and Pappert (1968) is an excellent example. The problem with these languages has always been that they lack in application to the problems encountered in perceiving complex and more natural events and scenes. We shall deal with

1

these various languages in Part II of this volume and, for the present, I shall deal with the "six-questions" of modern visual perception in the hope of illustrating the issues of language and processes underlying these specific areas of vision. These questions (I believe) are something like:

Q 1: To what extent are receptive field and response properties of individual cells determined by the complex neural connections in a specific area?

Q 2: What are the appropriate measures of neural activity?

Q 3: What features of an image are of specific interest to the visual system?

Q 4: What language(s) best describes these features and their detection processes?

Q 5: What relationships can be expected between individual cell activity and human psychophysical responses?

Q 6: What assumptions are necessary and sufficient in (5) to construct interpretable relationships?

I shall now deal with each question in some detail to illustrate the points made above, i.e. our implicit assumptions in research determine the experimental and theoretical outcomes as much as the explicit formulations.

Q. 1: *Single cells or networks.* One important aspect of vision research over the past 50 years is that the technology of electrophysiology has developed to such a stage that it is relatively simple to record electrical activity from individual cells along the visual pathways. From the discovery of lateral inhibition in *Limulus* (Hartline, 1949) to the feature extractors found in the frog's visual system (Lettvin *et al.*, 1959) and cortical feature extractors of Hubel and Wiesel (1962, 1968), the evidence clearly supports a correspondence between cell activity in specific cortical areas and stimulation of the visual field(s).

However, on further examination the interpretation problems become immense. Consider the initial conclusions of Hubel and Wiesel (even in 1968). They reported that cortical receptive fields, being driven by a contiguous collection of retinal ganglion cell fields, responded selectively to orientations of bars or slits of light. These "simple" cells were argued to lie in the same column structure of the cortex when close together in orientation selectivity. Hubel and Wiesel continued, of course, to postulate the complex and hypercomplex units, which, in turn, were driven by collections of simple cells as shown in Fig. 1.1.

Yet a series of recent experiments indicate that these results are, more properly, simple examples of a more general process in neurophysiological function. Results from intra-

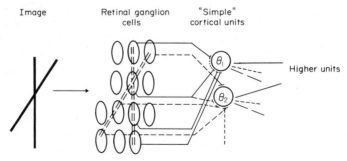

Image   Retinal ganglion   "Simple"
                     cells   cortical units

Higher units

FIG. 1.1. The orientation selective receptive fields in cat's visual cortex discovered by Hubel and Wiesel (1962, 1968).

cellular recordings by Creutzfeldt *et al.* (1974) and others indicate that, with directional sensitivity, the cells' responses are not solely determined by the spatial receptive field arrangement proposed earlier by Hubel and Wiesel. Rather, such results indicate that response is a function of intracortical inhibitory connections spreading over large areas of the visual fields of the cat.

In this way receptive fields of individual cells are proposed to be determined by the complex dendritic arborization processes of cortical cells, which, to some extent, have been theoretically examined by Leake and Anninos (1976) and anatomically studied by Valverde (1976). Recently, it has been proposed that the receptive field profiles of individual cortical cells represent the image profiles of two-dimensional spatial frequency filters of the image (see Spekreijse and van der Tweel, 1978: summary). As we shall see, although this approach has some advantages there are still problems and we shall deal with the issues in Chapters 6 and 7. At this stage it is sufficient to note this is a central problem of understanding how the visual system processes image information in the cortical areas: is the system fixed or dynamic?

Q.2: *Measures of neural activity.* Most microelectrode recordings are concerned with the measurement of spikes or the number of firings of the cell per second (pulses/second). However, it is not clear that this is a fundamental parameter of neural activity—certainly it is not clear that all information is transmitted via action potentials. For example, the firing probability is a function of the average potential and is not the same as the neuron's threshold function which depends on the membrane potential. That is, the firing probability is already a function of the average potential over the connecting cells (Sejnowski, 1976). Stein (1967) and Cowan (1971) have modelled the average firing rates by stochastic processes. Sejnowski (1976) summarizes these results by

$$\phi_a = N_a + \sum_b C_{ab} r_b,$$

where the average potential for cell a (ϕ_a) is determined by N_a, the average external input; r_b, the average firing rate of cell b; and C_{ab}, the neural connection matrix, where C_{aa} represents recurrent collaterals. The quantitative shape of C_{ab} is of fundamental importance to visual function and we shall continue with evidence for one form or another in Chapters 6 and 7. However, before these issues (in Q. 1 and Q. 2) are dealt with in more detail, the reader requires the technological background to filter theory and non-linear networks (Chapters 3 and 4).

Q. 3, 4: *Feature specificity and language problems.* These constitute the central problems in vision research today—maybe for all times. When research is conducted in visual perception the experimenter constructs, tests hypotheses, and measures responses from perspectives, which are considered valid in the specific area. However, what is viable from one perspective is not from another. For example, if the experimenter commences a project on cortical feature selectivity by assuming that the visual field is Euclidean in nature, having a coordinate system (etc.), then specific stimuli as lines, edges, angles, and motions will be considered as fundamental—a reasonable conclusion. Yet an optical or electrical engineer, in regarding the visual processes as a system, would probably regard sine-wave gratings or simple waveforms as appropriate input stimuli—also reasonable.

However, results so far indicate that from individual cortical cells to gross psychophysical responses, the visual system responds selectively to all these various types of image parameters. We may well ask whether these results imply that the visual system functions

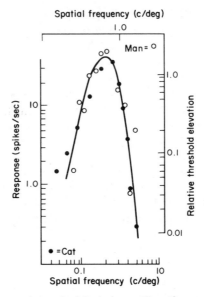

FIG. 1.2. Similarity between electrophysiological recordings from cat's cortical units (spikes/second) and human psychophysical responses (contrast sensitivity) for spatial frequency components of gratings. (From Campbell, 1976.)

on a coding strategy of which the above two code types must be examples. At this stage we have no answer to this equation—either in terms of neurophysiology or psychophysics—in cats or man!

As we shall see in Chapters 6 and 7, coding equivalences have to be established between various languages when a specific issue is being investigated. For example, what is the equivalent to orientation selectivity in the Fourier transform language? It is possible, by doing such, to arrive at what are epistemological criteria for one language as being more powerful than another.

Q. 5, 6: *Individual cells and psychophysics.* One of the amazing findings of vision research is the agreement between individual cell recording results and gross psychophysical responses on identical stimulus material. For example, the human visual contrast sensitivity function is very similar to frequency selectivity responses of individual cells in the cat's visual cortex (Fig. 1.2). Similar equivalences occur between orientation selective curves from visual cortex cells and orientation specific masking effects as measured with humans.

Why do these similarities exist? Various arguments have been posed to answer the question from various rubrics: probability summation, linear systems, etc. However, what still seems amazing to the author is that the great complexities of visual cortex, decision-making areas, etc., seem to be suppressed in such a way that an individual cell can reflect the total activity of the human brain in making a decision. Pribram (Pribram *et al.*, 1974) developed a holographic theory of visual function based on this type of observation. This type of process runs counter to other highly interactive processes in known neurophysiological structures, e.g., inhibition.

This is not to deny that in many instances such a simple connection could exist. We (Caelli and Julesz, 1979) have recently discovered one clear indication that decisions concerning texture discrimination can be made on such an additive assumption. As will be reported in Chapter 6, we have found that texture discrimination can be predicted from the addition of dipole orientation statistics for each texture—discrimination being based on the amplitude difference between these distributions.

Perhaps the more common justification of the association between the "local" individual cell response and gross psychophysical represses is "probability summation". This simply states that the probability of perceiving a difference, or detecting a signal, is the (Euclidean) sum of the probabilities of detecting each signal component. This, as well as other assumptions, will be discussed in Chapters 6 and 7.

It is clear that such questions just cannot be answered without some understanding of the technologies involved, which brings us back to the aim of this book. In visual perception the choice of even the appropriate language to use in which to embed issues is not clear. With this in mind we now proceed Part I. the methodology.

REFERENCES

CAELLI, T. and JULESZ, B. (1979) Psychophysical evidence for global feature processing in visual texture discrimination, *J. Opt, Soc. Am.* **69**, (5) 675–678.

CAMPBELL, F.W. (1976) The transmission of spatial information through the visual system, *Scient. Am.* 95–193.

COWEN, J. (1971) Stochastic models of neuroelectric activity. In Rice, S., Light, J., and Freed, K. (eds.), *Proceedings of the International Union of Pure and Applied Physics Conference on Statistical Mechanics*, pp. 109–127, University of Chicago Press, Chicago.

CREUTZFELDT, O., KHUNT, U., and BENEVENTO, L. (1974) An intracellular analysis of visual cortical neurones to moving stimuli: responses in a co-operative neuronal network, *Expl Brain Res.* **21**, 251–274.

HARTLINE, H. (1949) Inhibition of activity of visual receptors by illuminating nearby retinal areas in the Lumulus eye, *Fed. Proc.* **3**, 69.

HUBEL, D. and WIESEL, T. (1962) Recaptive fields, binocular interaction and functional architecture in the cat's visual cortex, *J. Physiol.* **160**, 106–154.

HUBEL, D. and WIESEL, T. (1968) Receptive fields and functional architecture of monkey striate cortex, *J. Physiol.* **195**, 215–243.

LEAKE, B. and ANNINOS, P. (1976) Effect of connectivity on the activity of neuronal net models, *J. Theor. Biol.* **58**, 337–363.

LETTVIN, J., MATURANA, H., MCCOLLOCH, W., and PITTS, W. (1959) What the frog's eye tells the frog's brain, *Proc. Inst. Radio Engrs* **47**, 1940–51.

MINSKY, M. and PAPERT, S. (1968) *Perceptrons*, MIT Press, Cambridge, Mass.

PRIBRAM, K., NUWER, M., and BARÓN, R. (1974) The holographic hypothesis of memory structure in brain function and perception. In *Contempory Developments in Mathematical Psychology* (Krantz, D., Atkinson, R., Luce, R., and Suppes, P., eds.), Freeman, San Fransisco.

SEJNOWSKI, T. (1976) On global properties of neuronal interactions. *Biol. Cybernetics*, **22**, 85–95.

SPEKREIJSE, H. and VAN DER TWEEL, L. (1978) *Spatial Contrast*, Akademie van Wetenschappen, Koninklijke Nederlandse.

STEIN, R. (1967) The frequency of nerve action potentials generated by applied currents, *Proc. Roy. Soc. B*, **167**, 64–86.

VALVERDE, F. (1976) Aspects of cortical organization related to the geometry of neurons with intra-cortical axons, *J. Neuroncytol*, **5**, 509–529.

PART I

Technology Relevant to Visual Perception

CHAPTER 2

Light and Introductory Optics

OUR knowledge about light and optics up to the beginning of the seventeenth century was little more than a collection of observations about the rectilinear nature of light, reflection and refraction, and various optical objects (lens, mirrors) inherited from the Egyptians, Greeks, Romans, and Arabs.

During the seventeenth century the processes of reflection and refraction were formally developed, the spectral decomposition of white light was formulated by Newton (1642–1727) and others including Hooke (1635–1703). In addition, Huygens (1629–95) discovered polarization. However, the wave theory was not redeveloped till Young (1773–1829), and the formulation that is now accepted was proposed by Maxwell (1831–79) in the famous Maxwell equations for electromagnetic waves. These wave equations, in conjunction with the relativistic kinematics of Einstein (1905), and the quantum considerations of Schrodinger (1922), constitute our present understanding of the nature of light—the input to the visual system.

This chapter is aimed at covering the more essential properties of light and optics relevant to visual perception. For those who want a more detailed knowledge of this subject, books such as Hecht and Zajac (1974) are strongly recommended.

2.1. ON THE NATURE OF LIGHT

Light is simply that part of the electromagnetic spectrum to which our visual system is sensitive. So, due to Maxwell (1831–79), we now regard light as being no different than radio, X-ray, or gamma radiations (Fig. 2.1). All such radiations are wave motions specified by a frequency and wavelength. Light rays can propagate in one, two, or three dimensions depending on the source employed. However, wavelengths and frequencies are preserved in each dimension (assuming uniform propagation media). The usual measurement units are microns (μ), millimicrons (mμ), or nanometres (nm); Angstroms (Å), where:

$$1\ \mu = 10^{-6}; \quad 1\ m\mu = 10^{-9}m = nm;$$

and $1\ \text{Å} = 10^{-10}m$.

The centre of the visible spectrum is about 555 nm (Fig. 2.1).

Although the quantum nature of light will be discussed, its waveform is of fundamental importance. This wave motion is usually illustrated by considering the motion of a moving wave along a string induced by vertical (up and down) movement of the string (Fig. 2.2). In this case the wave is sinusoidal, defined in position and time by $W(x,t)$. Since the wave

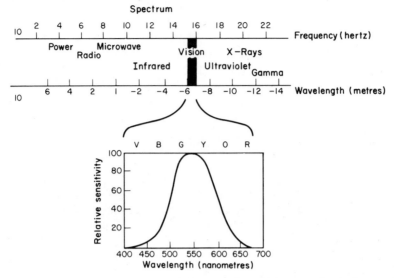

FIG. 2.1. The electromagnetic spectrum and the spectral sensitivity curve for the human visual system.

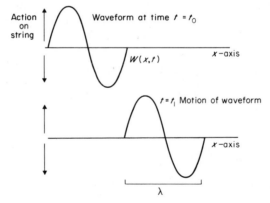

FIG. 2.2. Transverse wave motion exemplified in the motion of a wave along a string: $W(x, t)$.

repeats every wavelength λ:

$$W(x, t) = W(x \pm \lambda, t), \quad \text{for} \quad \lambda = 2\pi/k. \tag{2.1}$$

This also applies to temporal periods where $\tau = \lambda/v$ for wave velocity v. The period is the number of time units per wave, being the inverse of frequency. Two other measures often employed are angular velocity: $w = 2\pi/\tau$ (radians/second) and wave number $= 1/\lambda$. All these measures describe the repetitive nature of wave motion, which, in the case of light waves, is sinusoidal, harmonic motion.

Light must generally be treated as a wave motion propagating in two or three dimensions where the motion is orthogonal to the vibrating surface (essence of transverse waves). In these cases we replace x in (2.1) by a surface vector $\mathbf{r}$. If we define a motion vector $\mathbf{k}$, then we want the dot[†] product of $\mathbf{r}$ and $\mathbf{k}$ to be constant: $\mathbf{r} \cdot \mathbf{k} = a$. For harmonic (sinusoidal) waves we have

$$W(\mathbf{r}) = A \cos (\mathbf{k} \cdot \mathbf{r}) + i \sin (\mathbf{k} \cdot \mathbf{r}) = i\mathbf{k} \cdot \mathbf{r} \qquad (2.2)[‡]$$

With electromagnetic waves the transverse motion occurs as follows. We have two fields: an electric (E) and induction magnetic (B) field (Fig. 2.3). The E-field induces a force on any given charge q where $F_E = qE$. This increases the velocity of q which, in turn, defines the magnetic field $F_m = qv \times B$,[§] and the total force on q becomes $F = qE + qv \times B$. This moves q to a new position and the process recommences. That is, the time-varying E-field generates a B-field which is perpendicular to the direction in which E changes. B, in turn, generates a new E-field due to the induced electromagnetic field from B.

It is clear that the energy of light waves is a function of many variables including wave-

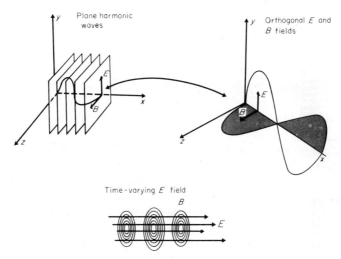

FIG. 2.3. Electromagnetic waves in two and three dimensions. Electric E and magnetic B fields are indicated.

[†] The dot, or scalar, product of two vectors a.b is defined by

$$(a_1 \ldots a_n) \cdot (b \ldots b_n) = \sum_{i=1}^{\tilde{n}} a_i b_i$$

being a number equal to the product of the vector lengths and the cosine of their intersection angle, or:

$$\mathbf{a} \cdot \mathbf{b} = |a||b| \cos \theta_{ab} \quad \text{(Chapter 4)}$$

[‡] This is a complex number or complex form of the wave equation having the general properties

$$z = x + iy, \quad i^2 = -1, \quad \text{and the polar length} \quad r = \sqrt{x^2 + y^2}$$

can be used with polar angles θ to give

$$z = re^{i\theta}, \quad e^{i\theta} = \cos \theta + i \sin \theta. \quad \text{(Chapter 4)}$$

[§] The cross product of two vectors $\mathbf{a}, \mathbf{b}$ is the orthogonal vector (to $\mathbf{a}$ and $\mathbf{b}$)

$$\mathbf{a} \times \mathbf{b} = (a_2 b_3 - a_3 b_2, \quad a_3 b_1 - a_1 b_3, \quad a_1 b_2 - a_2 b_1).$$

Its magnitude

$$|\mathbf{a} \times \mathbf{b}| = |a||b| \sin \theta_{ab} \quad \text{(Chapter 4)}$$

length, amplitude, propagation media, and distance travelled. However, Einstein (1905) did arrive at one simple energy condition:

$$E = hv, \qquad (2.3)$$

where v is the frequency and h is Planck's constant (6.624×10^{-27} erg-sec). This E is the energy of a photon or pocket in energy being transmitted along the transverse wave of the electromagnetic field. The time rate of flow of the radiant energy is the power or *radiant flux* (watts), which is (radiant) flux density when taken per unit area. If we have a monochromatic source of frequency v, then I/hv is the average number of photons crossing a unit area (normal to the beam) per unit time. This is termed the *photon flux density* and I is the irradiance or beam intensity (the time-averaged value of the Poynting vector: see Hecht and Zajac, 1974, for more details).

The photon flux for an area A is AI/hv, the average number of photons arriving per unit of time on A. Also, the irradiance from a point source is proportional to $1/r^2$, r being the distance from the source. This is termed the inverse-square law, which can be easily verified with a photometer.

Photons are defined as pockets (or states) of energy travelling along the light radiation wave which, in a vacuum, travels at about 299,792.9 km/sec. This speed retards in dense media.

In general there are two sources of photon emissions (or light waves): luminescence and incandescence.

(1) *Luminescence* is light generation by electron excitation where the photon frequency is a function of the generating substance. Each photon is emitted when one electron is displaced to a lower state level. A common luminescent source is the neon tube. Here the tube is closed and fitted with neon gas having a hot metallic cathode (negative side) at one end and an anode (positive side) at the other. On heating, the electrons are emitted from the cathode through the gas to the anode. The cathode rays (electrons) displace some of the electrons in the gas from their normal energy levels. The energy from this reaction is released as photons.

Fluorescence is another example of photon emission via the induction of electron state changes. With fluorescent lights the emitted electrons bombard mercury atoms resulting in ultraviolet light quanta. This light is directed at a phosphor coating which mainly emits

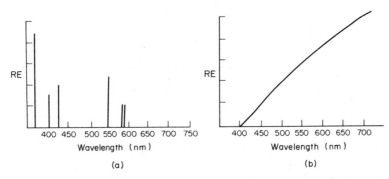

FIG. 2.4. (a) The discrete spectral response of a luminescent mercury vapor lamp compared to (b) the continuous spectrum of an incandescent source at 2854 K CIE, illuminant A. RE = relative energy.

visible light—quite an efficient use of quanta for lighting. Cathode-ray oscilloscopes function under these principles with the addition of a facility to direct the light at the phosphor with high accuracy in a small region at a time (see section 2.2).

(2) *Incandescence* is the high-temperature discharge of photons due to thermally agitated molecules. The total amount of radiation is proportional to the fourth power of the absolute (Kelvin) temperature scale and the energy (photon) distribution is typically continuous over wavelength in comparison to luminescent sources (Fig. 2.4). In particular the ("black body") radiation curves for various sources vary as a function of temperature.

2.1.1. The measurement of light

As implied by (2.3) and Fig. 2.4, the total energy radiating from any source is the sum of the energy of all the emitted photons or $h\upsilon$ values. A standard measure of this is power or watts (ergs/sec) and the photometric unit is luminous flux F which measures the total radiant energy in lumens, where (Riggs, 1965)

$$F = 685 \sum_0^\infty P_\lambda V_\lambda \Delta\lambda \text{ lumens.} \tag{2.4}$$

Here P_λ is the radiant flux (in watts) at each wavelength λ and $\Delta\lambda$ is the bandwidth over which the flux is summed. Finally, V_λ represents the relative photopic (or scotopic) luminosity coefficient of light at each wavelength set by the CIE (Commission Internationale de l'Eclairage) for a standard observer. This curve was devised to represent the effectiveness of light at each wavelength for stimulating cone-specific (photopic) and rod-specific (scotopic) vision in the standard observer (Fig. 2.5).

A steradian is defined as the solid angle subtended by an area of one square metre on the surface of a sphere centred at a radiation source. Hence a luminous intensity I of 4π lumens is one lumen per steradian or one candlepower. A surface one metre away would receive an illuminance of one lumen/square metre. In general a source, which has a luminous

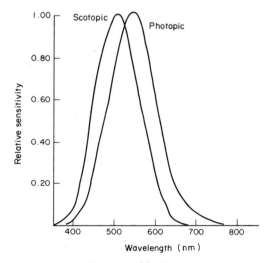

FIG. 2.5. Photopic and scotopic relative spectral luminosity curves so determined by the CIE.

TABLE 2.1. Illuminance and luminance values for some common sources.

Illuminance (lux)		Luminance (nits)
Direct sunlight	10^5	Sun's surface: 1.36×10^9 (dangerous)
Full daylight	10^4	50 W soft-white globe: 34×10^3
Overcast day	10^3	White paper on well-lit desk: 350
Full moon	10^{-1}	Absolute threshold (visual): 35×10^{-7}

intensity of one lumen per unit solid angle in a given direction, has a luminance of one candle/square metre (in that direction). Radiation emitted directly from a source (incident light) is measured by illuminance values, while reflected light is measured by luminance values: foot-candle (ft-c) and foot-lamberts (ft-L) respectively in the British system. However, the millilambert is the more common unit where 1 ml $= 0.929$ ft-L $= 0.296$ candle/ft$^2 = 3.183$ candles/m^2.

That is, for luminous flux, 1 lumen $= 0.00146$ W at 555mμ. For luminous intensity (candle-power) 1 candle (candela) $= 1$ lumen/steradian. With illuminance 1 $lux = 1$ $lumen/m^2 = 1$ metre-candle $= 0.0929$ ft-c. For luminance 1 $candle/m^2$ $(nit) = 1$ $lumen/$ $steradian/m^2 = 0.3142$ $ml = 0.2919$ ft-L.

Finally, one older measure—not employed so much these days—is the troland. One troland $=$ the luminance of 1 candle/m^2 on a surface viewed through an artificial pupil of area 1 mm^2. The problem with the measure is that light entering the peripheral areas of

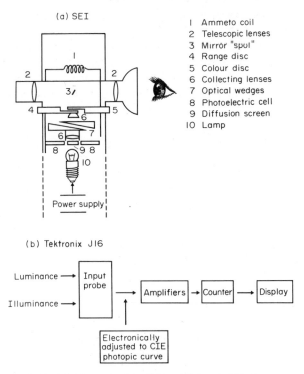

FIG. 2.6. Essential features of the SE1 and Tektonix J16 photometers.

the pupil is less effective as a retinal stimulant than centrally projected light. This is termed the Stiles–Crawford effect after Stiles and Crawford (1933).

Table 2.1 shows luminance and illuminance values for some common visual stimuli.

There are many commercially obtainable photometers having various degrees of accuracy in measuring luminance and illuminance sources. Many of the earlier types, as, for example, the SEI (Salford Electrical Instruments) photometer, were based on the visual comparison (by the experimenter looking through the device) of the target light source, with an adjustable light source controlled by a rheostat in the photometer (Fig. 2.6). This matching process required considerable practice and was subject to variance due to differences between observers (and within one observer) on what constituted a match, and the adaptation state of the eye.

Digital photometers, such as the Tektronix J16 series photometer, have replaced these earlier types and are more accurate in the objective performance—not requiring any

TABLE 2.2. Calculations required to ascertain the chromaticity of Wratten filter No. 75: (a) Tristimulus values according to the 1931 CIE standard observer, (b) tabulations from energy E_λ and transmittance T_λ values (λ = wave length, mv).

Wave length (mμ)	x	y	z	mμ	E_λ	T_λ	$(E_\lambda T_\lambda \bar{x})$	$(E_\lambda T_\lambda \bar{y})$	$(E_\lambda T_\lambda \bar{z}\lambda)$
380	0.0014	0.0000	0.0065	460	37.82	0.012	0.132	0.027	0.258
390	0.0042	0.0001	0.0201	470	42.87	0.045	0.377	0.126	2.484
400	0.0143	0.0004	0.0679	480	48.25	0.014	0.480	0.698	4.080
410	0.0435	0.0012	0.2074	490	53.91	0.122	0.210	1.368	3.060
420	0.1344	0.0040	0.6456	500	59.86	0.091	0.027	1.759	1.482
430	0.2839	0.0116	1.3856	510	66.06	0.048	0.029	1.595	0.502
440	0.3483	0.0230	1.7471	520	72.50	0.019	0.087	0.978	0.108
450	0.3362	0.0380	1.7721	530	79.13	0.009	0.118	0.614	0.030
460	0.2908	0.0600	1.6692	540	85.85	0.003	0.075	0.246	0.005
470	0.1954	0.0910	1.2876	550	92.91	0.001	0.040	0.092	0.001
480	0.0956	0.0390	0.8130						
490	0.0320	0.2080	0.4652			$X = 1.575$	$Y = 7.553$	$Z = 12.510$	
500	0.0049	0.3230	0.2720			$x = 0.073$	$y = 0.349$	$z = 0.578$	
510	0.0093	0.5030	0.1582						
520	0.0633	0.7100	0.0782						
530	0.1655	0.8620	0.0422						
540	0.2904	0.9540	0.0203						
550	0.4334	0.9950	0.0087						
560	0.5945	0.9950	0.0039						
570	0.7621	0.9520	0.0021						
580	0.9163	0.8700	0.0017						
590	1.0263	0.7570	0.0011						
600	1.0622	0.6310	0.0008						
610	1.0026	0.5030	0.0003						
620	0.8544	0.3810	0.0002						
630	0.6424	0.2650	0.0000						
640	0.4479	0.1750	0.0000						
650	0.2835	0.1070	0.0000						
660	0.1649	0.0610	0.0000						
670	0.0874	0.0320	0.0000						
680	0.0468	0.0170	0.0000						
690	0.0227	0.0082	0.0000						
700	0.0114	0.0041	0.0000						
710	0.0058	0.0021	0.0000						
720	0.0029	0.0010	0.0000						

(a)   (b)

matching on the part of the experimenter. These photometers function on the response of a photodiode sensor in the probe section. The sensors generate signal currents proportional to the intensity of the applied light source, within the 250–1200 nanometre wavelength range. The remainder of the circuitry is entailed in encoding the current as a function of the CIE relative luminosity curve, adjusting to zero, and digitizing the analogue response (Fig. 2.6).

Where white light consists of radiation roughly evenly distributed over the visible spectrum, coloured light consists of radiations restricted to specific areas of the spectrum — as illustrated in Fig. 2.1. The amount of radiant energy at each wavelength can be measured by a spectrophotometer, a device which can isolate each wavelength band usually by prism dispersion or the direct use of filters. The CIE has also set standards for the measurement of colours.

Since it is known that three primary colours are sufficient to match a given unknown colour, the CIE has set three distributions (tristimulus values) for an equal energy spectrum (the 1931 CIE standard observer). These are shown in Table 2.2a and denoted by $(\tilde{x}, \tilde{y}, \tilde{z})$. By taking a particular coloured source — a filter with known energy distribution E_λ and transmittance T_λ (Table 2.2b, left side) — the equivalent tristimulus values are determined at each wavelength by $E_\lambda T_\lambda (X, Y, X)$ (Table 2.2b). These numbers are then normed to give

$$x = \frac{X}{X + Y + Z}, \quad y = \frac{Y}{X + Y + Z}, \quad z = \frac{Z}{X + Y + Z}.$$

Since $x + y + z = 1$ it is sufficient to plot the two values (x, y) or the so-called CIE chromaticity diagram shown in Fig. 2.7.

This procedure enables one to compare sensitivities to various aspects of colour (e.g. colour matching) without having to continually standardize our differential sensitivity to spectral energy. The implications of this colour space to colour vision will be considered briefly in Chapter 8.

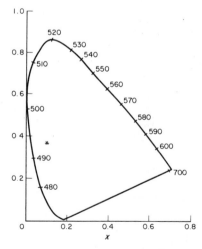

FIG. 2.7. The CIE chromasticity diagram. The asterisk indicates the location of light from illuminant A through Wratten filter No. 75 (adapted from Riggs, 1965).

2.2. COMMON LIGHT SOURCES IN VISION RESEARCH

In this section I intend to describe some of the essential features of common visual display devices that do not involve complicated lens systems (see section 2.3). We shall deal with coherent sources through polarization and lasers, and cathode-ray oscilloscopes (CRTs) and their associated digital drivers. Finally, for historical interest we shall consider the tachistoscope.

Polarized light. Whereas the light we normally experience is scattered in propagation directions, polarized light (linear or plane polarized) has a constant electric field orientation although its magnitude and sign varies over time (Fig. 2.3: top right). We can represent two orthogonal optical waves as sinusoidal waveforms:

$$E_x(z, t) = E_x^\circ \cos(Kz - wt),$$
$$E_y(z, t) = E_y^\circ \cos(Kz - wt + \varepsilon), \qquad (2.5)$$

where ε is the relative phase difference between the waves and E_x°, E_y° refer to the initial amplitudes (Fig. 2.3). For $\varepsilon = 0$ the sum of E_x and E_y reduces to

$$E = (E_x + E_y) \cos(kz - wt)$$

which is a plane-polarized wave having amplitude $(E_x + E_y)$ (Fig. 2.8). Conversely, all plane-polarized light waves can be decomposed into two orthogonal waveforms, as in (2.5).

There are two other common forms of polarization—circular and elliptical. Circular polarization occurs when the constituent waves have equal amplitude ($E_x^\circ = E_y^\circ$ in (2.5)) but are out of phase by $E = 2\pi m - \pi/2$ (m-integer valued). Here the direction field is not restricted to a single plane. The linear and circular forms are examples of elliptically polarized light (for more details consult Hecht and Zajac, 1974).

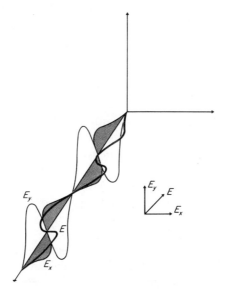

FIG. 2.8. Polarized light with two additive fields $E_x + E_y = E$.

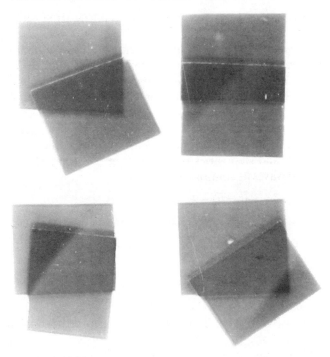

Fig. 2.9. Linear polarizers. The greyness is due to the absorption of the light by the polaroids. The black area demonstrates the action of the orthogonal grids.

The result of the above concepts of polarization is that it applies, in some degree, to all light. However, there are sources of polarized light that are purer than others. The most common form of polarization in everyday experiences or in a vision laboratory is that of polarization through filters. Due to the findings of Land and his predecessors (Land, 1951), particularly with the dichroic herapathite substance, we can now readily purchase polarized sheeting (linear polarized) made by heating polyvinyl alcohol and then stretching in orthogonal directions (two sheets) such that the long hydrocarbon molecules approximate two orthogonal grids. These grids act as linear polarizers (Fig. 2.9).

The output intensity of the filter is determined by Mauls' law:

$$I(\theta) = I(0)\cos^2\theta, \quad I(0) = \frac{c\varepsilon_\circ}{2}E_\circ^2\cos^2\theta \tag{2.6}$$

where $I(0)$ corresponds to the individual matched polarizers' intensities and θ the angle between polarized sources.

One common use for polarized filters, in visual perception, is in creating dichoptic images where each eye receives an image not registered by the other. Each image and each eye is allocated one of the polarizing filter pairs. For example, this method is particularly effective with stereopsis (Julesz, 1971).

Lasers. Whereas light can be made spatially coherent by polarization, there are light sources that naturally radiate coherent light. One such source is the laser (light amplification by simulated emission of radiation). An excited atom can revert to a lower energy state via two processes: spontaneous emissions and those induced by electromagnetic radiation of the appropriate frequency or simulated emission. In this case the photons are all in phase having the same polarization of the stimulating wave. The laser light is the same polarization of the stimulating wave. The laser light is highly collimated, spatially and temporally coherent, thus offering a highly directed monochromatic light source to the vision researcher.

The earlier lasers, as, for example, the original pulsed ruby lasers, were fixed in wavelength. However, the invention of the helium–neon gas laser by Maiman in 1960 has led to the availability of lasers that range in frequencies from infrared to ultraviolet emissions. One of the more well-known applications of lasers to vision research is in the generation of sine-wave gratings. By passing laser light through two small (vertical) slits, horizontally separated, an intensity distribution will be formed on the retina which approximates a sine-wave grating and is independent of corneal and lens features (Cornsweet, 1970; Campbell and Green, 1965).

Finally, lasers are used in the production of holograms. Although holograms are not currently employed in vision research as a method of presenting three-dimensional images to the eyes, holographic processes have been used to model the visual system (Pribram et al., 1974). They could be used to study phase encoding in vision as well as many phenomena concerning depth perception.

2.2.1. Cathode-ray tubes

A very common display source in vision research is the cathode-ray tube (CRT) largely due to its compatibility with digital computers and such analogue devices as wave generators. The modern CRT has an electron beam projected onto a phosphorous surface on the screen by electrostatic forces. The device usually consists of four sections: (1) the generator (triode), (2) a focusing device, (3) a guiding mechanism (deflector), and (4) the screen (Fig. 2.10).

The generator, or electron gun, accelerates particles which then pass through the focusing lens. The voltage difference between the anode and cathode is the determinant of the number of particles or the intensity of the point source of light. The focusing lens determines

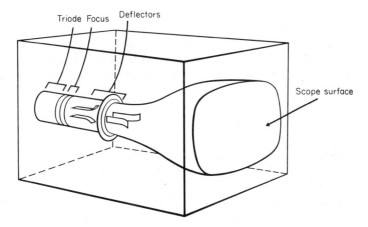

FIG. 2.10. Basic design principles of the cathode-ray oscilloscope.

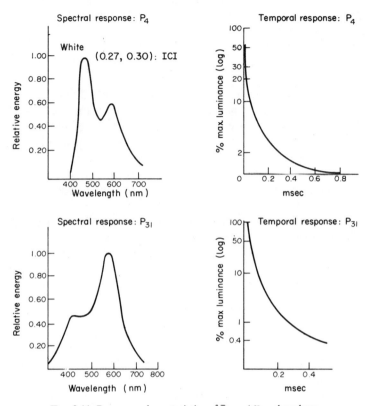

FIG. 2.11. Response characteristics of P_4 and P_{31} phosphoɪs.

the size of the phosphor spot on the screen. The various screen phosphors, having various colours and speed, are typically registered with the Joint Electron Device Engineering Council (JEDEC) having spectral response curves and rise/fall times specified. Figure 2.11 shows these curves for two common phosphors—P_4 and P_{31}—used in the Hewlett Packard scopes.

The P_4, P_{15}, and P_{31} phosphors are more suited to most vision research requirements due to their speed and colour. However, speed can often be a disadvantage, particularly when the CRT is computer-driven. This is because the computer usually cannot recycle through the set of image points of a speed greater than the flicker frequency of the phosphor. However, if a slower phosphor is employed the points displayed persist (in conjunction with visual persistence) and the image has a higher probability of remaining contiguous.

There are two types of CRTs in common use: the raster display and $X-Y$ or point–plot types. The former is identical to a television monitor which moves the beam across either 512 or 625 lines of the CRT at 50 or 60 Hz per complete cycle. This signal contains about a 10 MHz frequency bandwidth for picture information.

The point–plot scope is readily incorporated into a digital display system, particularly when interfaced with a digital computer. The typical system is illustrated in Fig. 2.12 accompanied by an example of a display subroutine (enabled by the digital-to-analogue (D/A) converter). This type of graphics system has replaced earlier systems like the tachisto-scope.

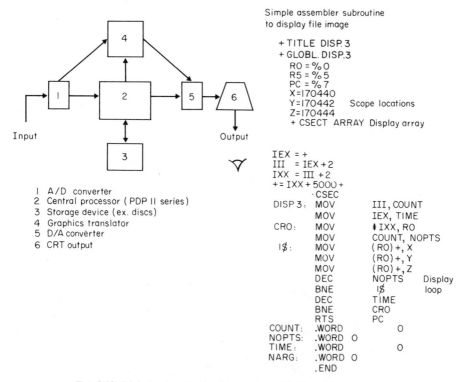

FIG. 2.12. Digital computer/graphics system with illustrative program.

A tachistoscope is a device for displaying various combinations of objects (usually up to three images) at given luminances, exposure, and interstimulus times. With the normal three-channel type (e.g. the Gerbrands version) fluorescent lamps are used to illuminate cards within each channel for a given time, intensity, and sequence. However, it should be noted that recent independent measurements by Mollon and Polden (1978) indicate that some of the time constants (rise and fall times of the fluorescent lamps) are poorer than generally assumed.

2.3. INTRODUCTORY OPTICS

So far we have dealt with some aspects of the nature of light and display conditions employed in vision research situations. However, to continue with this latter information it is necessary to consider an optical system and some of the properties of light when propagated through various media.

2.3.1. Reflection and refraction: plane surfaces

When light passes from one medium to another, two processes usually occur: reflection and refraction. We regard the propagating source or beam as the incident beam or ray (Fig. 2.13). This line is parallel to the propagating direction and normal to the wave front.

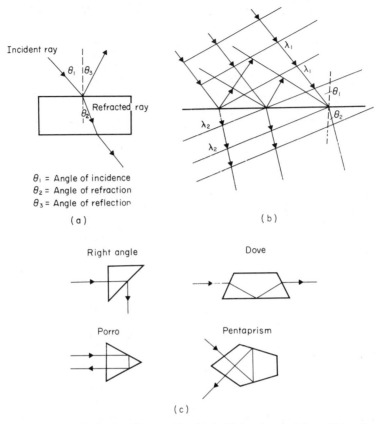

FIG. 2.13. (a) The laws of reflection illustrated by (b) the Huygen's principle and (c) various commonly used prisms where the dark line traces the beam path.

The angles of incidence θ_1, reflection θ_3, and refraction θ_2 are shown in Fig. 2.13 and are measured from the normal to the surface of the media. These angles are related by

$$\theta_1 = \theta_3 \tag{2.6}$$

and

$$\frac{\sin \theta_1}{\sin \theta_2} = N_{21}, \tag{2.7}$$

where N_{21} is termed the refractive index of the two media. The first of these laws (2.6) was known by Euclid; the second (2.7) was not discovered or deduced until Snell (1591–1626) and Descartes (1596–1650) respectively. It is consequently known as Snell's or Descartes' law. Table 2.3 illustrates the refractive indices of some well-known substances.

These laws can be derived from various propositions, in particular Fermet's principle[†], Huygens' principle[‡], and the Maxwell equations themselves (Hecht and Zajac, 1974).

[†] Fermet's principle: a light ray traverses an optical path length, between two points, which is stationary with respect to variations in the path. This is the principle of least time.

[‡] Huygens' principle: all points in a wave front can be considered as point sources for the production of spherical secondary wavelets, such that the new wave front will be the tangent surface of these wavelets.

TABLE 2.3. Refractive indices
of source common materials
(measured with respect to a
vacuum) $\lambda = 5890$ Å

Water	1.33
Air	1.0003
Crown glass	1.52
Dense flint glass	1.66
Ethyl alcohol	1.36

With Huygens' principle (Fig. 2.13b) the law of reflection is readily derived (through congruence) giving $\theta_1 = \theta_3$. The law of refraction in this case becomes:

$$\frac{\sin \theta_1}{\sin \theta_2} = \frac{\lambda_1}{\lambda_2} = N_{21}.$$

Although more complicated, the laws of reflection and refraction can be derived from Maxwell's equations (Hecht and Zajac, 1974). Light is totally reflected internally when the angle of incidence exceeds the critical angle θ_c such that the refracted rays point along the surface. This θ_c is determined by

$$N_1 \sin \theta_c = N_2 \sin 90°$$

or
$$\sin \theta_c = N_2/N_1$$

where N_1 and N_2 refer to the refractive indices of media with respect to a vacuum. For glass and air, $\theta_c = 41.8°$. The prisms shown in Fig. 2.13c use this property so that ray paths may be readily manipulated.

Figure 2.14a illustrates the relationship between reflected and refracted energies as a function of the incidence angle ($N_{21} = 1.5$). The relationship between photon transmissions, through interfaces of refractive indices greater than one, is not totally known (Hecht and Zajac, 1974). It is true, however, that as the speed of propagation decreases, moments increase and the relationship between incident and transmitted photon momenta P_i

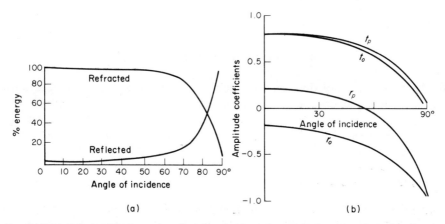

FIG. 2.14. (a) Relationship between reflected and refracted energies as a function of incidence angle ($N_{12} = 1.5$). (b) Shows amplitude components parallel p and orthogonal o to incoming E-fields.

and P_t is determined by the law of refraction:

$$N_{ti} = P_t/P_i.$$

The change in amplitude of light when transmitted through various media is represented by the Fresnel equations:

$$r_o = \frac{-\sin(\theta_i - \theta_t)}{\sin(\theta_i + \theta_t)},$$

$$r_p = \frac{\tan(\theta_i - \theta_t)}{\tan(\theta_i + \theta_t)},$$

$$t_o = \frac{2\sin\theta_t \cos\theta_i}{\sin(\theta_t + \theta_i)},$$

$$t_p = \frac{2\sin\theta_t \cos\theta_i}{\sin(\theta_t + \theta_i)\cos(\theta_i - \theta_t)},$$

where r and t refer to reflected and transmitted amplitudes, and subscripts o and p refer to the orthogonal and parallel directions of r and t with respect to the E fields. Figure 2.14b illustrates how these amplitudes vary as a function of the incidence angle.

The reflectance R and transmittance T are defined as the ratio of reflected (or incident) and refracted over incident flux respectively, or

$$R = \frac{I_r \cos\theta_r}{I_i \cos\theta_i} = \frac{I_r}{I_i},$$

$$T = \frac{I_t \cos\theta_t}{I_i \cos\theta_i}.$$

When no absorption occurs, $R + T = 1.0$.

Most white objects appear white due to a uniform reflection over the whole visible spectrum. On the other hand, most coloured objects are so due to selective absorption where all but the visible colour is absorbed by pigment molecules.

2.3.2. Spherical waves and surfaces

Most light sources are divergent in their radiations and such spherical waves are analogous to the ripples observed on the surface of water due to the dropping of a stone into the water. Since the wave direction is orthogonal to the wave front, then we can represent the spherical wave beam as a set of spokes radiating from the source (Fig. 2.15a).

Mirrors

In the case of a plane mirror (being totally reflective) the real image does not exist. Rather, all plane mirrors only have virtual images since the reflection process is divergent.

With mirrors the law of reflection also applies, requiring changes in the normal at each point of intersection (Fig. 2.15c). By restricting ourselves to paraxial rays (rays close to the

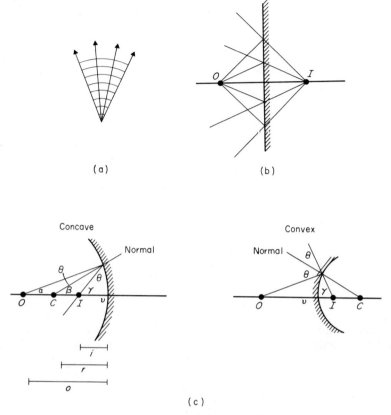

(a)   (b)

(c)

FIG. 2.15. Light propagation as spherical waves: note the radial line patterns as representative of the ray propagation directions (a). (b) Shows divergent rays reflected from mirror surface and imaginary images. (c) Spherical cases.

mirror axis) then we get:

$$\frac{1}{o} + \frac{1}{i} = \frac{2}{r},$$

(2.8)

where $o \equiv$ object distance, $i \equiv$ image distance, and $r \equiv$ radius of curvature for the mirror (Fig. 2.15c) from the mirror's vertex. This also applies to convex mirrors as shown in Fig. 2.15d except that all images are virtual, thus the i signs would change along with the r sign. When parallel light falls on a mirror the image point is called the focal point and is determined from (2.8) as $o \to \infty$, or $i = \frac{1}{2}r = f$, the focal length. This converts (2.8) to

$$\frac{1}{o} + \frac{1}{i} = \frac{1}{f}.$$

(2.9)

Parallel rays striking a mirror, in general, fall on the focal plane of the mirror (Fig. 2.15c).

With the principles that (a) a ray passing through the focal point emerges parallel to the axis (and vice versa), (b) a ray passing through the centre of curvature returns along itself, and (c) the law of reflection, we can readily determine the image of objects. Figure 2.16 illustrates image formation with concave and convex mirrors where the image magnitude

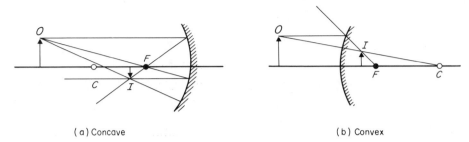

(a) Concave   (b) Convex

FIG. 2.16. Object images in (a) concave, and (b) convex mirrors. $O \equiv$ object, $I \equiv$ image, $F \equiv$ focus, $C =$ centre.

is determined by the magnification

$$m = \pm \frac{i}{o}.$$

The negative sign applies to inverted images. It can be seen that concave mirrors can give real inverted images, while convex mirrors give virtual erect images (Fig. 2.16).

Lenses

Whereas mirrors are reflecting surfaces, lenses are refracting surfaces. Again, using the law of refraction (locally) and interpreting the normal as perpendicular to the tangent of the (lenses) curve interface, we can determine the refracted path by (2.7). For paraxial rays (2.7) reduces to $N_1 \theta_1 \cong N_2 \theta_2$, and it follows that the equivalent to (2.7) is

$$\frac{N_1}{o} + \frac{N_2}{i} = \frac{N_2 - n_1}{r}, \tag{2.10}$$

where N_1 and N_2 refer to refractive indices (Fig. 2.17). The sign conventions must be observed where it is positive if the image (real, in contrast to mirrors) is on the refractive side of the lens. Similarly, r is positive if the centre of curvature is on the refractive side (or surface).

In most situations where spherical refraction is involved, there is more than one refracting surface. Consider the system in Fig. 2.17b. From the first surface, for $N_1 = 1$, $N_2 = n$,

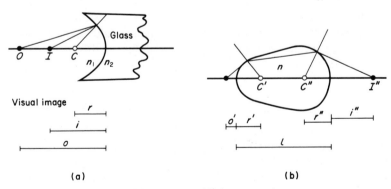

(a)   (b)

FIG. 2.17. Lenses and light propagation.

we obtain the virtual image by

$$\frac{1}{o'} - \frac{n}{i'} = \frac{n-1}{r'} \tag{2.11}$$

from (2.10). This virtual image is distance $l + i' = o''$ from the second surface and consequently the second (real) image distance i'' from the lens is determined by

$$\frac{n}{i'+l} + \frac{1}{i''} = \frac{1-n}{r''}, \tag{2.12}$$

where l is the lens thickness. For sufficiently thin lenses and large image-object distances, (2.12) reduces to:

$$\frac{n}{i'} + \frac{1}{i''} = -\frac{n-1}{r''}, \tag{2.13}$$

and it is readily shown from (2.11) and (2.13) that for original object distance o and final image distance i,

$$\frac{1}{o} + \frac{1}{i} = (n-1)\left(\frac{1}{r'} - \frac{1}{r''}\right). \tag{2.14}$$

This only applies for paraxial rays and thin lenses.

The focal length of a thin lens is computed by setting and $i = f$ in (2.14), that is,

$$\frac{1}{f} = (n-1)\left(\frac{1}{r'} - \frac{1}{r''}\right) = \frac{1}{o} + \frac{1}{i}. \tag{2.15}$$

This is termed the lens-maker's equation since focal lengths can be determined from refractive indices and radii of curvatures, noting, again, the sign conventions. Some common lenses are shown in Fig. 2.18.

The properties of lens combinations are readily calculated, even though it comes a complex ray-tracing exercise. Figure 2.19 illustrates two cases where two lenses are placed (a) closer than either focal length, and (b) further than either focal length. It can be seen here that in one case the image is minified and inverted, the other magnified and erect.

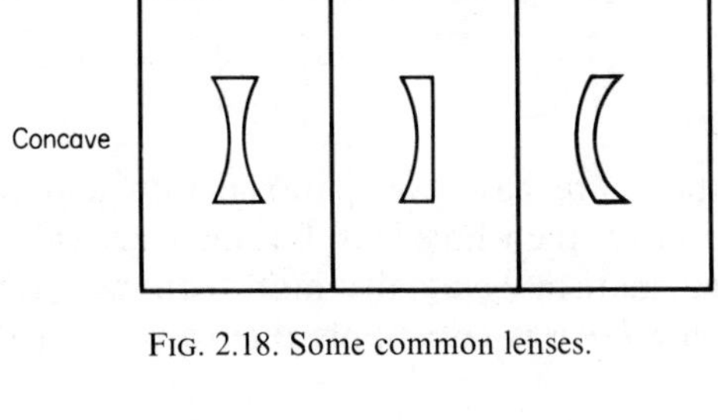

	BI	Planar	Meniscus
Convex			
Concave			

FIG. 2.18. Some common lenses.

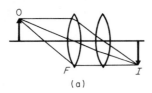

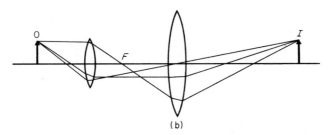

Fig. 2.19. Ray tracing for objects inside and outside the focal lengths of optical systems: (a) inside, (b) outside, $O \equiv$ object, $I \equiv$ image, $F \equiv$ focus.

In general it can be shown for two lenses that the distance of the image from the second lens is:

$$i^2 = \frac{f_2 d - f_2 i' f_1/(o' - f_1)}{d - f_2 - o' f_1/(o' - f_1)},$$ (2.16)

where $d \equiv$ distance between lenses, $f_1 \equiv$ focal length of lens 1, $f_2 \equiv$ focal length of lens 2, $o^1 \equiv$ object distance from lens 1, $i^1 \equiv$ image distance from lens 1, $i^2 \equiv$ image distance from lens 2.

Similarly, the total magnification M_t is the product of the individual lens magnifications

$$M_T = M_{T1} M_{T2}$$ (2.17)

or

$$M_T = \frac{f_1 i^2}{d(o' - f_1) - o' f_1}.$$

Finally, the effective focal length of the two lenses f_T is determined by

$$\frac{1}{f_T} = \frac{1}{f_1} + \frac{1}{f_2}$$ (2.18)

and this also applies for N lenses.

Aberrations

All the calculations above are based on paraxial rays and the assumption that the refractive index is constant over the whole lens. But there are various types of aberrations: spherical, coma, and astigmatism being the more common forms of monochromatic aberrations. *Chromatic aberration* is commonly due to the fact that the refractive index is dependent on frequency. It should be noted that most lenses have some degree of propagation differences between various colours.

Spherical aberrations refer to the deviations observed in rays' paths from paraxial paths. This deviation increases as the square of the distance from the axis so that the simplest way to preclude it is by using stops to decrease the aperture. Coma or comatic aberrations are due to the fact that the principle planes of a lens are actually curved surfaces— particularly outside the paraxial region. This is more related to thick lenses having two principle planes where each plane is defined as the locus of points within the lens where refraction is intended to operate critically.

Astigmatism

By defining the meridion plane as that generated by the optical axis and the chief ray (the ray passing through the centre of the aperture) and the sagittal plane as that containing the chief ray and being perpendicular to the meridion plane, astigmatism is generally understood to be an effective focal length difference between meriodional and sagittal sections of the lens. Consequently as the light source becomes more oblique, this difference is accentuated.

We should, finally, mention the essential properties of diffraction and interference phenomena as they also are relevant to the use of optical systems in vision research.

Diffraction is the bending of light around an obstacle such as a slit or edge. The effect is due to rays passing through a slit (or touching an edge, etc.) at differing amplitude and phase values (slight as they may be). This causes the various parallel rays to leave the slit at different angles. *Fresnel diffraction* occurs when the light source or image screen for

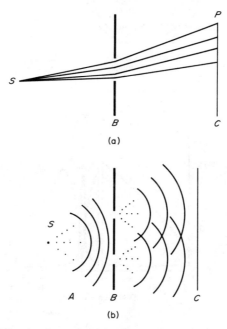

FIG. 2.20. (a) Fresnel diffraction from source *S*, using screen *B*, and projecting onto screen *C*. (b) Interference patterns.

the diffraction pattern are a finite distance from the aperture (slit). Neither sets of rays are parallel (Fig. 2.20a). *Fraunhofer diffraction* occurs when the source and image screen are moved large distances from the aperture resulting in a parallel wave front at the aperture (Fig. 2.20). At a circular aperture the diffraction patterns generally are concentric annuli of undulating amplitude. This pattern will be considered in more detail in Chapter 3 on Fourier analysis.

Interference refers to how two light waves interact to produce various interference patterns. Of course, when both sources are polarized no interference effects would occur. Thomas Young, in 1801, demonstrated interference patterns by allowing diffraction waves from two apertures to overlap on the image screen. Depending on the phase and amplitude differences between the sources, the interference effects may enhance or inhibit the resultant intensity distribution (Fig. 2.20b).

2.4. SOME OPTICAL SYSTEMS

2.4.1. The human eye

The eyeball is a spherical object of about 20 mm in diameter. It is covered by the sclera which at the front is the transparent membrane of the cornea (Fig. 2.21). The cornea is about

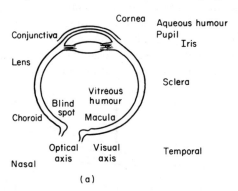

(a)

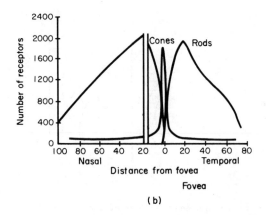

(b)

FIG. 2.21. The human eye and associated rod and cone receptor distributions.

12 mm in diameter and about 0.8 mm thick at the centre and 1 mm thick at the surround of the visible sclera ("white" at the eye). The aperture (pupil) varies in diameter between 1.5 and 9 mm, depending on luminance or focusing constraints, and is determined by the muscular action of the iris. The lens is composed of about 22,000 lamina of fine fibrous transparent material varying in refractive index from 1.406 for the centre and to 1.386 for the outer lamina. The aqueous and vitreous humours have indices of about 1.336 and 1.337 respectively.

The choroid is a dark layer, pigmented with melanin inside the inner sclerotic wall of the eye. It absorbs stray light as the black paint inside a camera. The retina covers the chroid as a thin layer of rod and cone receptors whose retinal distributions are shown in Fig. 2.21b. The rods are not colour sensitive like the cones are; however, the rods are more sensitive to light than the cones, being related to peripheral vision (scotopic vision). Many rods drive the retinal ganglion cells, which, in turn, convey information to the visual cortex. The cones are less sensitive to light and are directly related to foveal or central vision (photopic vision) where down to one cone may drive one ganglion cell. However, the purpose of this book is not to deal with these details, which are assumed to be known to the reader. An excellent reference on the anatomy and physiology of the human and vertebrate retinae is Davson (1949).

In physiological optics the power of a lens is defined as the reciprocal of the focal length. The unit of power is the inverse metre, or diopter, such that a lens with a 1 m focal length has 1 diopter power. From (2.18) we can see that lenses sum in their power. The total of about 59 diopters' power of the human eye is composed of 43 diopters for the cornea. The lens itself, surrounded by air, is about 19 diopters.

The normal eye focuses light into the retina through the process of accommodation whereby the ciliary muscles increase or decrease the curvature of the lens (Fig. 2.21). It can focus parallel rays on the retina (the far point is at infinity) down to sufficient contractions to focus objects at 7–100 cm (near point) for teenagers to the middle-aged respectively. When the second focal point does not lie on the retina for near or far objects the eye is termed ametropic (the normal eye is termed emmetropic).

There are various forms of ametropia, the more common being hyperopia (hypermetropia), myopia, presbyopia, and astigmatism. Myopia (or shortsightedness) occurs when parallel rays are focused in front of the retina (Fig. 2.22) due to increased lens power resulting in a far point closer than infinity. Distant images beyond this point are blurred. In this case a negative (concave) lens is used to decrease the total power of the system. Accommodation for near objects is not affected by this process; nor is magnification due to the fact that eyeglasses are kept at the first focal point distance from the eye (about 16 mm from the cornea). Hyperopia (or farsightedness) is a refractory error which causes the unaccommodated eye to focus parallel rays behind the retina (Fig. 2.22). A positive (convex) lens is used to increase the power of the system. The hyperopic eye can accommodate to focus far objects but is limited with near ones. Astigmatism is generally due to a non-uniform curvature of the cornea. It is regular if normal, myopic, or hyperopic in either of the meridional planes of the eye and, under these conditions, can be corrected by use of cylindrical lenses. If both axes are affected sphero-cylindrical or toric lenses are used (Fig. 2.22).

Presbyopia refers to refractive errors induced by ageing which usually takes the form of an ever-increasing near point (of focus) distance from the eye. This is due to the decrease in lens elasticity and hence accommodation. Figure 2.23 illustrates this loss over age.

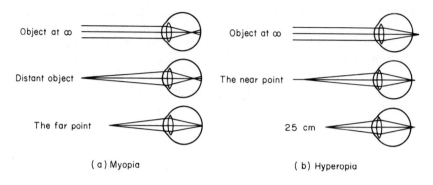

(a) Myopia   (b) Hyperopia

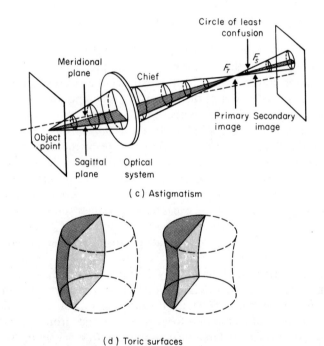

(c) Astigmatism

(d) Toric surfaces

FIG. 2.22. Optical features of (a) myopia, (b) hyperopia, and (c) astigmatism as usually corrected by (d) toric lenses (Adapted from Hecht and Zajac, 1974.)

2.4.2. Maxwellian viewing system

This device is illustrated in Fig. 2.24 and is used for focusing light on a small region of the natural pupil. It thus overcomes effects due to pupil dilation and guarantees a uniform field of light. It is a particularly useful device when dealing with visual phenomena related to intensity differences in the visual field. An artificial pupil (small stop or aperture of

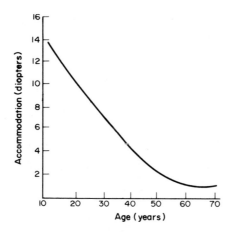

Fig. 2.23. Presbyopia as measured by accommodation facility over age.

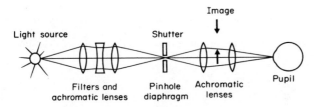

Fig. 2.24. Maxwellian viewing system to avoid pupil dilation.

between 2 and 4 mm diameter) may also be used to prevent some dilation effects in conjunction with or independent of the Maxwellian viewer.

2.4.3. Collimators

A collimating lens is one which transforms light into parallel rays, particularly from the viewing position of the observer. This can be accomplished by placing the source at the focal plane of a convex lens such that to the observer the image appears to be focused at infinity.

This device is necessary when conducting experiments in the interaction between motion and depth perception, in particular when the motion is displayed on the surface of an oscilloscope.

2.5. CONCLUSIONS

In this chapter we have reviewed some of the basic properties of light and optical systems. Although light was treated as part of the electromagnetic spectrum, it was also viewed as a quantum phenomenon and so measured by photon emissions. Such emissions are Poisson distributed over time (Cornsweet, 1970). We then dealt with the measurement of light intensity and colour, the latter being a complex issue with reference to the CIE standards. Some geometric implications of this colour space will be considered in Chapter 8.

We then considered a variety of light sources including polarized, laser light, and CRT display sources. These types of devices are becoming more important in vision research in the study of a variety of phenomena from diffraction patterns on the retina to pattern-recognition in humans.

REFERENCES

CAMPBELL, F. and GREEN D. (1965) Optical and retinal factors affecting visual resolution, *J. Physiol.* (*London*) **181**, 576–593.

CORNSWEET, T. (1970) *Visual Perception*, Academic Press, New York.

DAVSON, H. (1949) *The Physiology of the Eye*, McGraw-Hill, New York.

HALLIDAY, D. and RERNICK, R. (1966) *Physics*, Wiley, New York.

HECHT, E. and ZAJAC, A. (1974) *Optics*, Adison-Wisely, London.

JULESZ, B. (1971) *Foundations of Cyclopean Perception*, University of Chicago Press, Chicago, Illinois.

LAND, E. (1951) Some aspects of the development of Sheet polarizers, *J. Opt. Soc. Am.* **41**, 957.

MOLLON, J. and POLDEN P. (1978) On the time constants of tachistoscopes, *Q. Jl Exp. Psychol.* **30**, 555–458.

PRIBRAM, K., NUWER, M., and BARON, R. (1974) The holographic hypothesis of memory structure in brain function and perception. In *Contempory Developments in Mathematical Psychology* (Krantz, D., Atkinson, R., Luce, R., and Suppes, P., eds.), Freeman, San Franscisco.

RIGGS, L. (1965) Light as a stimulus in vision. In *Vision and Visual Perception* (C. H. Graham, ed.), Wiley, New York.

STILES, W. and CRAWFORD, B. (1933) The luminous efficiency of rays entering the pupil at different points, *Proc. Roy. Soc.* (*London*) *B*, **112**, 428, 450.

CHAPTER 3

Convolutions and Fourier Methods

3.1. INTRODUCTION

As indicated in Chapter 1, one aim of modern perception research is to provide an adequate language to represent many varied properties of visual function—from the profiles of individual cell responses to more gross psychophysical behaviour. Over the past two decades some have phrased this problem in terms of how the visual system may filter the incoming image to extract "local" features (features related to specific retinotopic locations) or even detect shapes, contours, and edges. This filtering process is represented by convolutions or product functions, and is particularly suited for Fourier methods.

In this chapter we shall consider these methods and how they may be enacted on an image via digital computers. In particular, we shall show how these methods are examples of linear systems and have a great amount of similarity. Perhaps the most common means of image analysis is the Fourier transform and its frequency domain properties. The reason for interest in this method lies in the clear relationships between contrast sensitivity and the spatial frequency components of grating stimuli—both at the psychophysical and individual cell response levels. These types of findings will be examined in detail in Part II of this book, while in this chapter we shall expose the languages so that the reader can make an informed decision about its appropriate uses.

In most of these methods the image, or function, is decomposed into a set of basic wave forms whose sum, sometimes product, is the total image. We shall first deal with the simplest one of all—the Fourier decomposition.

3.2. FOURIER SERIES AND FOURIER TRANSFORM

In Chapter 2 we dealt with situations where the resultant wave form was the sum of a series of harmonic (or sine) waves, e.g. with interference and polarization. Let us consider this case in more detail. Take two harmonic waves,

$$\left. \begin{aligned} W_1(t) &= a_1 \sin(wt + b_1), \\ W_2(t) &= a_2 \sin(wt + b_2), \end{aligned} \right\} \tag{3.1}$$

having the same frequency wt and differing in amplitude a_1, a_2 and phase b_1, b_2. Adding W_1 to W_2 gives

$$\begin{aligned} W_T = W_1 + W_2 &= a_1 \sin(wt + b_1) + a_2 \sin(wt + b_2) \\ &= a_1(\sin wt \cos b_1 + \cos wt \sin b_1) + a_2(\sin wt \cos b_2 + \cos wt \sin b_2) \\ W_T &= (a_1 \cos b_1 + a_2 \cos b_2) \sin wt + (a_1 \sin b_1 + a_2 \sin b_2) \cos wt. \end{aligned} \tag{3.2}$$

Since the coefficients of sin wt and cos wt are independent of time, let

$$a \cos b = a_1 \cos b_1 + a_2 \cos b_2 \tag{3.3}$$

and
$$a \sin b = a_1 \sin b_1 + a_2 \sin b_2. \tag{3.4}$$

So, by squaring and adding (3.3) and (3.4) we obtain.

$$a = [a_1^2 + a_2^2 + 2a_1 a_2 \cos(b_2 - b_1)]^{1/2}$$

and
$$b = \tan^{-1}\left(\frac{a_1 \sin b_1 + a_2 \sin b_2}{a_1 \cos b_1 + a_2 \cos b_2}\right)$$

Hence (3.3) and (3.4) reduces (3.2) to:

$$W_T = a \cos b \sin wt + a \sin b \cos wt$$

or
$$W_T = a \sin(wt + b). \tag{3.5}$$

This (3.5) demonstrates that the sum of two harmonic waves of the same frequency results in an harmonic wave having a composite amplitude and phase but identical frequency as the original waves (Fig. 3.1).

In reverse, this result indicates that we can always decompose an harmonic wave into constituent waves of the same frequency. The generalization of this process raises the question as to whether we can break up any wave form into a sum of various harmonic waves of differing amplitudes, frequencies, and phase. It was Fourier (1768–1830) who answered this question in the affirmative in what is called the Fourier theorem. The theorem states that any function $f(x)$, which is smooth and having a period λ (or frequency, repetition rate, of $1/\lambda$), can be constructed from the sum of harmonic waves whose wavelengths (periods) are integer fractions of the original (i.e. $\lambda/2$, $\lambda/3$, etc.).

In particular, the Fourier series of $f(x)$ is

$$f(x) = \frac{A_0}{2} + \sum_{j=1}^{\infty} A_j \cos jkx + i \sum_{j=1}^{\infty} B_j \sin jkx^{\dagger}. \tag{3.6}$$

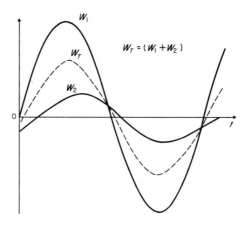

FIG. 3.1. The addition of waves having the same frequency results in a composite wave differing in amplitude and phase.

† Here we use the imaginary component i in the sine series. The Fourier series has real and imaginary components, the latter prefixed by i, where $i^2 = -1$.

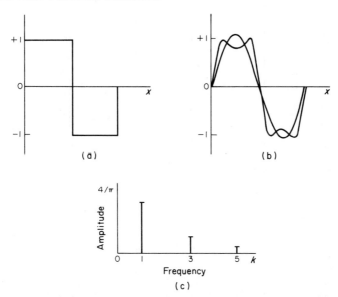

FIG. 3.2. (a) square wave and (b) associated first two terms of its Fourier series approximation and (c) frequency spectrum.

where the Fourier coefficients A_i and B_i are

$$A_j = \frac{2}{\lambda} \int_0^\lambda f(x) \cos j\,kx\,dx,$$

$$B_j = \frac{2}{\lambda} \int_0^\lambda f(x) \sin j\,kx\,dx. \tag{3.7}$$

The k is introduced here simply to transform the x variable in radian measures: $kx = 2\pi x/\lambda$.

By defining an even function as one where $f(x) = f(-x)$ and an odd function as one where $f(-x) = -f(x)$, it can be seen that $\cos x$ is even (symmetrical about zero) and $\sin x$ is odd. Consequently the Fourier series breaks down to the sum of even and odd functions, the former being the "real" components, the latter "imaginary". Symmetrical patterns only have cosine series, but, in general, most images have both even and odd components, thus requiring the full complex Fourier series decomposition.

Let us consider the Fourier series representation of the square wave as shown in Fig. 3.2a and defined by

$$f(x) = \left\{ \begin{array}{ll} 1 & 0 < x \le \lambda/2, \\ -1 & \lambda/2 < x \le \lambda. \end{array} \right\} \tag{3.7a}$$

This is an odd function, hence $A_j = 0$ for all j. Thus for

$$B_i = \frac{2}{\lambda} \int_0^{\lambda/2} (1) \sin j\,kx\,dx + \frac{2}{\lambda} \int_{\lambda/2}^\lambda (-1) \sin j\,kx\,dx$$

we obtain

$$B_j = \frac{2}{j\pi} (1 - \cos j\pi)$$

$f(t) = \int_{-\infty}^{\infty} F_F(i\omega)e^{i\omega t}\dfrac{d\omega}{2\pi}$		$F_F(i\omega) = \int_{-\infty}^{\infty} f(t)e^{-i\omega t}\,dt$	
	$\text{rect}\,\dfrac{t}{T} = \begin{cases} 1 & (|t| < T/2) \\ 0 & (|t| > T/2) \end{cases}$	$T\,\text{sinc}\,\dfrac{\omega T}{2\pi} \equiv T\,\dfrac{\sin\dfrac{\omega T}{2}}{\dfrac{\omega T}{2}}$	
	$\text{sinc}\,\dfrac{t}{T} \equiv \dfrac{\sin\dfrac{\pi t}{T}}{\dfrac{\pi t}{T}}$	$T\,\text{rect}\,\dfrac{\omega T}{2\pi} = \begin{cases} 0 & (|\omega| < \dfrac{\pi}{T}) \\ T & (|\omega| > \dfrac{\pi}{T}) \end{cases}$	
	$\begin{cases} 1 - \dfrac{|t|}{T} & (|t| < T) \\ 0 & (|t| \geqslant T) \end{cases}$	$T\,\text{sinc}^2\,\dfrac{\omega T}{2\pi} \equiv T\left(\dfrac{\sin\dfrac{\omega T}{2}}{\dfrac{\omega T}{2}}\right)^2$	
	$e^{-\frac{|t|}{T}}$	$\dfrac{2T}{(\omega T)^2 + 1}$	

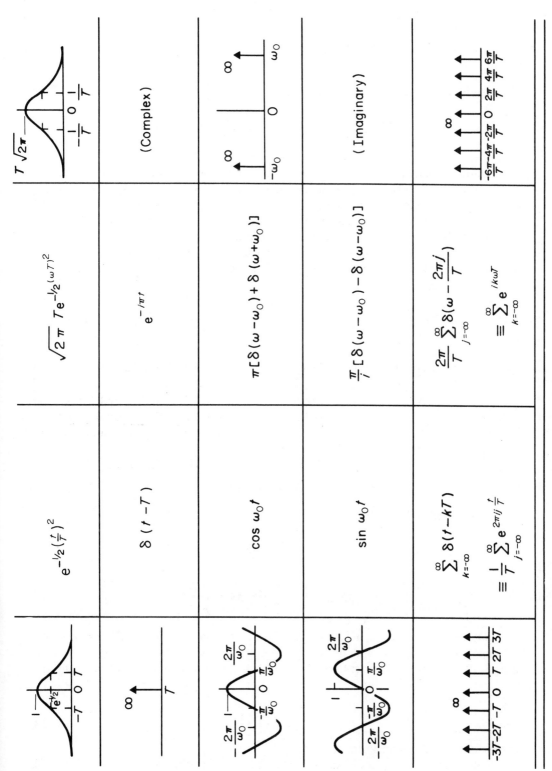

The table below transcribes the Fourier transform pairs shown in Fig. 3.3:

Time function	Fourier transform
$e^{-1/2\left(\frac{t}{T}\right)^2}$	$\sqrt{2\pi}\,T e^{-1/2(\omega T)^2}$
$\delta(t-T)$	$e^{-j\omega T}$ (Complex)
$\cos\omega_0 t$	$\pi[\delta(\omega-\omega_0)+\delta(\omega+\omega_0)]$
$\sin\omega_0 t$	$\dfrac{\pi}{j}[\delta(\omega-\omega_0)-\delta(\omega-\omega_0)]$ (Imaginary)
$\displaystyle\sum_{k=-\infty}^{\infty}\delta(t-kT) \equiv \frac{1}{T}\sum_{j=-\infty}^{\infty}e^{2\pi ij\frac{t}{T}}$	$\dfrac{2\pi}{T}\displaystyle\sum_{j=-\infty}^{\infty}\delta\!\left(\omega-\frac{2\pi j}{T}\right) \equiv \sum_{k=-\infty}^{\infty}e^{jk\omega T}$

Fig. 3.3 Fourier transform pairs of common occurrence.

or

$$B_1 = \frac{4}{\pi}, \quad B_2 = 0, \quad B_3 = \frac{4}{3\pi}, \dots$$

This results in the Fourier series of the square wave:

$$f(x) = \frac{4}{\pi}\left[\sin kx + \frac{1}{3}\sin 3kx + \frac{1}{5}\sin 5kx + \dots \right], \tag{3.8}$$

where $k = 2\pi/\lambda$. The series approximation is shown in Fig. 3.2b.

The fundamental $(k = 2\pi/\lambda)$ occurs when $j = 1$, and the harmonics are defined as $2k$, $3k, \dots$, where κ/λ corresponds to the spatial frequency values. The spatial frequency spectrum of the square wave is the plot of jk against each B_j value in (3.8) (Fig. 3.2c). This spectrum is a means of denoting the appropriate amplitudes for the various sine wave components (frequencies) of the Fourier series decomposition.

Now if we have a function, which has possibly infinite frequency values, then we would change the summations in (3.5) to integral forms where

$$f(x) = \frac{1}{\pi}\left[\int_0^\infty A(k)\cos kx \, dk + iB(k)\sin kx \, d\,k \right] \tag{3.9}$$

given that

$$A(k) = \int_{-\infty}^\infty f(x)\cos kx \, dx \quad \text{and} \quad B(k) = \int_{-\infty}^\infty f(x)\sin kx \, dx. \tag{3.10}$$

Here, again, the function $f(x)$ is represented by the sum (infinite and compact, hence the integral) of the values $A(k)\cos kx$ and $B(k)\sin kx$ for each small dk value, commanding a continuous spectrum profile. These latter two equations are called the Fourier cosine and sine transforms (3.10).

By substituting (3.10) into (3.9), and noting the exponential form (Chapter 2),

$$e^{\pm ikx} = \cos kx \pm i\sin kx, \tag{3.11}$$

it is readily deduced that (3.9) becomes

$$f(x) = \frac{1}{2\pi}\int_{-\infty}^\infty F(k)e^{-ikx}\, dx, \tag{3.12}$$

where

$$F(s) = \int_{-\infty}^{a\infty} f(x)e^{isx}\, dx. \tag{3.13}$$

Equations (3.12) and (3.13) are termed the Fourier transform pair — both being complex transforms involving real and imaginary components of the form $x + iy, i^2 = -1$. In turn, (3.12) is the inverse Fourier transform to (3.13), since if we define the Fourier transform as $\mathcal{F}$,

$$\mathcal{F}[f(x)] = F(s),$$

then

$$\mathcal{F}^{-1}[F(s)] = f(x) \tag{3.14}$$

represents the inverse transform, or (3.12).

Consider the narrow square wave (or "impulse" wave) shown in Fig. 3.3. Here the

Fourier transform is

$$F(s) = \int_{-\infty}^{\infty} f(x)e^{isx}\,dx = \int_{-\alpha}^{\alpha} \frac{1}{2\alpha}e^{isx}\,dx$$

or

$$F(s) = \frac{1}{2\alpha}\int_{-\alpha}^{\alpha} \cos sx\,dx + \frac{i}{2\alpha}\int_{-\alpha}^{\alpha} \sin sx\,dx,$$

since this is an even function $[f(x) = f(-x)]$ the imaginary term vanishes, leaving (Fig. 3.3a).

$$F(s) = \frac{\sin \alpha s}{\alpha s}. \tag{3.15}$$

This is termed a sinc function (which, in its limit, is a Bessel function of order 1). Similarly, the inverse transform of the sinc function is the impulse function. We shall see in Chapter 6 how this relationship between images and their spectral profiles has led to specific conjectures about the receptive field properties of cortical cells, particularly related to sinc functions.

As stated above, there are two components to the Fourier transform: a real (even) component, $F_R(s)$, and imaginary (odd) component, $F_I(s)$. Here

$$F(s) = F_R(s) + F_I(s). \tag{3.16}$$

These components are usually represented in polar form $r(s)$ and $\theta(s)$ where

$$r(s) = \sqrt{F_R^2(s) + F_I^2(s)}, \quad \theta(s) = \tan^{-1}\left(\frac{F_I(s)}{F_R(s)}\right), \tag{3.17}$$

or

$$F(s) = r(s)e^{i\theta(s)} \tag{3.18}$$

Since $r(s)$ is the Euclidean metric, $r(s)$ is termed the *amplitude spectrum* of $f(x)$ while $\theta(s)$ is the *phase spectrum*—the product of both constituting the Fourier transform (3.18).

The Fourier series and transform need not be restricted to one variable and, in general, the transform applies to n-dimensional functions. Of course, in vision research the two-dimensional case is most relevant where the transform pair are defined by

$$f(x, y) = \frac{1}{4\pi^2}\int_{\infty}^{\infty}\int_{-\infty}^{\infty} F(s, t)\exp\left[-i(sx + ty)\right]\,ds\,dt. \tag{3.19}$$

for the inverse and

$$F(s, t) = \int_{-\infty}^{\infty}\int_{-\infty}^{\infty} f(x, y)\exp\left[i(sx + ty)\right]\,dx\,dy \tag{3.20}$$

for the Fourier transform. As before, s and t correspond to the appropriate frequencies along the two axes of the transform plane, while (x, y) corresponds to the coordinate system of the original two-dimensional input function $f(x, y)$.

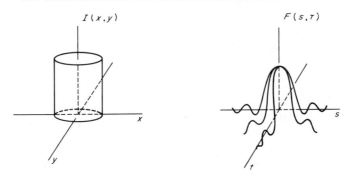

FIG. 3.4. Fourier transform of the cylindrical function showing sinc function ("Mexican hat") spectrum profile.

An important example of the two-dimensional transform is the cylindrical function (Fig. 3.4):

$$f(x, y) = \begin{cases} 1 & \sqrt{x^2 + y^2} \leq r, \\ 0 & \text{elsewhere.} \end{cases} \quad (3.21)$$

By making the polar coordinate transforms,

$$x = a \cos \theta, \quad y = a \sin \theta,$$

and

$$s = \alpha \cos \phi, t = \alpha \sin \phi, \text{ and noting } dx \, dy = a \, da \, d\theta,$$

$ds \, dt = \alpha \, d\alpha \, d\phi$, (3.20) becomes

$$F(a, \phi) = \int_0^{2\pi} \int_{-\infty}^{\infty} f(a, \theta) \exp \left[ia\alpha \cos (\theta - \phi) \right] a \, da \, d\theta.$$

Now the cylinder is circularly symmetric i.e., is only dependent on r (3.21) for a change in value and therefore independent of ϕ. This reduces $F(\alpha, \phi)$ to,

$$F(\alpha) = \int_0^r \int_0^{2\pi} \exp \left[i\alpha a \cos \theta \right] d\theta \, a \, da$$

whose solution is termed a Bessel function of first order J_1, where

$$F(\alpha) = 2\pi r^2 \left[\frac{J_1(\alpha r)}{\alpha r} \right], \quad J_1(z) = \frac{1}{2\pi i} \int_0^{2\pi} \exp \left[i(\theta + z \cos \theta) \right] d\theta.$$

This has the familiar shape of a Mexican-hat as shown in Fig. 3.4. We should note that this only refers to the amplitude, or frequency, domain and not the less-definitive phase domain.

The two-dimensional transform (3.19) states that a pattern $f(x, y)$ can be constructed by the addition of the product of two functions $e^{-i(sx + ty)}$ and $F(s, t)$: the latter being complex valued. The phase components along the line

$$sx + ty = \text{const} \quad (3.21a)$$

are constant. Those constant phase angle lines are useful in determining edge or line information in an image. In fact it is often noted that phase information (relative position of elements) is not easily discriminated from high-frequency component image information since both portray edges and detail.

It is not generally true that the two-dimensional transform is separable into s and t

components. This only occurs when

$$F(s, t) = F_g(s) F_h(t)$$

or

$$f(x, y) = g(x) h(y)$$

a condition called separability.

We may ask what other properties of the input function $f(x, y)$ can be traced through to specific features of the amplitude and phase spectra. Consider a general rigid transformation of the image:

$$\left. \begin{array}{l} x' = a_1 x + a_2 y + a_3, \\ y' = b_1 x + b_2 y + b_3, \end{array} \right\} \tag{3.22}$$

where $a_1 b_2 - a_2 b_1 = 0$. When a_i and b_i convert (3.22) to

$$x' = x \cos \theta + y \sin \theta + a_3,$$
$$y' = - x \sin \theta + y \cos \theta + b_3,$$

the image is rotated through an angle θ and translated by (a_3, b_3) with respect to (x, y) axes respectively (Fig. 3.5).

The resultant Fourier transform.

$$F(s, t) = \int \int f(x', y') \exp \left[i(sx' + ty') \right] dx' sy'$$

can be broken down as follows. From (3.22)

$$sx' + ty' = (sa_1 + tb_1)x + (sa_2 + tb_2)y + (sa_3 + tb_3)$$

and by letting

$$\left. \begin{array}{l} s' = sa_1 + tb_1, \\ t' = sa_2 + tb_2, \\ \alpha_{st} = sa_3 + tb_3, \end{array} \right\} \tag{3.23}$$

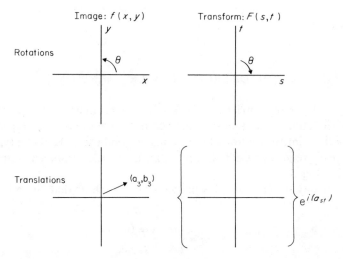

FIG. 3.5. Some relationships between image transforms and Fourier transform domain changes.

we obtain

$$F(s, t) = \int \int f(x', y') \exp \left[i(s'x' + t' y' + \alpha_{st}) \right] dx' \, dy'$$

or

$$F(s, t) = \exp (i\alpha_{st}) \int \int f(x', y') \exp \left[i(s'x' + t'y') \right] dx' \, dy'. \tag{3.24}$$

But (3.23) corresponds to a rotation in the opposite direction to that of (3.22). Hence an image rotation corresponds to an opposite direction rotation in the transform domain, and the translation corresponds to the modulation factor $\exp (i\alpha_{st})$.

Other relationships are also clear. A contraction or expansion of the image corresponds to similar effects in the spectrum since

$$s(\alpha x) + t(\beta y) = (\alpha s)x + (\beta t)y.$$

A reflection of one image about one axis, say $g(x, y) = f(-x, y)$ representing the image as a mirror reflection of $f(x, y)$ by $g(x, y)$ about the y-axis, is also represented in the spectrum since $s(-x) + ty = (-s)x + ty$.

In general the Fourier transform of a linear combination of functions is equal to the linear combination of their transforms

$$\mathscr{F}(\alpha A + \beta B) = \alpha \mathscr{F}(A) + \beta \mathscr{F}(B) \tag{3.25}$$

for α, β being arbitrary constants. Secondly, the Fourier transform of the product of two functions is equal to the product of their transforms

$$\mathscr{F}(A \times B) = \mathscr{F}(A) \mathscr{F}(B), \tag{3.26}$$

where $A \times B$ denotes

$$A \times B = \int_{-\infty}^{\infty} A(x) B(x - t) \, dx,$$

which is called the convolution of A and B. This second property is sometimes called the convolution theorem.

3.3 THE DISCRETE FOURIER TRANSFORM

Often in applications of Fourier transforms, and particularly with spectrum analyses, the image to be investigated consists of a finite collection of events to be regarded as pulses solely encoding the relative position of the events. A good example of this type of stimulus is the point display image on a CRT (Chapter 2), where each luminance source is regarded as a narrow pulse (Fig. 3.6).

A conventional way to represent this image is via the Dirac delta function (δ-function) defined by

$$\delta(x) = \begin{cases} 0 & x \neq 0. \\ \infty & x = 0, \end{cases}$$

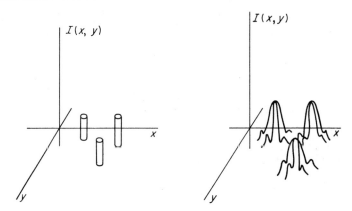

FIG. 3.6. (a) Discrete image composed of impulse functions and (b) their filtered profiles.

and having the properties that:

(i)
$$\int_{-\infty}^{\infty} \delta(x)\,dx = 1,$$

and

(ii)   for any function $f(x)$:

$$\int_{-\infty}^{\infty} f(x)\,\delta(x)\,dx = f(0),$$

the value of the function at the origin.

The two-dimensional form of the δ-function is defined by

$$\delta(x, y) = \begin{cases} 0 & x \neq, y \neq 0, \\ \infty & x = y = 0, \end{cases} \tag{3.27}$$

and
$$\int_{-\infty}^{\infty}\int_{-\infty}^{\infty} \delta(x, y)\,dx\,dy = 1.$$

Also
$$f(x_0, y_0) = \int_{-\infty}^{\infty}\int_{-\infty}^{\infty} \delta(x - x_0)\delta(y - y_0)f(x, y)\,dx\,dy, \tag{3.28}$$

where (x_0, y_0) corresponds to an arbitrary position on the image plane.

For discrete images $f(x, y)$ reduces to

$$f(x, y) = \sum_k \sum_l \delta(x - x_k)\,\delta(y - y_l)$$

and the Fourier transform becomes

$$F(s, t) = \sum_k \sum_l \exp\left[i(sx_k + ty_l)\right]. \tag{3.29}$$

This discrete form of the Fourier transform is employed in the various programs available to compute Fourier spectra and analyses of images. In particular, the fast Fourier transform (FFT) algorithm devised by Good (1958) and Cooley and Tukey (1965), employs an integer representation of the input image, where the image resolution is restricted to a multiple of 2, 2^m, for both x- and y-axis. This increases the speed of computation since the sine and cosine terms generally consume considerably less computer time (see Rabiner and Rader, 1972, for more details).

3.4. LINEAR SYSTEMS, MODULATION TRANSFER FUNCTIONS, AND FILTERING

The Fourier transform pair does not only provide an approximation to a function, but also introduces us to the concept of a linear system. In this system we have an input–output relationship governed by a transformation $\mathscr{F}$, where for input functions f_1, f_2.

$$\mathscr{F}(\alpha f_1 + \beta f_2) = \alpha \mathscr{F}(f_1) + \beta \mathscr{F}(f_2). \tag{3.30}$$

Here the input functions are carried through the system (represented by $\mathscr{F}$) such that linearity is preserved between them. In this sense the Fourier transform pair constitute a linear system (3.25). This concept is illustrated in Fig. 3.7. The system is termed stationary if the input–output relationship is unaffected by changes in image position.

One way of determining the output of a system to arbitrary inputs is through observing the system's response to impulses or δ-functions. This is called the *impulse response* of the system, and the *point-spread function* corresponds to this output function. With the Fourier transform this happens to be the sine or Bessel function (Mexican hat function): Figure 3.6.

In many systems, particularly optical systems, the concept of modulation is most important. In general, *modulation M* is defined as the difference between maximum and minimum intensities divided by their sum, or

$$M = \frac{I_{max} - I_{min}}{I_{max} + I_{min}}. \tag{3.31}$$

Since both input and output modulations can be calculated for a system (being a number from 0 to 1), interest lies in how modulation is transferred through the system. With the case of a Fourier transform these transmission properties are represented by the *modulation transfer function*, or MTF.

In general, an image is never transmitted through a system without the loss of some information. That is, by equating modulation with contrast, the transmission always implies some contrast loss. An alternative way to think of this is in terms of the Fourier spectrum. From the Fourier transform pair we know that the forward transform produces amplitude (frequency) and phase spectra. If no operations are performed on either spectrum then

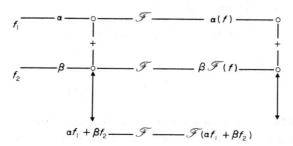

FIG. 3.7. Basic properties of a linear system.

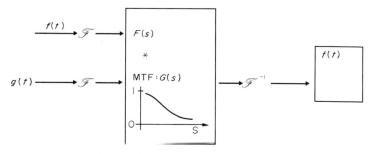

FIG. 3.8. The modulation transfer function and linear systems for Fourier transforms.

the inverse transform produces the original image (Fig. 3.8). However, it is known—certainly with optical systems — that there is always attenuation of the upper frequency components. This is represented by the MTF function shown in Fig. 3.8, where values of 1.0 imply no change in frequency transmission and 0.0 implies that the frequency is not transmitted.

Consequently the frequency spectrum is changed to a "new" spectrum via the MTF: and, upon reconstruction of the image (phase unchanged or unmodulated) it is readily seen as lacking detail or high-frequency components according to the MTF characteristics (Fig. 3.8).

The MTF is an example of a filter where various frequencies are modulated according to the filter profile in the amplitude spectrum. The most common forms of filters are low-pass, high-pass, and band-pass types, and are represented in Fig. 3.9. These filters only allow the specified frequency range to be transmitted through the system. For example, the band-pass filter defined by

$$g(s) = \begin{cases} 1 & s_L \leq s \leq s_u, \\ 0 & \text{elsewhere}, \end{cases}$$

allows only frequencies between s_L and s_u to be transmitted.

Many of the "internal mechanisms" of linear systems are composed of filters or MTF

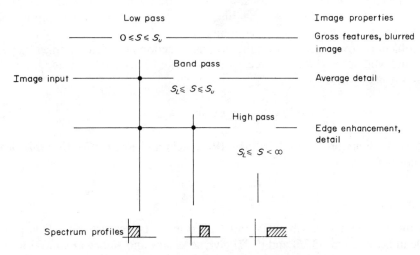

FIG. 3.9. Filter characteristics and profiles.

functions as defined above. Yet a filter or MTF is a function and consequently the inverse Fourier transform (two-dimensional case) is

$$f(x, y) = \int_{-\infty}^{\infty} \int_{-\infty}^{\infty} g(s, t) F(s, t) \exp \left[i(sx + ty) \right] \mathrm{d}s \mathrm{d}t, \tag{3.32}$$

where $g(s, t)$ represents the filter. But (3.32) is a convolution of g and F. So the output function $f(x, y)$ must also be equal to the product of the inverse Fourier transform of the filter with the inverse Fourier transform of the signal or input, due to the convolution theorem (3.26).

We shall see in Chapter 6 how the properties of filters in the frequency domain, coupled with the image phase spectrum, are currently being employed to describe the functional properties of cortical receptive fields and the psychophysics of visual image processing.

3.5. DIGITAL IMAGE PROCESSING AND THE FOURIER TRANSFORM

In most applications of the Fourier transform in image processing the discrete Fourier transform (two-dimensional case)

$$F(s, t) = \frac{1}{MN} \sum_{m=0}^{M-1} \sum_{n=0}^{N-1} f(m, n) \exp \left[-2\pi i \left(\frac{ms}{M} + \frac{nt}{N} \right) \right] \tag{3.33}$$

is used, where $s = 0, 1, 2, \ldots, M - 1; t = 0, 1, 2, \ldots, N - 1$. The inverse transform is determined by

$$f(m, n) = \sum_{s=0}^{M-1} \sum_{t=0}^{N-1} F(s, t) \exp \left[2\pi i \left(\frac{ms}{M} + \frac{nt}{N} \right) \right]. \tag{3.34}$$

These discrete transforms have the same properties as the continuous case, e.g. the convolution theorem holds and hence filtering can be readily handled. However, there are some important problems which do arise using discrete transforms. These are sampling and "aliasing" problems. Consider the one-dimensional case, where $f(x)$ is represented by samples $f(kx)$, $-\infty < k < \infty$, is the sampling period.

The problem is how to reconstruct the original function $f(x)$ from samples $f(kx)$. From Peterson and Middleton (1962) this reconstruction can be attained by using interpolation functions, say $g(x)$, where

$$f(x) = \sum_{k=-\infty}^{\infty} f(kx) g(x - kx). \tag{3.35}$$

By employing s-functions it can be shown (Rosenfeld and Kak, 1976) that this produces the relationship

$$F(s) = \frac{G(s)}{T} \sum_{n=-\infty}^{\infty} F \left(s - \frac{2\pi n}{x} \right) \tag{3.36}$$

between the Fourier transforms of g and f ($G(s)$ and $F(s)$ respectively). This process is reversible indicating that (3.36) and (3.37) give necessary and sufficient conditions for the reconstruction of the original image by such interpolation procedures.

Now if $f(x)$ is such a function that its Fourier transforms is zero above a certain frequency $2\pi f_c$ ("bandlimited"), and the period $X \le 1/2f_c$, then (3.36) is satisfied when

$$G(s) = \begin{cases} X & |s| < 2\pi f_c, \\ 0 & \text{elsewhere.} \end{cases} \tag{3.37}$$

This condition has led to the Whittaker–Kotelnikov–Shannon theorem (sometimes simply called Shannon's sampling theorem[†]), which states that:

If the Fourier transform of a function $f(x)$ is zero for $|s| \ge 2\pi f_c$, then $f(x)$ can be exactly reconstructed from samples of its values taken $1/2f_c$ apart or closer.

This also applies to two-dimensional sampling lattices often used in image processing,

Fig. 3.10. Aliasing effects in patterns.

[†] The more general form of the sampling theorem states that if the Fourier transform is zero above a certain frequency f_c, then $f(x)$ can be uniquely determined from the values $f_n = f(n\pi/f_c)$ at a sequence of equidistant points, distance π/f_c apart (Shannon, 1949; see also Papoulis, 1962).

where we obtain the conditions

$$F(s,t) = \frac{G(s,t)}{Q} \sum_p \sum_q F\left(s - \frac{2\pi p}{Q}, t - \frac{2\pi q}{Q}\right) \tag{3.38}$$

between the Fourier transform pairs, where Q is the area of the parallelogram formed by four adjacent sampling points. The analogue to the one-dimensional sampling theorem is in two-dimensions (Rosenfeld and Kak, 1976).

A function $f(x, y)$, whose Fourier transform $F(s,t)$ is zero everywhere except for a bonded spatial frequency region, can be reproduced from values taken from a lattice of points as long as the spectrum $F(s,t)$ does not overlap with its images on a periodic lattice of points.

If we sample $f(x,y)$ at intervals of X and Y along x- and y-axes respectively, then this causes replication of $F(s,t)$ at intervals of $1/X$ and $1/Y$ along the s- and t-axes. So if $F(s,t) = 0$ for $|s| < 1/2X$ and $|t| < 1/2Y$, then no overlapping will occur. So, in general, the aim of any reconstruction technique is to minimize overlapping of the (periodic) duplicates of the spectral image of the input. Their overlapping is sometimes called "aliasing" since when overlapping occurs spurious frequencies are generated which, when inverted, induce noticeable differences in the image, e.g. moiré patterns (Fig. 3.10) are induced by aliasing. So for signals bandlimited to W hertz, the sampling rate should be not slower than $2W$ hertz. The $2W$ hertz rate is called the Nyquist rate.

There are many other issues related to Fourier methods, such as the consideration of various types of filters, phase spectral analyses, and non-linear systems. These will be dealt with partially in Chapters 4, 6, and 7 when they arise in vision research issues.

3.6. CONVOLUTIONS, AUTOCORRELATIONS, AND OTHER TRANSFORMS

We have seen that the Fourier transform has powerful applications in the area of image processing. Yet we have not compared it with other types of transforms available that analyse functions or images for various components. In this section we shall show how these various transformations are related — and differ.

The Fourier transform (3.13) is an example of a convolution since it involves the product of two functions $f(x)$ and e^{isx} with a small increment in the domain dx and then summed.

In general, a convolution is defined by

$$G(t) = \int_{-\infty}^{\infty} f(x)g(x + t)dx, \tag{3.39}$$

where $f(x)$ and $g(x)$ are two functions defined over the x-domain. In the case of the Fourier transform $g(x) = e^{isx}$, $t = 0$, making G a function of s, or $G(s)$. This is also called the "characteristic" equation of $f(x)$ since, when differentiated about $s = 0$, it generates the moments of $f(x)$ (see Lukacs, 1960, for more details).

When $g(x + t) = f(x + t)$, (3.39) is termed the autocorrelation function of $f(x)$, or

$$C_a(t) = \int_{-\infty}^{\infty} f(x)f(x + t)dx. \tag{3.40}$$

For $g(x + t) = e^{sx}$, (3.39) becomes the Laplace transform which is extensively used in control theory (see Chapter 4).

From the convolution theorem (3.26) it is readily seen that the Fourier transform of the autocorrelation function $A(t)$ is equal to the square of Fourier transform of $f(x)$. That is, the amplitude spectrum of the autocorrelation function is equal to the square of the amplitude spectrum of $f(x)$. In addition, if we regard the Fourier transform as the product of amplitude and phase spectra by (3.18),

$$F(s) = A(s) \exp [i\phi(s)],$$

then it is also true (Papoulis, 1962) that

$$\int_{-\infty}^{\infty} |f(x)|^2 dx = \frac{1}{2\pi} \int_{-\infty}^{\infty} A^2(s) ds. \tag{3.41}$$

This is called Parseval's formula. The Wiener–Khintchine relation also states that the spectrum of the autocorrelation function is equal to the square of the modulus of the Fourier transform, or

$$C_a(t) = \int_{-\infty}^{\infty} (f(x))^2 e^{itx} dx. \tag{3.42}$$

Of course, since $(f(x))^2$ is always an even function, the Wiener–Khintchine relation reduces to the autocorrelation function, being equal to the cosine Fourier transform of its power spectrum.

It will be shown in Chapter 6 how these various convolutions extract different aspects of images, e.g. periodicities, symmetries, linearities, and thus how they have been used to model various properties of human vision.

Yet there are other transforms that are used in image processing which have particular relevance to digital configurations. In particular we shall consider the Radamacher, Haar, and Walsh functions and their associated transforms. Other non-linear transforms will be considered in Chapter 4.

The three more common orthogonal functions used in place of the Fourier transform with digital signal processing are the Radamacher, Haar, and Walsh functions. These functions consist of sequences of square or rectangular waves as shown in Fig. 3.11, where periodicity is not assumed—as it was in the Fourier case. The concept of sequency, or generalized frequency, replaces the Fourier frequency components. Sequency is usually defined as half the average number of zero crossings per unit time (Fig. 3.11).

The Radamacher function is a periodic rectangular pulse having only $(+1, -1)$ values (amplitudes) with 2^{m-1} cycles in the interval between 0 and 1—including 1, not 0 (Fig. 3.11):

$$\text{rad}(m, t) = \text{rad}(m, t+1) = \text{rad}(1, 2^{m-1}t) \tag{3.43}$$

and $\qquad \text{rad}(m, t) = \text{rad}(m, t + n2^{1-m}), \quad m = 1, 2, \ldots; \quad n = \pm 1, \pm 2, \ldots.$

The Haar function, having non-constant amplitude, is periodic and defined by

$$\text{har}(r, m, t) = \begin{cases} 2^{r/2}, & \dfrac{m-1}{2^r} \le t < \dfrac{m-\frac{1}{2}}{2^r}, \\[2ex] -2^{r/2}, & \dfrac{m-\frac{1}{2}}{2^r} \le t < \dfrac{m}{2^r}, \\[2ex] 0 & \text{elsewhere,} \end{cases} \tag{3.44}$$

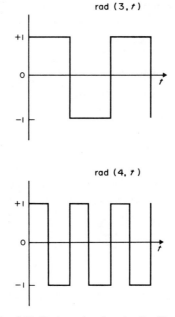

FIG. 3.11. Rademacher function for $N = 3, 4$.

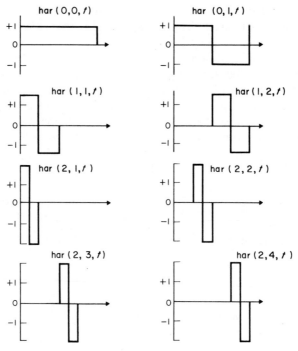

FIG. 3.12. Haar function for $N = 8$.

and $\mathrm{har}(0,0,t) = 1$; $0 \le r < \log_2 N$; $1 \le m \le 2^r$. This function is illustrated in Fig. 3.12.

The Walsh function has three forms: Walsh ordering, dyadic or Paley ordering, and natural or Hadamard ordering. These various forms are all related and are simply different ways of manipulating the basic Walsh function.

The Walsh ordering function is defined by

$$S_w = \{\mathrm{wal}_w(i,t), \quad i = 0, 1, \ldots, N-1\}, \quad N = 2^n; n = 1, 2, \ldots, \tag{3.45}$$

where $w \equiv$ Walsh ordering, $i \equiv i$th element of s_w.

$$S_i = \begin{cases} 0, & i = 0, \\ i/2, & i \text{ even}, \\ (i+1)/2, & i \text{ odd}. \end{cases} \tag{3.46}$$

and the Walsh equivalents to sine and cosine are defined by

$$\mathrm{cal}(s_i, t) = \mathrm{wal}_w(i,t), \quad i \text{ even},$$

$$\mathrm{sal}(s_i, t) = \mathrm{wal}_w(i,t), \quad i \text{ odd}.$$

Figure 3.13 shows an example of the Walsh function for $N = 8$. The table or matrix on the right is called a Hadamard matrix $H(n)$ having, in general, the properties:

(a) each element is $+1$ or -1;
(b) H is symmetric;
(c) the inverse is proportional to the original;
(d) it is orthogonal;[†]
(e) $H(k)$ is defined by

$$H(k) = \begin{bmatrix} H(k-1), & H(k-1), \\ H(k-1), & -H(k-1), \end{bmatrix} \tag{3.47}$$

for $H(o) = 1$, $n = \log_2 N$.

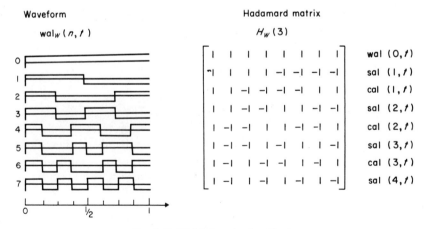

FIG. 3.13. Walsh function for $N = 8$.

[†] See Chapter 5 for formal definition of orthogonality.

The Walsh–Hadamard transform is the Walsh transform equivalent to the discrete Fourier transform most commonly used. The Walsh series representation of a function is

$$x(t) = \sum_{k=0}^{\infty} d_k \, \mathrm{wal}_w(k,t), \quad d_k = \int_0^1 x(t) \, \mathrm{wal}_w(k,t) dt, \tag{3.48}$$

$$k = 0, 1, 2, \ldots .$$

which has odd and even series (in comparison to the Fourier series):

$$x(t) = a_0 \, \mathrm{wal}_w(k,t) + \sum_{k=1}^{\infty} \left[a_k \, \mathrm{cal}(k,t) + b_k \, \mathrm{sal}(k,t) \right], \tag{3.49}$$

where $a_0 = d_0$, $a_k = d_{2k}$, $b_k = d_{2k-1}$. For $N = 2^m$ the series truncates to

$$x(t) \approx a_0 \, \mathrm{wal}_w(0,t) + \sum_{k=1}^{N/2-1} \left[a_k \, \mathrm{cal}(k,t) + b_k \, \mathrm{sal}(k,t) \right] + b_{N/2} \, \mathrm{sal}(N/2,t). \tag{3.50}$$

This (3.50) is the Walsh transform. Walsh–Hadamard transforms are used for the Walsh functions, which can be expressed as Hadamard matrices $H(n)$ as defined above. The Walsh–Hadamard transform (WHT) has the exponential form

$$B_x(u) = \frac{1}{N} \sum_{m=0}^{N-1} X(m)(-1)^{\langle m,n \rangle},$$

where $u = 0, 1, \ldots, N-1$; $\langle m,n \rangle = \sum_{s=0}^{n-1} u_s m_s$ for u_s and m_s being the coefficients of the binary representation of u and m respectively. $X(m)$ is the sampled input data while $Bx(u)$ is the Walsh transform domain.

This readily generalizes to n-dimensional Walsh transforms. In particular, the two-dimensional case is:

$$B(u_1, u_2) = \frac{1}{N_1 N_2} \sum_{m_2=0}^{N_2-1} \sum_{m_1=0}^{N_1-1} X(m_1, m_2)(-1)^{\langle m_1, u_1 \rangle + \langle m_2, u_2 \rangle} \tag{3.51}$$

for

$$\langle m_i, u_i \rangle = \sum_{s=0}^{n_i-1} m_i(s) u_i(s), \quad i = 1, 2,$$

where $m_i(s)$ and $u_i(s)$ are the binary representation coefficients.

The inverse is thus

$$X(m_1, m_2) = \sum_{u_2=0}^{N_2-1} \sum_{u_1=0}^{N_1-1} B(u_1, u_2)(-1)^{\langle m_1, u_1 \rangle + \langle m_2, u_2 \rangle}. \tag{3.52}$$

The reader is referred to Ahmed and Rao (1975) for more details on these functions and transforms. However, we should note that the WHT transform compares favourably with the discrete Fourier transform—the fast Fourier transform (FFT) routine developed by Cooley and Tookey.

Finally, the Haar transform is defined as

$$Y(n) = \frac{1}{N} H^*(n) \times (n), \tag{3.53}$$

where $X(n)$ is the input data and $H^*(n)$ is an $N \times N$ Haar matrix obtained by sampling the set of Haar functions $\{ \mathrm{har}(r,m,t) \}$.

3.7. FOURIER TRANSFORM ROUTINES

We should briefly consider some properties of the FFT algorithm developed by Cooley and Tookey (1965) since it is used extensively in computer-based Fourier routines for image processing. The underlying problem is to find an efficient algorithm to compute the harmonic waveforms particularly when large numbers of points are used. The transform is

$$C_x(k) = \frac{1}{N} \sum_{m=0}^{N-1} X(m) W^{km}; \quad k = 0, \ldots, N-1 \tag{3.54}$$

for $m = 0, \ldots, N-1$; $W = e^{-2\pi i/N}$; $i^2 = -1$.

Now the decimal numbers m may be expressed in binary form as

$$m = \sum_{i=0} m_i 2^i, \tag{3.55}$$

where $m_i = 0$ or $1, n = \log_2 N$. This is also true for k, where

$$k = \sum_{j=0}^{n-1} k_j 2^j; \quad k_j = 0 \quad \text{or} \quad 1, n = \log_2 N.$$

A binary form for the input data $X(m)$ $(\tilde{X}(m))$ becomes

$$\tilde{X}(m) = \tilde{X}(m_{n-1}, \ldots, m_1, m_0)$$

reducing (3.54) to

$$C_x(k) = \frac{1}{N} \sum_{m_0 m_1} \sum \cdots \sum_{m_{n-1}} \tilde{X}(m_{n-1}, \ldots, m_1, m_0) W^{k \left[\sum_{j=0}^{n-1} m_1 w^i \right]}. \tag{3.56}$$

Consider (3.56) for $N = 4$. Here

$$C_x(k) = \frac{1}{4} \sum_{m_0 m_1} \sum \tilde{X}(m_1, m_0) w^{k[2m_1 + m_0]}$$
$$= \tfrac{1}{4} [\tilde{X}(0,0) + \tilde{X}(0,1) W^k + \tilde{X}(1,0) W^{2k} + \tilde{X}(1,1) W^{3k}].$$

The algorithm is best expounded by considering the case of $N = 8$. Here

$$C_x(k) = \frac{1}{8} \sum_{m} X(m) W^{km}; \quad k = 0, 1, \ldots, 7,$$

where $W = e^{-\pi i/4}$. Now, $m = m_2 2^2 + m_1 2^1 + m_0 2^0$, and so

$$8C_x(k) = \sum_{m_0 m_1 m_2} \sum \sum \tilde{X}(m_2, m_1, m_0) W^{k(4m_2 + 2m_1 + m_0)} \tag{3.57}$$

Let $M_2 = \sum_{m_2} \tilde{X}(m_2, m_1, m_0) W^{4km_2}$,

and since $W^4 = -1$, and using the binary form of k, we obtain

$$m_2 = \sum_{m_2} \tilde{X}(m_2, m_1, m_0)(-1)^{m_2(4k_2 + 2k_1 + k_0)}.$$

But

$$(-1)^{m_2(4k_2 + 2k_1 + k_0)} = 1,$$

so

$$m_2 = \sum_{m_2} \tilde{X}(m_2, m_1, m_0)(-1)^{k_0 m_2} = \tilde{X}_1(k_0, m_1, m_0). \tag{3.58}$$

Substituting (3.58) into (3.57) gives

$$8C_x(k) = \sum_{m_0} \sum_{m_1} \tilde{X}_1(k_0, m_1, m_0) W^{2km_1} W^{km_0}.$$

Employing the same notation we also obtain

$$M_1 = \sum_{m_1} \tilde{X}_1(k_0, m_1, m_0)(-i)^{(2k_1 + k_0)m_1} = \tilde{X}_2(k_0, k_1, m_0),$$

$$M_0 = \sum_{m_0} \tilde{X}_2(k_0, k_1, m_0) \left(\frac{1-i}{\sqrt{2}} \right)^{(4k_2 + 2k_1 + k_0)m_0} = \tilde{X}_3(k_0, k_1, k_2).$$

These equations for M_0, M_1, M_2 determine the Fourier transform for $N = 8$, and, in general, there are $\log_2 N$ such functions. This is sometimes called the radix method and is well adapted to digital computers. This method only requires $\log_2 N$ iterations (from above) involving $N \log_2 N$ arithmetic operations for N data points. The normal or "direct" method has operations proportional to N^2 while the FFT operations are only proportional to N—a considerable time saving.

The FFT routine requires a basic $2N$ storage locations while the direct method needs about $2N^2$ locations. It also has better round-off error characteristics than the direct method. Large images can consequently be analysed by the FFT routine with the use of disc storage on relatively small minicomputers (see Piotrowsky, 1979, for one such programme).

3.8. SUMMARY AND CONCLUSIONS

In this chapter we have considered the basic properties of the Fourier representation of systems, systems as such, and other transforms which may be related to image processing. As will be seen in Part II, concepts of filtering, MTF, and image decompositions in accord with linear systems are, at present, popular in vision research, particularly in relation to contrast perception.

REFERENCES

AHMED, N. and RAO, K.R. (1975) *Orthogonal Transforms for Digital Signal Processing*, Springer-Verlag, New York.

COOLEY, W. and TOOKEY, J. (1965) An algorithm for machine computation of complex fourier series, *Mathematics of computation*, **19**, 297–301.

GOOD, I (1958) The interaction algorithm and practical Fourier series, *J. Roy. Statist. Soc. B*, **20**, 361–372.

HECHT, C. and ZAJAC, A (1974) *Optics*, Addison–Wesley, London,

LUKACS, E. (1960) *Characteristic Functions*, Griffin, London.

MAURICE, R.D.A. (1976) *Convolution and Fourier Transforms for Communications Engineers*, Pentech Press, London.

PAPOULIS, A. (1962) *The Fourier Integral and its Application*, McGraw-Hill, New York.

PEARSON, D.E. (1975) *Transmission and Display of Pictorial Information*, Pentech Press, London.

PETERSON, D. and MIDDLETON, D. (1962) Sampling and reconstruction of wave number—limited functions in *N*-dimensional Euclidean spaces, *Information and Control* **5**, 279–323.

PIOTROWSKY, L. (1979) Image enhancement using a visual model, MSc thesis, University of Sydney, Sydney.

RABINER, L. and RADER C. (1972) *Digital Signal Processing*, IEEE Press, New York.

ROSENFELD, A. and KAK, A. (1976) *Digital Picture Processing*, Academic Press, New York.

SHANNON, C. (1949) *Communication in the Presence of Noise*, Proc. IRE.

CHAPTER 4

Network Theory and Systems

4.1. INTRODUCTION TO NETWORKS

Although the vertebrate visual system is a most complex structure, *a fortiori*, the processes of human psychophysics—some principles have emerged over the past few decades which do enable us to predict perceptual behaviour on a variety of events. These principles relate the known electrophysiological responses of individual cortical units to the decision-making properties of psychophysical judgements both involving network models and decision theory. The aim of this chapter is to introduce the reader to these areas of research and technology.

What is a network or system? In its most general form a network can be conceived of as a directed graph: a set of nodes whose interconnections represent transmission or energy flow. These nodes may be resistors, capacitors, or even nerve cells in the visual system—the interconnections being the axonal and dendritic tree structures.

Possibly due to the great developments in electrophysiology, most network models for neural function involve concepts of electronic components used in general electrical networks. For this reason the following series of definitions and functions should prove useful.

(a) Basic units

Charge: relates to the energy of an electron, where each electron has a charge of 1.6021×10^{-19} coulomb.

Electric current: transferring charge from one point to another. The current is usually measured in amperes as the change in charge over time, or

$$i = \frac{dq}{dt},$$

where q is in coulombs and t in seconds.

Here a current of 1 ampere corresponds to the motion of $1/(1.6021 \times 10^{-19})$ electrons in one second.

Voltage: represents work (or energy) per unit charge:

$$v = w/q,$$

where w is in joules, q in coulombs.

57

Power: the time rate change of energy, or

$$p = \frac{dw}{dt},$$

where power is the product of voltage and current:

$$p = v \times i.$$

Capacitance: it was Coulomb who found that charges repel or attract as a function of

$$F = \frac{q_1 q_2}{4\pi E d^2}, \quad \text{in newtons,}$$

where d corresponds to the distance between charges q_1 and q_2 (in metres) and E is permittivity: free-space value of 8.854×10^{-12} farad per metre. Applying this to two plates distance d apart and having surface areas A, the capacitance is

$$C = \frac{EA}{d}, \quad \text{in farads}$$

This may be expressed as

$$C = q/v = \frac{1}{v} \int i \, dt$$

where q is the charge on input plate and v is the voltage between plates. This is sometimes called the circuit parameter as it relates q and v.

Inductance: the interpretation of inductance L, the induction of current due to magnetic fields, is expressed through Faraday's law as

$$v = \frac{d(Li)}{dt},$$

or, for constant inductance,

$$v = L \frac{di}{dt}.$$

Resistance: resistance is the reciprocal of conductance $(1/R)$ and is encapsulated in Ohm's law:

$$R = v/i.$$

The conventional representations for these elements are shown in Fig. 4.1a.

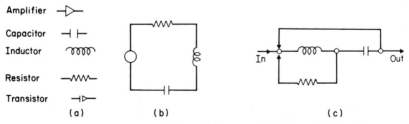

FIG. 4.1. Some codes for (a) network devices and (b) general *RLC* network (c) with one specific example.

(b) Basic electrical currents

Kirchhoff's current and voltage law states that the sum of all branch currents (and voltages) leaving a circuit mode is zero at all instances of time. With the additional properties that resistances sum when in series, and inductances combine accordingly, it is possible to derive the network conditions for simple circuits. Consider the circuit shown in Fig. 4.1b—the *RLC* network. Here the voltage $v(t)$ has three components (by Kirchhoff's laws):

$$v = L\frac{di}{dt} + Ri + \frac{1}{c}\int i \, dt = v_t + v_R + v_C. \tag{4.1}$$

Equations like (4.1) lead to the concept of a *linear system* where the input $f(t)$ and output $g(t)$ signals are related by the linear relationship

$$g(t) = \sum_{i=1}^{n} a_i(t)\frac{df^i(t)}{dt^i} = T(f); \tag{4.2}$$

$d^k f/dt^k$ represents the kth derivative[†] of $f(t)$ with respect to time and $a_k(t)$—a variable coefficient. These coefficients are often constant over time and, then, denoted by $a_i(t) = \alpha_i$. The system is linear since each term is independent of all others and not raised to any power other than unity.

The principle of superposition holds for linear systems. That is, for any input signals f_m, f_n, there is a corresponding output signal defined by

$$g = T(f_m + f_n) = T(f_m) + T(f_n).$$

The *RLC* system is a linear system.

There are many other ways of representing the input–output relations than the direct way described above, which involves complex solutions of differential equations. We have already seen (Chapter 3) how the Fourier transform can represent the transfer function when frequency modulation occurs.

In network analyses the Laplace transform is more appropriate than the Fourier. It is defined by[‡]

$$\mathscr{L}(f(t)) = \int_0^{\infty} f(t)e^{-st}dt = F(s), Re(s) > \sigma_0, \tag{4.3}$$

having an inverse

$$\mathscr{L}^{-1}(F(s)) = \frac{1}{2\pi j}\int_{c-j\infty}^{c+j\infty} F(s)e^{st}ds = f(t), \quad c > \sigma_0, \tag{4.4}$$

where s is the complex variable $s = \sigma + jw, \sigma_0$ is some constant. The Laplace transform differs from the Fourier in so far as the exponent s is a full complex number in the former. Consequently S is a plane (the s-plane) having real and imaginary axes. By defining the Laplace transform as operating on inputs $f(t), g(t)$ we obtain the following useful properties:

(i) Linearity: $\mathscr{L}(\alpha f(t) + \beta g(t)) = \alpha F(s) + \beta G(t)$.

[†] The kth derivative of a function: $d^k f(t)dt^k$ represents the kth rate of change of the function with respect to time.

[‡] This only applies for when $\int_0^{\infty} f(t)e^{-st}dt$ is absolutely convergent.

(ii) Scale change: $\mathscr{L}(f(t/\alpha)) = \alpha F(\alpha s)$

(iii) Time translation: $\mathscr{L}(f(t + \alpha)) = F(s)\,e^{\alpha s}, \alpha > 0.$

(iv) Differentiation: $\mathscr{L}(\mathrm{d}^k f(t)/\mathrm{d}t^k) = \mathscr{L}(f^{(k)}(t)) = s^k F(s) - s^{k-1}f(0) - f^{k-1}(0).$

(v) Integration: $\mathscr{L}\left(\displaystyle\int_{-\infty}^{t} f(u)\mathrm{d}u \right) = \mathscr{L}(f^{(-1)}(u)) = F(s)/s + \dfrac{1}{s}f^{(-1)}(0).$

(vi) Convolutions: $\mathscr{L}\left(\displaystyle\int_{0}^{t} h(t - u)\, g(h)\mathrm{d}u \right) = H(s)\,G(s).$

Just as the output function in the Fourier system was specified by the input and transfer function, so the system response function $h(t)$ is determined by the input $f(t)$ and system function $g(t)$, where, in Laplace domain, from (vi),

$$H(s) = F(s)\,G(s). \tag{4.5}$$

Alternatively, the transfer function is defined by $H(s)/F(s)$, or, output/input when zero initial conditions are assumed. If we consider the RLC network shown in Fig. 4.1c, the transfer characteristics are defined from individual transfer functions

$$\frac{f}{v_l} = \frac{1}{Ls}; \quad \frac{v_R}{f} = R; \quad \frac{v_C}{f} = \frac{1}{Cs}. \tag{4.6}$$

In this example

$$v_l = v_{\text{input}} - v_R - v_C = v_{\text{input}} - v_l\left(\frac{1}{LCs^2} + \frac{R}{Ls} \right)$$

or

$$v_{\text{input}} = v_l\left(1 + \frac{1}{LCs^2} + \frac{R}{Ls} \right). \tag{4.7}$$

So

$$\frac{v_C}{v} = \frac{1}{LCs^2 + RCs + 1} \tag{4.8}$$

corresponds to the total transfer function of the network in Fig. 4.1c. In this way (4.8) can be seen to operate on any input function to produce an output consistent with the network performance (see McFarland, 1971, for more details).

Standard Laplace transform pairs are found in most introductory books on network theory and so we shall not include them here.

Clearly one of the most important properties of Laplace transforms is that it reduces integration and differentiation to division and multiplication respectively.

In the following section we shall investigate some of the specific networks and systems associated with visual perception.

4.2. NETWORKS IN VISION

In this section we shall consider network models for retinal, cortical, and eye-movement systems in order to illustrate how specific network properties are representative of visual function.

With the development of microelectrode recording techniques it has become possible to record the electrical activity of cells within the visual system. However, due to the small

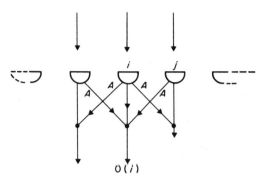

FIG. 4.2. Simple form of lateral inhibition with inhibitory coefficients $A(\leq 1.0)$. Output at cell i, $0(i)$ is determined by $0(i) = I(i) - \sum_j A(J)$.

currents involved, almost all recordings are of spike, or action, potentials and not of the small electrotonic voltage changes, which constitute the action potential. For this reason most microelectrode recording results are in terms of number of recorded spikes per unit of time, or spike frequency.

That single retinal cells of *Limulus* (horseshoe crab) could exhibit electrical activity was demonstrated by Hartline and Graham (1932). However, Hartline and Ratliff (1957) also discovered that the activity of one cell can be inhibited by another cell whose receptive fields impigned upon each other. This is termed lateral inhibition and is illustrated in Fig. 4.2.

Here (Fig. 4.2) the net output of cell j is determined by three components: the input η_i, the input to neighbouring cells i, and the inhibitory coefficient (or gain, 0–1.0) of the inhibitory synaptic connection. Such mechanisms are usually contingent on a threshold below which inhibitory action would not occur. So the output of cell j would become, in this case,

$$R_i(t) = \eta_i(t) - \sum_{j=1}^{n} C_{ij}[R_j(t) - C_{ij}^0(t)], \qquad (4.9)$$

where C_{ij} is the inhibitory coefficient, C_{ij}^0 is the threshold value, R_i being the firing rate of neuron i, and η_i is the external excitatory input to cell j.

The relationship between the action potential and passive electronic conduction (i.e., current flow along cell axons and dendrites, which is below threshold) is akin to that of the *RC* circuit, where the capacitor is analogous to the synaptic function (see Rodieck, 1970, for more details). It can be seen from (4.9) that the effect of one cell on another is largely determined by the "gain control" parameter C_{ij}. This mechanism has been used to explain perceptual phenomena as Mach bands and simultaneous contrast effects. The essence of the argument is illustrated in Fig. 4.3, where the apparent contrast change at each edge is predictable from (4.9) in terms of luminance diferences and gain values.

The cytoarchitecture of the vertebrate visual cortex also indicates that cells mutually interact through their dendritic aborizations. However, it is not clear whether such inter-actions are restricted to inhibitory types. Even the proposal by Hubel and Wiesel (1962) that cells in the primary projection area have interactions restricted to columns would seem to be too limited a range (Valverde, 1976). Recently, Kreutzfeldt *et al.* (1974) have also demonstrated through electrophysiological recordings that interactions occur between retinoptic domains at greater distances than originally thought.

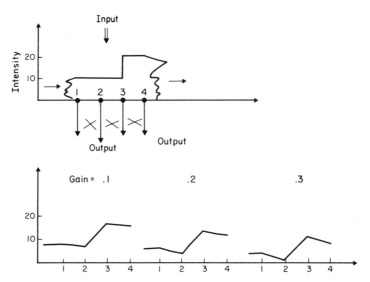

FIG. 4.3. Edge enhancement and Mach band for three different inhibitory gain A coefficients.

Perhaps the most common way of representing such interactions is in terms of a generalized version of (4.9), where c_{ij} can be excitatory or inhibitory (Sejnowski, 1976):

$$\phi_i = \eta_i + \sum_j C_{ij} r_j. \tag{4.10}$$

Here ϕ_i is the output of cell i, η_i is the external input to cell i, and r_j is the average firing rate of cell j, C_{ij} being the connectivity matrix representative of the dendritic arborizations of the neural net. When $i = j$ we have recurrent collaterals, while positive C_{ij} and negative C_{ij} correspond to excitatory and inhibitory gains (or contributions) respectively. ϕ_i, being the net output, corresponds to a membrane potential.

A network is in equilibrium if the output of each element is consistent, and so a field of interacting neurons is in equilibrium if the average membrane potentials are constant.

By letting $P(x)$ represent the probability that a neuron of (normalized) potential x will fire during a specific period, and σ_j be the standard deviation of the firing rate for the period θ_j, the mean, then, (4.10) reduces to the "equilibrium equation":

$$\phi_i = \eta_i + \sum_{j=1}^{n} C_{ij} p[(\phi_j - \theta_j)/\lambda_j] \tag{4.11}$$

for $\lambda_j =$ transition width. Under uniform conditions $\lambda_j = \lambda$, for all j. Of course, it should be noted that firing rate varies directly with membrane potential.

If we consider just two interacting cells having outputs ϕ_1 and ϕ_2 and we define the equilibrium condition by $\phi_i' = \phi_i$, then it is true that the inequalities in magnitudes ($\|\ \ \|$) occur:

$$\| \phi_i' - \phi_j' \| \le \frac{1}{\lambda} \| C_{ij} \| \cdot \| \phi_i - \phi_j \| \tag{4.12}$$

for constant mean firing rates θ and range σ over all cells. If $\| C_{ij} \| < \lambda$, then the output difference is smaller than the input difference. This is termed "weak coupling" as no single connection can dominate the firing rate of any neuron.

Recently, Leake and Anninos (1976) have investigated the effects of various C_{ij}—connectivity matrices—on the neural network's equilibrium conditions. In their formulation five assumptions are made which are representative of current network assumptions:

(1) All cells have the same synaptic delay τ and fire only at integral multiples thereof.
(2) Overall synaptic input to any cell can be expressed as an algebraic sum of excitatory and inhibitory inputs and this sum is recorded with negligible time delay.
(3) The absolute refractory period r of any cell varies between τ and 2τ.
(4) The effect of an excitatory postsynaptic potential (EPSP) or an inhibitory postsynaptic potential (IPSP) remains for a period less than τ so that summation is essentially spatial.
(5) The refractoriness of a cell at twice t is independent of the probability that it receives threshold excitation at time t.

From assumptions (3–5) the probability that a cell fires at time $t = (n + 1)\tau$, is the product of the probabilities that it is not refractory and that it receives at least threshold excitation from cells firing one synaptic delay earlier. If we also define the variable $Y_{i,n}$ as

$$Y_{i,n} = \begin{cases} 0 & \text{if the } i\text{th cell is resting at } t = n\tau, \\ 1 & \text{if the } i\text{th cell is firing at } t = n\tau, \end{cases}$$

then it can be shown for activity X_n at time $n\tau$ $(0 < X_n < 1)$

$$p(Y_{i,n+1} = 1/X_n) = (1 - X_n)p(Z_{i,n+1} \geq \theta/X_n) \quad \text{for} \quad 1 \leq i \leq N, \tag{4.13}$$

where $Z_{i,n}$ is the overall input to the ith cell at time $t = (n + 1)\tau, \theta = $ common firing threshold. From (4.13) the expected activity at time $\tau(n + 1)$, given time τn activity, is

$$E(X_{n+1}/X_n) = (1 - X_n)P(Z_{n+1} > \theta/X_n). \tag{4.14}$$

Leake and Anninos (1976) consider the case of networks with randomly interconnected elements—uniformly distributed over the constituent cell bodies. For u^+ and u^- representing the number of excitory and inhibitory axon collaterals resulting from the firing of one cell, then at time $(n + 1)\tau$ there are $N(1 - h)X_n u+$ and $Nh X_n u-$ active excitatory and inhibitory collaterals. This results in the number of EPSPs and IPSPs impinging on a cell at time $(n + 1)\tau$ having Poisson distributions with means $\lambda_1 = X_n u^+(1 - h)$ and $\lambda_2 = X_n u^- h$ respectively. Combining these two processes results in the new variable z:

$$f(z) = e^{-(\lambda_1 + \lambda_2)} \lambda_1^z \sum_{j=0}^{\infty} \frac{(\lambda_1 \lambda_2)^j}{(z + j)! j!}, \quad z = 0, 1, 2, \ldots$$

where z has mean

$$\lambda_1 - \lambda_2 = X_n[u^+(1 - h) - u^- h]$$

and variance

$$\lambda_1 + \lambda_2 = X_n[u^+(1 - h) + u^- h].$$

As X_n approaches zero so do both these expressions, indicating that zero is an equilibrium point.

In a series of reports Grossberg (1976, 1978) has applied similar analyses to more perceptual aspects of visual feature extraction, pattern discrimination, and memory. Here the concern has been with the development of neural networks, which can adapt and eventually stabilize as "mature" information processing units. We shall consider the interaction between two network regions V_1 and V_2 as done by Grossberg (1976) to exemplify the concepts.

Assume region v_1 has n elements v_{1i}, $i = 1, n$, where the input intensity $I_i(t)$ to v_{ij} depends on a specific image feature, e.g. an area of the visual field, orientation, spatial frequency, etc., v_{ii} has output response $x_{ii}(t)$. If we normalize $I_i(t)$ by

$$I = \sum_i I_i(t), \quad \theta_i = I_i/I, \tag{4.15}$$

the inputs are now relative to each other. Now when the output response of v_{1i} is divergent, i.e. propagates to more than one cell, or element, in V_2, Grossberg (see Grossberg and Levine, 1975) showed that the interactions have to be encoded in some way. The problem is that each element saturates for constant θ_i values and some form of disinhibition of regeneration is required. The network

$$\dot{x}_{1i} = -Ax_{1i} + (B - x_{1i})I_i - x_{1i}\sum_k I_k \tag{4.16}$$

represents a non-recurrent $(k \neq i)$, on-centre off-surround network $[(B - x_{1i})\,I_i - Ax_{1i}]$ undergoing shunting (mass action $x_{1i}\sum_k I_k$); x_{1i} represents the change in response $(dx/dt = \dot{x})$ over time. The response $0 \leq x_{1i}(0) \leq B$ and equilibrium conditions $\dot{x}_{1i} = 0$ reduce (14.16) to

$$x_{1i} = \theta_i \frac{BI}{A + I}.$$

Here the inhibitory inputs A and I restrict the response x_{1i}, or, as Grossberg concludes, the response adapts due to the automatic gain control of the inhibitory inputs.

The case where V_2 elements are driven by a series of V_1 elements has also been considered by Grossberg (1976). Here it is suggested that a third layer V_3 mediates the excitatory and inhibitory effects of V_2 due to the multiple V_1 inputs. The V_3 elements, in turn, are driven by divergent V_2 elements and would simply feed back a modulation signal to V_{2i} elements as to set their respective gains so that saturation would be minimized according to network forms like (4.16). In this way adaptive on-centre and off-surround structures could be established (A and B values in (4.16)).

These networks are important to consider since they attempt to relate known neurophysiological processes to perceptual function, as we shall see in Part II. Other non-linear networks have also been applied to modelling neural function—particularly those related to Volterra expansions (Palm and Poggio, 1977). However, for the moment we shall consider one clear application of network and control theory to visual function—the pupil-control system.

The pupil (in man) is controlled by two antagonistic muscles: the sphincter pupillae and the dilator pupillae, being *para*-sympathetically and sympathetically innervated respectively. Retinal illumination varies with pupil size, and thus the information transmitted along the optic nerve. However, some fibres (the pupillomotor ones) go directly to the brain stem where they innovate the Edinger–Westphal nuclei that, in turn, control the pupil size—a closed-loop system (Fig. 4.4).

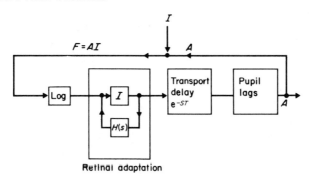

Fig. 4.4. Block diagram of the pupillary light-reflex system. (From McFarland, 1971.)

Assuming the Weber–Fechner law, retinal sensitivity is a function of the logarithm of light intensity. In addition the retina has slow dark adaptation in comparison to fast light-adaptation behaviour. This subcontrol system is shown in Fig. 4.4. A second source is the delay time in transmitting the signal through to the brain stem and back again T, such that the response

$$y(t) = x(t - T) \qquad (4.17)$$

yields Laplace transform

$$y(s) = e^{-ST} \int_{T^-}^{T^+} x(t - T)dt. \qquad (4.18)$$

Start (1959) proposed that the relationship between pupil area a and nerve signal m is

$$G_m = T^3 \frac{d^3 a}{dt^2} + 3T^2 \frac{d^2 a}{dt^2} + 3T \frac{da}{dt}, \qquad (4.19)$$

where G is the pupil gain and T is the time constant (Fig. 4.4).

Pupil-size changes can be readily measured by means of a pupillometer where infrared light is reflected from the iris onto a photocell to result in an index of pupil size in terms of the amount of reflected light. Results from Clynes (1961) indicate that a transport delay of about 250 msec accounts for the delay in pupil response. Also, that there is a response proportional to illumination changes in both direction, and a rate response sensitive only to increases in illumination.

In the above analysis the system (Fig. 4.4) was analysed as a function of time: events were analysed sequentially and various mechanisms are seen to have specific positions in the network. There is another way to analyse systems, i.e., as a function of frequency (McFarland, 1971). Frequency analysis is based on the principle that a sinusoidal input will result in another sinusoidal output if the system is linear. Phase and frequency differences between input and output waveforms reflect system features. The "amplitude ratio" (AR), being the ratio of output to input amplitudes, is one such measure of system behaviour. Of course, when frequency is varied and AR values are obtained from each frequency, this becomes the modulation transfer function (MTF) used in Fourier analysis (see Chapter 3). A similar tabulation is done with phase differences between input and output signals ϕ.

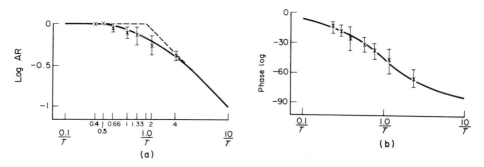

FIG. 4.5. Bode (a) relating AR (amplitude ratio of output to input) to frequencies: (b) is the Nyquist diagram relating AR to phase differences between input and output ϕ: case of animal's response rate as function of temperature, (See McFarland, 1971, p. 78.)

Bode plots and Nyquist diagrams are used to relate AR and ϕ values to frequency differences. In Bode plots logarithmic AR and linear ϕ values are plotted against logarithmic frequency values (Fig. 4.5). Consider, for example, a simple integrator k/s. For a sinusoidal input function

$$x(t) = A \sin (wt)$$

the integrator results in

$$\frac{A}{w} \sin \left(wt - \tfrac{1}{2}\pi\right)$$

or a phase shift of 90° and amplitude modulation of $1/w$. So

$$\log AR = \log k - \log w$$

is the Bode plot being a line of slope -1, intersecting the frequency axis $w = 1$. This is a first-order system. Second-order systems result in a slope of -2. This curve is called the high-frequency asymptote and its slope reflects the order of the system (McFarland, 1971). The "break frequency" is defined by extrapolating the high-frequency Bode plot to intersect with the constant low-frequency line (Fig. 4.5). The slope of this line approximates the system order and the frequency value corresponds to the "time constant" of the system $(T = 1/w)$.

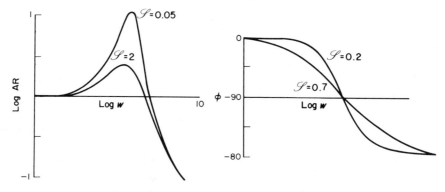

FIG. 4.6. (a) Bode, and (b) Nyquist plots for typical second-order systems with different damping ratios $\mathscr{S}$.

Second-order systems

$$H(s) = As^2 + Bs + C \qquad (4.20)$$

are usually defined by two parameters of "natural frequency" $= w = \sqrt{C/A}$ and "damping ratio" $\mathscr{S} = B/2\sqrt{A/C}$. For $B = 0$ damping is absent, and w_n reduces to $s = iw_n$ when $H(s) = 0$. The system response to a step function input is then a sine wave whose frequency is the "natural frequency" of the system. When the damping ratio $\mathscr{S}$ is less than 1 (corresponding to imaginary roots of (4.20)) the system is "underdamped"; $\mathscr{S} > 1$, it is "overdamped", taking longer for the system to stabilize on a final value. The frequency and phase responses of a typical second-order system are shown in Fig. 4.6.

In this section we have briefly dealt with network and control systems which are currently employed in modelling various functions of the visual system. However, we still employ the traditional methods of analysing data or modelling response parameters in a statistical way. This is necessary for systems evaluations. In the following section we shall deal briefly with this topic.

4.3. STATISTICAL AND PROBABILITY ANALYSES OF SYSTEMS

One essential property of systems analyses is that we can quantitatively evaluate one model against others. This involves assumptions about signal samples and response populations—the linearity and non-linearity of the system, and, above all, the application of specific statistical decision models. We shall deal with the two more common forms of analysis: the linear model (analysis of variance and regression) and decision theory.

Probably the most popular type of model posed in perception research is that a particular stimulus parameter value $S_i(t)$ (on parameter i at time t) determines a response $[R(t)]$ in such a way that all stimulus parameters combine to determine a total response

$$R(t) = \sum_{i,j=0}^{n,m} \alpha_i s_i(t) \, S_j(t) + E_n(t) \qquad (4.21)$$

for n stimulus parameters and residual error term $E_n(t)$. Typically $R(t)$ is percentage correct, reaction time, spikes per second, threshold contrast, etc.—usually a real bounded number. In addition the $S_i(t)$ terms are often equated with various treatment groups and both (R, S) parameters are converted to variance values. In this sense the total response variance (or experiment variance), by (4.21), is decomposed into group, interaction, and residual error variance as

$$\sigma_T^2 = \left[\sum_i \sigma_{A_i}^2 \right] + \left[\sum_{ij} \sigma_{A_i A_j}^2 + \sum_{ijk} \sigma_{A_i A_j A_k}^2 + \cdots + \right] + \sigma_{\text{error}}^2 \qquad (4.22)$$

or $\text{TOTAL} = \text{FACTORS} + \text{INTERACTIONS} + \text{ERROR}$

By assuming that each treatment group sample is independently drawn from a normal population (or distribution) it is possible to test statistical hypotheses as the interaction effects contribute little (or an insignificant amount) to the total variance, that factors differ in their contributions. These tests are feasible due to the fact that the ratio of two such variances from an F (Snedecor F) distribution statistic (Winer, 1971). This is called analysis of variance, and is a powerful tool or establishing the importance of specific predictor variables in performance.

Regression analysis extends (4.22) by asking the statistical question as to whether the total variance can be explained by a linear combination of individual factors, or

$$R(t) = \sum_{i=1}^{n} \alpha_i S_i(t) + \alpha_{n+1} E_{n+1}, \tag{4.23}$$

where $\alpha_i \ldots \alpha_{n+1}$ are constants and E_{n+1} corresponds to the error term or total residual error. This form of regression (4.23) is termed multiple regression, the simplest form being the linear regression equation

$$R(t) = \alpha S(t) + \beta. \tag{4.24}$$

This can be rephrased as a "least-square" problem where the squared distance between dependent y and independent or predictor x variables is minimized with respect to α, β by

$$\psi = \sum_t [y(t) - (\alpha x(t) + \beta)]^2$$

for

$$\frac{\partial \psi}{\partial \alpha} = 0, \quad \frac{\partial \psi}{\partial \beta} = 0.$$

Regression/multiple regression is a powerful data analytic model since it is linear. It is ideally suited to multivariate systems applications where, for example, a specific psychophysical response is conjected to be a linear fraction of network features, as in MTF and Bode plot functions, or stimulus parameters.

Yet in many psychophysical and neurophysiological areas of vision research the response structure involves much more than merely a predictor variable parameter value. Specifically, some decision is made or threshold reached before an overt response is recorded.

The most common form of a decision problem in perception research occurs when there are two states of the stimulus—noise N or signal-plus-noise SN, and there are just two responses—signal is present s or not n. In this context the four outcomes of hit $[p(ns/S)]$, miss $[p(n/S)]$, correct rejection $[p(n/N)]$, and false alarms $[p(S/N)]$ must be considered.

Typically the N and SN distributions, as registered in the sensory decision system, are assumed to be Gaussian as illustrated in Fig. 4.7. These are *a priori* probabilities in so far as response probabilities are contingent on their shape. If we now consider a position along the "sensory axis" (Green and Swets, 1966), then the likelihood ratio $l(x)$ is defined

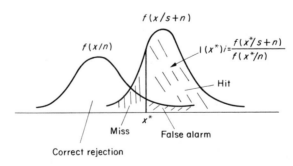

FIG. 4.7. Likelihood ratio $l(x)$ defined over signal and noise, and noise alone distributions. Notice the response types associated with each area.

as the ratio of the signal and noise function values, or

$$l(x) = \frac{f(x/s)}{f(x/n)} \tag{4.25}$$

as shown in Fig. 4.7. This line determines the four response outcomes and also reflects a criterion, even threshold value, above which a signal response occurs, and below which noise is reported.

Whereas the likelihood ratio is the ratio of the ordinates of hit and false alarm probabilities (sometimes called response criterion, or β) the other type of determinant of responses is the degree of overlap of the signal and noise distributions shown in Fig. 4.7. This is termed the sensitivity, or detectability value d', and is measured by the distance between the standardized scores for the hit and false alarm values

$$d' = z\,(\text{hits}) - z\,(\text{false alarms}) \tag{4.26}$$

or the distance between the means of the signal and noise distributions. If responses are made consistent with likelihood ratios then they are said to obey the Neyman–Pearson objective.

Under the Gaussian assumptions of signal and noise distributions, with equal variance, the relationship between hit and false alarm probabilities, as a function of different likelihood ratios, is termed the Receiver-operating-characteristic (Roc curve, Fig. 4.8).

The area of decision theory is complex and cannot be even adequately summarized here. However, two points should be noted from what has already been discussed. Firstly, most threshold techniques assume zero false alarms and are thus "high threshold" estimation methods. Secondly, it is often assumed in visual psychophysics that response probabilities $p(R)$ summate according to

$$P(R) = \left[\sum_{i=1}^{n} p_i^n(R) \right]^{1/n} \tag{4.27}$$

and is sometimes called probability summation. In decision theory this is called the

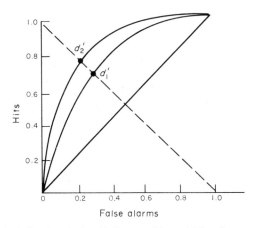

FIG. 4.8. Roc curves depicting the relationship between hits and false alarm probabilities for different criteria (likelihood ratios).

integrator model where

$$d'_t = \left[\sum_{n=1}^{n} d_i^n \right]^{1/n}$$

These models assume that (a) each detection observations are statistically independent such that the joint likelihood ratios are products of individual criterions, and, secondly, such that observes endeavour to optimize correct detection rates (see Green and Swets, 1966).

4.4 SUMMARY

We briefly conclude this chapter by noting that the technology of network theory and decision theory has applications in many areas of vision research from basic biophysical models of cell response profiles to more overt human psychophysical response systems.

REFERENCES

CLYNES, M. (1961) Unidirectional rate sensitivity: a biocybernetic law of reflex and humoral systems as physiological channels of control and communication, *Annual of New York Academy of Science* 93.

CREUTZFELDT, O. D., KHUNT, U., and BENEVENTO, L. (1974) An intracellular analysis of visual cortical neurones to moving stimuli: responses in a co-operative neuronal network, *Exp. Brain Res.*, **21**, 251–274.

GREEN, D. M. and SWEETS, J. A. (1966) *Signal Detection Theory and Psychophysics*, Wiley, Sydney.

GROSSBERG, S. (1976) Adaptive pattern classification and universal recoding: parallel development and coding of neuronal feature detectors, *Biol. Cybernetics* **23**, 121–134.

GROSSBERG, S. (1978) A theory of visual coding, memory and development. *Formal Theories of Visual Perception.* In (E. L. J. Leeuwenberg and H. F. J. M. Buffart, eds.), Wiley, New York.

GROSSBERG, S. and LEVINE, P. S. (1975) Some developmental and attentional biases in the contrast enhancement and short term memory of recurrent neural networks. *J. Theoret. Biol.*, **53**, 341–356.

HARTLINE, M. K. and GRAHAM, C. H. (1932) Nerve impulses from single receptors in the eye, *J. Cell. Comp. Physiol.* **1**, 277–295.

HARTLINE, M. K. and RATLIFF, F. (1957) Inhibitory interaction of receptor units in the eye of *Limulus.*, *J. Gen. Physiol.*, **40**, 357–376.

HUBEL, D. Y. and WIESEL, T. N. (1962) Receptive fields, binocular interaction and functional architecture in the cat's visual contex, *J. Physiol.* (*London*) **160**, 106–154.

LEAKE, B. and ANNINOS, P. A. (1976) Effects of connectivity on the activity of neuronal net models, *J. Theoret. Biol.*, **58**, 337–363.

MCFARLAND, D. J. (1971) *Feedback Mechanisms in Animal Behaviour*, Academic Press New York.

PALM, G. and POGGIO, T. (1977) Wiener-like system identification in physiology, *J. Math. Biol.*, **4**, 375–381.

RODIECK, R. (1970) *The vertebrate Retina*, Academic Press New York.

SEJNOWSKI, T. J. (1976) On global properties of neuronal interactions, *Biol. Cybenetics*, **22**, 85–95.

START, L. (1959) Stability, oscillations and noise in the human pupil servomechanism. *Proc. IRE* 47, 1925–1936.

VALVERDE, F. (1976) Aspects of critical organization related to the geometry of neurons with intra-cortical axons, *J. Neurocytol.* **5**, 509–529.

WINER, B. J. (1971) *Statistical Principles in Experimental Design*, McGraw-Hill, New York.

CHAPTER 5

Introduction to Geometric Structures

In the previous chapters we have briefly, often too briefly, considered various aspects of networks, optics, Fourier, and other transforms that are used to model processes in visual perception. However, all these languages do not contain an implicit geometry. In this chapter geometries of various types will be considered in order to fill this gap. After all, of all senses, vision is the most geometric—relating directly to distances, angles, perspective, and geometric transformations that all constitute our visual environment. That many perceptions do not accord to our simple geometric concepts, say the geometry of flat surfaces, was even noted by Euclid and further investigated by Vetruvius and others through the ages (Pedoe, 1976).

Most of us would readily agree that judgements of length, angle, and motion are "natural" to the visual components of perception. However, it is not clear whether this implies that, in visual perception, we assume that all such judgements are made with respect to an unchanging reference frame or "perceptual aether" (see Caelli et al., 1978a, for more details on this issue). Rather, it can be easily demonstrated that such geometric estimates are a function of the visual context. In particular, results from experiments on illusions of motion, angle, and length indicate that these parameters are overestimated and underestimated as specific functions of the context parameters (Robinson, 1972).

The above at least implies a changing or variable curvature geometry for visual perception and that visual space–time geometries are not all of the same kind. That is, particular geometries apply for different experiences and there is no primary and invariant geometry for visual perception. Perspective or projective geometry is relevant for judging depth and motions in depth while more metric geometries are obviously involved in judging size, length, and orientations of objects in the fronto-parallel plane. Given this situation, then, it would seem important that we know something about the various geometric systems developed over the centuries to describe different kinds of spatial events—some even directly perceptual.

So we may well ask: What is a geometry, or geometric space? The reader may respond that geometry is the study of measurement—the measurement of length, angle, and other spatial properties. Although this is true, geometry is more than that. Geometry is concerned with the study of spatial relations or relations which can be described in a formal way. It is not necessarily concerned with measurement, as we shall see with projective geometry.

Of particular interest to perceptionists, geometry is largely concerned with the study of the types of transformations that do not change the defined spatial relationship(s) between objects (object invariance). For example, we shall see that affine geometry preserves

71

FIG. 5.1. Relationships between the more common geometries.

parallelism, while projective geometry only preserves cross-ratios. In this chapter we shall review the major geometries and their interrelationships. Figure 5.1 illustrates the hierarchical order between these structures from projective to the metric Euclidean and Riemannian geometries.

The geometry we inherited from the Egyptians and Greeks was summarized by Euclid into the axiomatic system of Euclidean geometry. The postulates are five in number (Coxeter, 1962):

E_1 : *A straight line may be drawn from any point to any other point.*
E_2 : *A finite straight line may be extended continuously in a straight line.*
E_3 : *A circle may be described with any centre and any radius.*
E_4 : *All right angles are equal to one another.*
E_5 : *If a straight line meets two other straight lines so as to make the two interior angles on one side of it together less than two right angles, the other straight lines, if extended indefinitely, will meet on that side on which the angles are less than two right angles.*

The fifth postulate implies the parallel axiom:

Through any point P not on a given line ρ there exists one and only one line parallel to ρ in the plane determined by P and ρ.

From these axioms the Euclidean plane (and solid geometry) was deduced—the geometry taught to us in school and probably the only geometry that most know anything about. This is understandable due to the great correspondence between this system and physical reality itself—at least as we simply *conceive* of it. Yet exceptions to these postulates have been recognized throughout the ages and include the early observations that, under perspectives, parallel lines do meet at the horizon. Saccheri (1667–1733) had constructed an example which demonstrated that more than one (or no) line(s) can be drawn through the point P parallel to a line (being early examples of hyperbolic and elliptic geometries respectively). In fact Riemann (1826–66) realized that Saccheri's results could be made consistent with the axioms for geometry if E_1, E_2, and E_5 in the Euclidean system were replaced by:

H_1 : *Any two points determine at least one line.*
H_2 : *A line is unbounded.*
H_5 : *Any two lines in a plane will meet.*

The great circles of a sphere provide an example of such a space since they always intersect, etc. This is the elliptical space where no lines are parallel.

We shall see that in these non-Euclidean geometries various metric properties differ from the Euclidean geometry of solid objects. For example, in elliptical geometry the sum of the internal angles of a triangle is greater than 180°, while in hyperbolic geometry the sum is less than 180°. The shortest line (geodesic) between two points is not a straight line, etc. However, before dealing with such metric geometric properties we shall deal with the more abstract geometries—projective and affine. It should be noted that, in all cases, the geometry is well identified by the types of transformations that leave objects invariant, i.e. objects permitted by the geometry. If the reader can appreciate this concept, then he/she has some insight into the geometric structures.

5.2. PROJECTIVE AND AFFINE GEOMETRIES

Contrary to our concept of geometry being related to measurement, projective geometry is concerned with the properties of objects under perspective and without ruled surfaces. It is concerned with what invariances, objects, can be constructed when the geometer has simply an unscaled ruler at his disposal: no units of measurement. In Euclidean geometry objects only stay the same (are invariant) under rigid transformations—rotations and translations. With perspective views of physical objects the angles, lengths of lines, do not remain the same when projected; a circle can appear to be an ellipse and vice versa. So projective geometry does not consider the rigidity of an object. Projective geometry models projection phenomena, where, due to the optical projections, parallel lines meet at a point so that there are no parallels or measurement in terms of a coordinate system. In this sense projective geometry is sometimes termed the geometry of photography. The postulates of this geometry are simply:

P_1: *Any two distinct points determine one and only one line.*
P_2: *Any three distinct non-collinear points, also any line and a point not on the line, determine one and only one plane.*
P_3: *Any two distinct coplanar lines intersect in one and only one point.*
P_4: *Any line not in a given plane intersects the plane in one and only one point.*
P_5: *Any two distinct planes intersect in one and only one line.*

The intersection point of any two planar lines is either a "normal" point or a "point at infinity" (point on the horizon in our visual analogy). In projective geometry both types of points are treated identically and the resultant "line at infinity", defined by the points at infinity, is treated as a normal line subject to the above axioms. In this sense the plane of projective geometry is the Euclidean-augmented to include the line and points (ideal points) at infinity.

Projective points and lines (lines and planes, etc.) are interchangeable. That is, all the theorems of projective geometry are true if we interchange lines and points, etc. For example, any two distinct points determine a line and vice versa. However, a line in projective space is not limited as the Euclidean straight line. Since it has a "point at infinity" (ideal point) it can be represented by a closed circle, and the segment AB can have two senses or correspond to two arcs of the circle, as shown in Fig. 5.2.

The objects of projective geometry are any collection of points, lines, or planes, the more basic being pencils of points (lines) and projectivities. A pencil of points is simply the totality of points on a line while a projectivity is a relationship between two pencils through a set

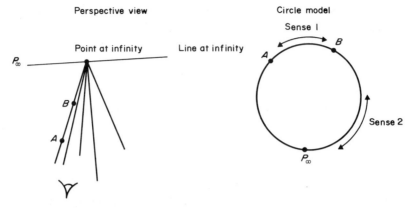

FIG. 5.2. Two senses of segment AB and the circle model for a projective line.

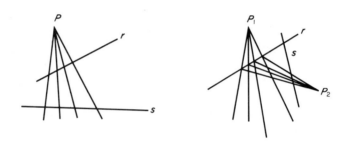

(a) Perspectivity between r, s through P (b) General projectivity between r, s through P_1, P_2

FIG. 5.3. Perspective relationships between pencils of points.

of points of projectivity (Fig. 5.3). The most elementary type of projectivity is the perspective relationship where two pencils are related through one point of perspectivity (Fig. 5.3).

In fact the "fundamental theorem" of projective geometry is a statement about projectivities. That is:

> *Given in the projective plane three distinct collinear points and another three distinct points on the same or a different line, there is only one projectivity carrying the first triple into the second.*

Other relationships between pencils of points (lines) and projectivities have been discovered. For example, for the four points (A, B, C, D) on a line there exists separate projectivities which carry $ABCD$ into $BADC$, $DCBA$, and $CDAB$.

So in projective geometry (plane, that is) the transformations consist of projections and sections, just as in Euclidean geometry the invariant transformations are rotations and translations (leaving objects rigid). When these projective transformations are applied to the segments in the Euclidean (for example) plane it is readily seen that lengths are not necessarily preserved. What is? The answer is cross-ratios.

The cross-ratio between four collinear points $(A, B; C, D)$ is defined by the segment ratios

$$(A, B; C, D) = \frac{AC}{AD} \frac{BD}{BC}, \tag{5.1}$$

and it can readily be shown that this quantity is invariant under projection and section (Ayres, 1967). For every set of four points there are six distinct cross-ratio values out of the twenty-four possible orderings. It should also be noted that a projectivity between four points (denoted by $\overline{\wedge}$)

$$(A, B, C, D) \overline{\wedge} (A', B', C', D')$$

implies equality in their cross-ratios

$$(A, B; C, D) = (A', B'; C', D),$$

and vice versa. In turn, this implies that for four points on a line there is a projectivity that will carry these four into another ordering of these same points, since

$$(A, B'; C, D) = (B, A; D, C) = (D, C; B, A) = (C, D; A, B).$$

Two of the important theorems of projective geometry are Desargues' two-triangle theorem and the theorem of Pappus given by him in the third century AD. Desargues' theorem states that:

If two coplanar triangles are perspective from a point, then they are also perspectives from a line; and, conversely.

This is illustrated in Fig. 5.4.

Whereas Desargues' theorem is concerned with plane projective geometry, Pappus'

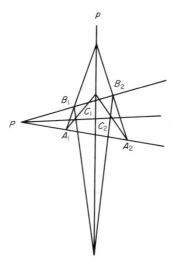

FIG. 5.4. Desargues' theorem, where triangles ABC and $A_2B_2C_2$ are perspective through P and hence the line P, and conversely.

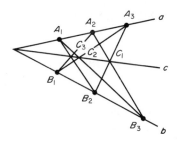

FIG. 5.5. The theorem of Pappus: C_1, C_2, and C_3 are collinear.

theorem is concerned with projective geometry between lines. The theorem states that (Fig. 5.5):

If A_1, A_2 A_3 are three distinct points on a line a; B_1, B_2, B_3 are distinct points on line b, the three points: $C_1 = A_2 B_3 \cdot A_3 B_2$; $C_2 = A_1 B_3 \cdot A_3 B_1$; $C_3 = A_1 B_2 \cdot A_2 B_1$ are collinear.

Other relationships between points on projective lines are important. For example, an involution is a property of projectivities where correspondences are reciprocal (points A, A' in Fig. 5.6). That is, consider a projectivity

$$p(A, B, C, \ldots) \overline{\wedge} p(A', B', C', \ldots)$$

between points on the same line p, then if we have

$$p(A, B, C, \ldots) \overline{\wedge} p(B', A', C', \ldots),$$

the projectivity is called an involution. Consider Fig. 5.6. There

$$p(A'_1, B_1, B'_1, C_1) \overset{P_1}{\overline{\wedge}} p(A', B, B', C),$$

where $\overline{\wedge}$ denotes perspectivity. Now let $P_2 = B' B \cdot A' P, P_3 = B' C_1 \cdot A' P$ and $C' = B_1 P_3 \cdot p$. Then

$$(A, A', B_1, B', C) \overset{P_1}{\overline{\wedge}} (A, A'_1, B_1, B'_1, C_1) \overset{B_1}{\overline{\wedge}} (A', A'_1, P_2, P_1, P_3) \overset{B_1}{\overline{\wedge}} (A', A, B', B, C').$$

So here $A \leftrightarrow A', B \leftrightarrow B', C \leftrightarrow C'$, indicating that $(A A')$, $(B B')$ are reciprocal in the projectivity.

A related structure in projective geometry is that of the harmonic set. Consider the four

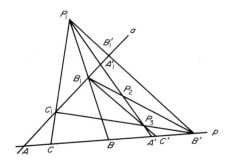

FIG. 5.6. An involution on the line p with two reciprocal pairs (A, A'), (B, B').

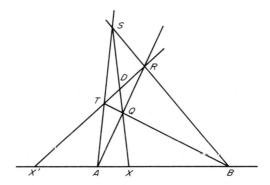

FIG. 5.7. Harmonic set $(A, B; X, X')$ determined by the quadrangle $QRST$.

points $QRST$ in Fig. 5.7 (a complete quadrangle). The set $H(A, B; X, X')$ is called an harmonic set where X separates A and B and B separates X and X'. It can be seen that the sets of points (A, B, X, X') form an involution having double points (A, B). That is

$$(A, B, X, X') \barwedge (A, B; X', X).$$

When there are two double points ($A \leftrightarrow A, B \leftrightarrow B$), the involution is termed hyperbolic.

The point about what we have just discussed is that the initial five axioms of projective geometry can be extended to ten and the fundamental theorem can be proved without using the extended Euclidean plane as a model. That is, axioms 1–5 and the Euclidean plane are required in conjunction with the "line at infinity" to prove the theorem that:

For three distinct collinear points A, B, C and another three such points A', B', C' on the same, or another, line—there is one and only one projectivity which carries triples into triples.

These additional axioms are:

P_6 :   *If two triangles are perspective from a point, they are perspective from a line.*
P_7 :   *Diagonal points of a complete quadrangle are never collinear (see points A, B, D in Fig. 5.7).*
P_8 :   *If $H(A, B; X, X')$ then the point pairs A, B and X, X' separate each other.*
P_9 :   *If the pairs of points A, B and D, E separate each other, then A, B, D, E are distinct points.*
P_{10} :   *If the pairs A, B and D, E_1 separate each other and if the pairs A, E_1 and B, E_2 separate each other, then the pairs A, B and D, E_2 separate each other.*

It can also be shown (Ayres, 1967) that a one-to-one correspondence between the real number system and projective lines can be established by means of harmonic set constructions.

Whereas projectivities are determined by three points correspondences, conics are uniquely determined by five points, since the conic is generated from the intersection of two non-perspective projectivities having thus two centres of projectivities and three other intersections, which uniquely determine the projectivity—and conic.

It is possible to establish coordinate systems for the projective plane by choosing a

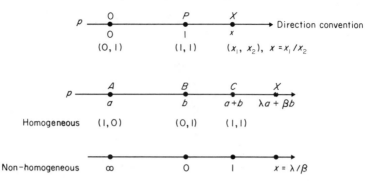

FIG. 5.8. Homogeneous and non-homogeneous coordinate systems on a projective line.

fundamental element as the point and line. Projective coordinates are defined on the line (say) by choosing a zero point (0) and a direction convention on p. This involves selecting two points 0 and p with coordinates 0 and 1 respectively (Fig. 5.8). What is termed the *non-homogeneous* coordinate of a point X is the directed distance of X from 0. In turn, a *homogeneous system* on p may be established by assigning coordinates $(0, 1)$ to 0 and $(1, 1)$ to p, and to the point X the coordinates (x_1, x_2) such that $x_1/x_2 = X$, the x distance from 0 (Fig. 5.8).

In this sense the relative homogeneous projective coordinates of any point $X:(x)$ on p are (α, β) for $(x) = \alpha(a) + \beta(b)$, where (a) corresponds to A, (b) to B being two other distinct points. The relative non-homogeneous projective coordinate of the same point is $x = \alpha/\beta$. It should be noted that here we do not have a uniform coordinate system for the total projective plane. Since A and B correspond to $(1, 0)$ and $(0, 1)$ there is always a third point C having coordinates $(1, 1)$.

The cross-ratio of any four points on a line is independent of the coordinate system established on the line (Coxeter, 1961). Any two lines in the projective plane have coordinates defined by (A, B, C) and (A', B', C') respectively. If there is a projectivity between both pencils, then for the pair X on p, X' on p', the cross ratios are equal:

$$(A, B; C, X) = (A', B'; C', X').$$

That is,

$$\frac{a-c}{a-x}\frac{b-x}{b-c} = \frac{a'-c'}{a'-x'}\frac{b'-x'}{b'-c'}$$

and for

$$s = \frac{a-c}{b-c}, \quad s'_1 = \frac{a'-c'}{b'-c'},$$

$$\alpha = sa' - s'b', \quad \beta = ab's' - a'bs,$$

$$\gamma = s - s, \quad \delta = as' - bs,$$

we obtain

$$x' = (\alpha x + \beta)/(\gamma x + \delta). \tag{5.2}$$

This is termed the projective transformation, being a linear transformation where $\alpha\delta - \gamma\beta \neq 0$, and preserving cross-ratios.

If the lines p (containing X) and p' (containing X') coincide, then the projective transform may be interpreted as a transformation of coordinates such that points do not change (passive or alias transform), or, as a transformation of points into other points (x to x') of the same line (active or alibi transformation). This latter interpretation is called a collineation that has at least one point that does not change — $M : \infty$ is always a double point.

When $x' = x$ we obtain

$$x_1 = \frac{(a-d) + \sqrt{(d-a)^2 + 4bc}}{2c}, \quad x_2 = \frac{(a-d) - \sqrt{(d-a)^2 + 4bc}}{2c}.$$

For $(d-a)^2 + 4bc > 0$ there are two distinct double points and the projectivity is termed hyperbolic. For $(d-a)^2 + 4bc = 0$ it is parabolic and for $(d-a)^2 + 4bc < 0$ it is elliptical, having no real double points.

Similarly, an involution occurs if and only if $a + d = 0$. This reduces the projective transform to

$$fx'x + g(x' + x) + h = 0, \quad g^2 - fh \neq 0,$$

and hence is determined by any two reciprocal pairs of points.

Homogeneous point coordinates can be introduced to the projective plane by taking four points no three of which are collinear. We choose $A_1 : (a)$, $A_2 : (b)$, $A_3 : (c)$, $A_4 : (a + b + c)$. A_1 to A_3 are termed the triangle of reference, fixed by A_4 — the unit point. So A_1, A_2, A_3, A_4 may assume relative coordinates $(1, 0, 0)$, $(0, 1, 0)$, $(0, 0, 1)$, $(1, 1, 1)$, and any planar point $Y : (y)$ has coordinates $(y) = \alpha(a) + \beta(b) + \gamma(c)$. The projective transform is

$$x' = \frac{ax + by + c}{dx + ey + f}, \quad y' = \frac{gx + hy + i}{dx + ey + f}, \tag{5.3}$$

and consequently three pairs of non-collinear points determine the planar projectivity. This transform preserves collinearities and cross-ratios.

The planar projective transformations are either parallel or central depending on whether the projectivity is from a point at infinity or from a normal planar point, respectively. Such transforms preserve the following properties:

(a) collinearities;
(b) cross-ratios;
(c) rectilinearity of shapes;
(d) conics — conics are transformed into conics.

Hence the "identity" of an object, i.e. its rigid features, are not necessarily preserved.

Perhaps the most useful form of the planar projection transformation of any three-dimensional configuration onto a projective plane (x', y') is

$$\begin{bmatrix} x' \\ y' \end{bmatrix} = [r - f] \begin{bmatrix} x/(r - z) \\ y/(r - z) \end{bmatrix}$$

where (x, y, z) is a point in three-dimensional Euclidean space, (x', y') is the projected position on projection plane, f is the distance of projection plane from origin, and r is the distance of point of projectivity from origin. This is illustrated in Fig. 5.9.

Affine geometry is derived from projective geometry by, as in Euclidean geometry,

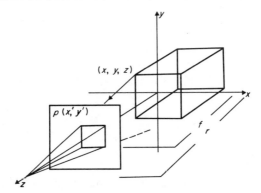

FIG. 5.9. Reference system for the projection of three dimensional objects onto a projection plane p.

separating lines and points of infinity from other planar points. This permits the definition of parallel lines, as we know it, and consequently, in affine geometry, segments between parallel lines may be compared. Affine transformations so preserve:

(a) segments;
(b) parallel lines;
(c) angles;
(d) n-sided polygons;
(e) pairs of equal vectors;
(f) ratios of areas between any two triangles.

All triangles are affinely equivalent and measurement is strictly unidimensional.

However, the relationships between projective, affine, and Euclidean geometries are readily seen in the following algebraic representations.

The general projective transformation can be represented in non-homogeneous coordinates by

$$\begin{aligned} x'_1 \\ x'_2 = \\ x'_3 \end{aligned} \begin{bmatrix} e_{11} & e_{12} & e_{13} \\ e_{21} & e_{22} & e_{23} \\ e_{31} & e_{32} & e_{33} \end{bmatrix} \begin{bmatrix} x_1 \\ x_2 \\ x_3 \end{bmatrix} \qquad (5.4)$$

or $X' = EX$, where E is a matrix whose determinant $\neq 0 (|E| \neq 0)$, i.e. E is non-singular. When $e_{31} = e_{32} = 0$ the transformation is called a collineation. When

$$X' = \begin{bmatrix} x'_1 \\ x'_2 \\ x'_3 \end{bmatrix} = \begin{bmatrix} e_{11} & 0 & e_{13} \\ 0 & e_{11} & e_{23} \\ 0 & 0 & e_{33} \end{bmatrix}, \quad e_{11} - e_{33} \neq 0, \qquad (5.5)$$

the transformation is an homology when $e_{11} \neq e_{33}$, and an elation for $e_{11} = e_{33}$. All are subgroups[†] of the projective transformation group.[‡]

[†] The determinant of a matrix E above is defined by

$$|E| = e_{11}(e_{22}e_{33} - e_{32}e_{23}) - e_{12}(e_{21}e_{33} - e_{31}e_{23}) + e_{13}(e_{21}e_{32} - e_{31}e_{22}).$$

When E is such that $|E| \neq 0$, there is an inverse transformation.

[‡] See section 5.6.

Since in affine geometry the line at infinity is removed from the projective plane, then the collineation in homogeneous form ($e_{31} = e_{32} = 0$) becomes

$$x' = a_{11}x + a_{12}y + a_{13}, \quad \begin{vmatrix} a_{11} & a_{12} \\ a_{21} & a_{22} \end{vmatrix} \neq 0, \qquad (5.6)$$
$$y' = a_{21}x + a_{22}y + a_{23},$$

the affine transformation. For

$$x' = ax + b_1, \quad a \neq 0,$$
$$y' = ay + b_2,$$

the affine transformation is called a *homothetic* transformation containing dilations a and translations b. Similar triangles are homothetic.

Whereas affine geometry preserves parallels, Euclidean transformations preserve parallels and perpendiculars and, of course, rigidity. It can be shown (Ayres, 1967) that these rigid transforms reduce to (from 5.6)

$$x' = ax - by + c \quad a^2 + b^2 = 1.$$
$$y' = bx + ay + d$$

or, in explicit form, for rotation θ in the plane, and translations c, d,

$$x' = x \cos\theta - y \sin\theta + c, \quad y' = x \sin\theta + y \cos\theta + d.$$

5.3. VECTOR ANALYSIS AND METRICS

Before discussing the usual metric geometries we should review some of the more import-ant properties of vectors and metrics. We shall stick largely to two- and three-dimensional Euclidean spaces (E^2, E^3, respectively), but all the following properties may be applied to n-dimensional spaces.

We can all probably remember that vectors have magnitude and direction; and we represent them as ordered numbers $(x_1, x_2, x_3) = X$ in E^3, having magnitude $\|X\| = \sqrt{x_1^2 + x_2^2 + x_3^2}$. However, vectors have many more properties; in particular they form an abelian group under scalar multiplication and vector addition, since for any three vectors A, B, C and scalars α, β, γ (a scalar is simply a constant or real number):

(i) $A + B = B + A$.
(ii) $(A + B) + C = A + (B + C)$.
(iii) $\alpha(A + B) = \alpha A + \alpha B$.
(iv) $\alpha(\beta A) = \alpha \beta A$.
(v) $(\alpha + \beta)A = \alpha A + \beta A$.
(vi) $\|\alpha A\| = |\alpha| \|A\|$.

The unit vector $\mathbf{u}_A$ is defined by $A/\|A\|$, thus guaranteeing that its magnitude is unity. The graphical representation of these vector properties are illustrated in Fig. 5.10.

Vectors are what is termed linearly dependent if there exists scalars $\alpha_1 \dots \alpha_n$, not all zero, such that

$$\alpha_1 \mathbf{A}_1 + \dots + \alpha_n \mathbf{A}_n = 0.$$

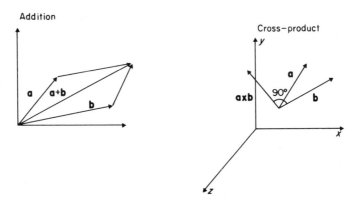

FIG. 5.10. Vectors and their properties.

These vectors are linearly independent if they are not linearly dependent, or (5.20) implies $\alpha_1 = \alpha_2 = \ldots = \alpha_n = 0$.

In order to generate any vector in E^3 (or E^n) it is necessary to construct three independent vectors such that any vector can be derived from a linear combination of these "basis" vectors. In this case $e_1 = (1, 0, 0)$, $e_2 = (0, 1, 0)$, $e_3 = (0, 0, 1)$ is the usual basis, since $\mathbf{X}$ (any vector) can be obtained by

$$\mathbf{X} = \alpha e_1 + \beta e_1 + \beta e_2 + \gamma e_3,$$

The basis is "orthonormal" if $\| e_i \| = 1$, $i = 1, 3$; and $e_i e_j = 0, i \neq j$. In this sense the dimensionality of a vector space is equal to the number of independent vectors.

Vectors can be "multiplied" in two different ways—each having a different geometric interpretation. The first, dot or scalar product of two vectors $\mathbf{A} = (a_1, a_2, a_3)$, $\mathbf{B} = (B_1, b_2, b_3)$, is a scalar

$$A \cdot B = a_1 b_1 + a_2 b_2 + a_3 b_3 .$$

and it satisfies:

(i) $A \cdot A = \| A \|^2 \geq 0$, is positive definite ($= 0$ if and only if $\mathbf{A} = \mathbf{0}$).
(ii) $A \cdot B = B \cdot A$.
(iii) $(\alpha A)B = \alpha(AB) = A(\alpha B)$.
(iv) $A(B + C) + AB + AC$.
(v) $AB = \| A \| \cdot \| B \| \cos \theta$; and, finally, it satisfies the Cauchy–Schwartz inequality
(vi) $\| AB \| \leq \| A \| \cdot \| B \|$.

Property (v) indicates that the dot product represents the scalar projection of A onto B since it equals $(A \cdot B)/|B|$. Secondly, perpendicular (orthogonal) vectors have zero dot product, $A \cdot B = 0$.

The second type of product is called the cross (or vector) product defined by

$$\mathbf{A} \times \mathbf{B} = (a_2 b_3 - a_3 b_2)e_1 + (a_1 b_3 - a_3 b_1)e_2 + (a_1 b_2 - a_2 b_1)e_3 .$$

For $\| \cdot \|$ representing magnitude of a vector, the following cross-ratio properties may be found:

(i) $\| A \times B \| = A \| \cdot \| B \| \sin \theta$, θ being the angle between the two vectors.
(ii) $A \times B = - B \times A$.

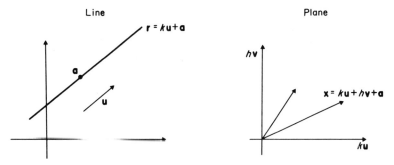

FIG. 5.11. The line $\mathbf{x} = k\mathbf{u} + \mathbf{a}$ through $\mathbf{a}$ parallel to $\mathbf{u}$; and the plane $\mathbf{x} = k\mathbf{u} + h\mathbf{v} + \mathbf{a}$.

(iii) $A \times (B + C) = A \times B + A \times C$.
(iv) $(\alpha A) \times B = \alpha(A \times B)$.
 (v) $A \times A = 0$.
(vi) $A \times B = 0$ if and only if A and B are linearly dependent.

Both scalar and cross products are related as follows:

$$A \cdot B \times C = C \cdot A \times B = B \cdot C \times A = A \times B \cdot C = -(B \cdot A \times C)$$
$$= -(C \cdot B \times A) = -(A \cdot C \times B).$$

This is sometimes called the mixed or triple product. The product $A \cdot B \times C$ is zero only if the three vectors are linearly dependent.

Consider the lines in Fig. 5.11. Here the line x through $\mathbf{a}$ parallel to $\mathbf{u}$ can be represented by

$$\mathbf{x} = k\mathbf{u} + \mathbf{a} \quad \text{for} \quad -\infty < k < \infty,$$

where k-values determine specific positions along the curve. This is called the parametric equation of a straight line. The two-parameter equation of a plane becomes (Fig. 5.11)

$$\mathbf{x} = k\mathbf{u} + h\mathbf{v} + \mathbf{a}.$$

However, the properties of curves and surfaces will be discussed in detail in the following two sections.

5.4. SOME PROPERTIES OF CURVES

In general, a curve in three-dimensional Euclidean space is defined by

$$f(u) = f_1(u)e_1 + f_2(u)e_2 + f_3(u)e_3, \tag{5.7}$$

where $f_i(u)$ are scalar functions assuming different values at each point u of the curve (Fig. 5.12).

The slope, or derivative, of such a vector function is defined by

$$f'(u) = \lim_{\Delta u \to 0} \frac{f(u + \Delta u) - f(u)}{\Delta u}. \tag{5.8}$$

In this way the properties of differentiation, or the calculus, can be applied to vector functions. For example, the tangent (vector) to a curve is

$$f'(u) = \frac{df}{du} = \left(\frac{df_1(u)}{du}, \quad \frac{df_2(u)}{du}, \quad \frac{df_3(u)}{du} \right) \tag{5.9}$$

and the unit tangent vector is

$$t(u) = f'(u)/\|f'(u)\|, \tag{5.10}$$

where $\|f'(u)\|$ corresponds to the magnitude of the slope vector.

For example, the tangent vector to a circle of radius r:

$$\mathbf{X}(u) = (r \cos u, r \sin u)$$

is

$$\mathbf{X}'(u) = (-r \sin u, r \cos n)$$

having unit tangent vector

$$\mathbf{t}(u) = \mathbf{X}'(u)/\sqrt{r^2 \sin^2 u + r^2 \cos^2 u},$$

so,

$$\mathbf{t}(u) = (-\sin u, \cos u).$$

Whereas tangents deal with the slope, or rate of change of position, curvature encodes the rate of change of slope with respect to arc length. That is, the curvature vector is defined by

$$\mathbf{k}(u) - \mathbf{t}'(u) = \frac{d\mathbf{t}(u)}{du}. \tag{5.11}$$

This is a vector whose magnitude is the curvature (Fig. 5.12)

$$K(u) = \|\mathbf{k}(u)\|. \tag{5.12}$$

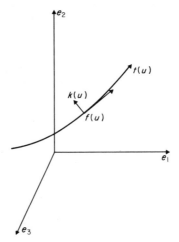

FIG. 5.12. Parametric form of a curve $f(a)$ with respect to the coordinate system (e_1, e_2, e_3) showing tangent $(t(u))$ and curvature $(k(u))$ vectors.

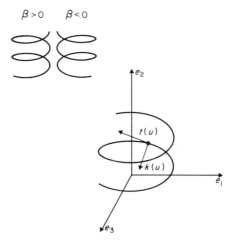

FIG. 5 13. Tangent and curvature vectors for helix. The helix is left-handed for $\beta < 0$, right-handed for $\beta > \lambda 0$.

The reciprocal of curvature is called the radius of curvature,

$$\rho(u) = 1/K(u).$$

When $k(u) = 0$, u is called a point of inflection where curvature is really undefined.

Consider the helix (Fig. 5.13):

$$X(a) = (\alpha \cos u)e_1 + (\alpha \sin u)e_2 + \beta u e_3, \quad \alpha > 0, \quad \beta \neq 0. \tag{5.13}$$

The derivative is $\mathbf{X}'(u) = (-\alpha \sin u, \alpha \cos u, \beta)$

having the unit tangent vector

$$\mathbf{t}(u) = (-\alpha \sin u, \alpha \cos u, \beta)/\sqrt{\alpha^2 + \beta^2},$$

and curvature vector

$$\frac{dt(u)}{du} \bigg/ \left\| \frac{dX(u)}{du} \right\| = \frac{-\alpha}{\alpha^2 + \beta^2}(\cos u, \sin u, 0),$$

where tangent and curvature vectors are perpendicular (orthogonal)—as always (Fig. 5.13).

The curvature vector continuously varies along a curve but as a point of inflection it is not defined. Here the unit curvature vector

$$U_k(u) = \mathbf{k}(u)/K(u)$$

is replaced by a vector parallel to $k(u)$ called the principal normal $n(u)$, where (usually)

$$\mathbf{k}(u) = K(u)\,\mathbf{n}(u). \tag{5.14}$$

Since $\mathbf{n}(u)$ and $\mathbf{t}(u)$ are orthogonal, their cross-product, defined as the binormal vector

$$\mathbf{b}(u) = \mathbf{t}(u) \times \mathbf{n}(u), \tag{5.15}$$

gives three orthogonal vectors: $[\mathbf{t}(u), \mathbf{n}(u), \mathbf{b}(u)]$ known as the right-handed orthonormal triple or moving trihedron of a curve (Fig. 5.14). The vector pairs (t, n), (t, b), and (n, b) form the osculating, rectifying, and normal planes respectively (Fig. 5.14).

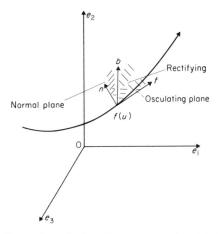

FIG. 5.14. The moving trihedron of a curve at each point of the curve.

The torsion of a curve is the rate of departure of a curve from its osculating plane— sometimes conceived of as the rate of change of curvature or screw action of a curve. It is defined by

$$\tau(u) = -\mathbf{b}'(u)\,\mathbf{n}(u)$$

or, generally,

$$\tau(u) = -\mathbf{b}'(u)\,(\mathbf{k}(u)/K(u)),$$

where $\mathbf{b}(u)$ is the binormal and $\mathbf{k}(u)$ the curvature vectors. The torsion vector is independent of direction. It is also zero for all planar curves. A classical example of two curves which differ only in torsion is the helix. A left-handed helix and a right-handed helix are represented from (5.13) by $\beta < 0$ and $\beta > 0$, respectively. We have already seen that these two conditions result in identical curvatures. However, torsion is derived by

$$t(u) = \frac{1}{\sqrt{\alpha^2 + \beta^2}}(\beta \sin u, -\beta \cos u, \alpha)$$

and

$$b'(u) = \frac{1}{\alpha^2 + \beta^2}(\beta \cos u, \beta \sin u, 0),$$

where

$$\tau(u) = -b'(u)\,n(u) = \beta/(\alpha^2 + \beta^2).$$

It can be shown that once tangents, curvature, and torsion parameters of a curve are known, then the curve is completely (uniquely) specified (Coxeter, 1961). These vectors are also related by the Serret–Frenet equations:

$$\begin{aligned}
t' &= kn, \\
n' &= -kt + \tau b, \\
b' &= -\tau n.
\end{aligned} \qquad (5.16)$$

So it is these local geometric features of slope, curvature, and torsion that define a curve.

As will be shown in Part II, these exact vector quantities are not always encoded unequivocally in contour perception, and it is this equivocation that may be at the basis of many effects in depth and motion perception.

5.5. PROPERTIES OF SURFACES

We have seen that a curve has a one-parameter representation:

$$\mathbf{X}(u) = X_1(u)e_1 + X_2(u)e_2 + X_3(u)e_3.$$

In Fig. 5.15 we show how when this same parametrization is changed to two variables we obtain a surface.

Here the surface $X(u, v)$ has the parametric form

$$X(u, v) = X_1(u, v)e_1 + X_2(u, v)e_2 + X_3(u, v)e_3$$

such that each coefficient has at least a non-zero first derivative in each parameter. This guarantees smoothness and continuity of the surface to some degree[†]. If the surface coefficients have non-zero derivatives up to order m, then the surface is called a surface of class C^m. We should also note the relationship between the parameter space and the surface itself. Since u, v are independent they can be represented as two axes as shown in Fig. 5.15, and a motion (rectilinear) in this space corresponds to a motion on the surface in the "embedding" Euclidean space E^3.

The sphere, illustrated in Fig. 5.15, has the parametric form

$$X(\theta, \phi) = (\cos \theta \sin \phi)e_1 + (\sin \theta \sin \phi)e_2 + (\cos \phi)e_3 \tag{5.17}$$

and has θ-parameter and ϕ-parameter curves as shown.

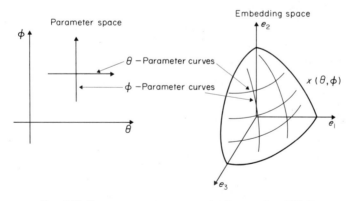

FIG. 5.15. Two-parameter representation for a surface $X(\theta, \phi)$,

[†] Other conditions are also necessary. One, in particular, is that the rank of matrix $M = 2$, i.e.

$$\text{rank} (M) = \text{rank} \begin{bmatrix} \partial X_1/\partial u & \partial X_1/\partial u \\ \partial X_2/\partial u & \partial X_2/\partial u \\ \partial X_3/\partial u & \partial X_3/\partial u \end{bmatrix} = 2.$$

$Xu = \partial x/\partial u$ corresponds to the rate of change of the vector function $X(u, v)$ only with respect to the parameter u. This is called the partial derivative of $X(u, v)$.

We now consider a curve on the surface $X(u, v)$ as being a one-parameter form $X[u(s), v(s)] = Y(s)$. Since $Y(S)$ is on the surface it is of the same class C^m as the surface. The non-zero vector $\mathbf{T}$ is *tangent* to the surface at a point p if there is a regular curve $Y(s)$ on the surface at p such that $T = dY\,ds$. But since $Y(s) = X[u(s), v(s)]$ it can be readily seen that T must be a linear combination of the two derivatives (independent)

$$X_u = \partial X/\alpha u, \quad X_v = \partial X/\alpha v$$

or

$$T = X_u \frac{du}{ds} + X_v \frac{dv}{ds}$$

as shown in Fig. 5.16. This is called the tangent plane at p.
The tangent plane at p has the general form

$$Y = X + hX_u + kX_v, \quad -\infty < h, k < \infty. \tag{5.18}$$

As with the unit normal to a curve, we can define the *unit normal vector* to a surface, at p, by

$$N = \frac{X_u \times X_v}{\| X_u \times X_v \|}. \tag{5.19}$$

This results in the normal line

$$Y = X + kN, \quad -\infty < k < \infty$$

as illustrated in Fig. 5.16.

Again, consider the sphere (5.17). Here the tangent plane assumes the form

$$
\begin{aligned}
Y(h, k) &= X(\theta, \phi) + hX_\theta(\theta, \phi) + kX_\phi(\theta, \phi) \\
&= (\cos\theta\sin\phi, \sin\theta\sin\phi, \cos\phi) + h(-\sin\theta\sin\phi, \cos\theta\sin\phi, 0) \\
&\quad + k(\cos\theta\cos\phi, \sin\theta\cos\phi, -\sin\phi), \\
Y &= (\cos\theta\sin\phi - h\sin\theta\sin\phi + k\cos\theta\cos\phi, \sin\theta\sin\phi \\
&\quad - h\cos\theta\sin\phi + k\sin\theta\cos\phi, \cos\phi - k\sin\phi).
\end{aligned}
$$

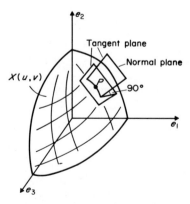

FIG. 5.16. Tangent and normal planes to a surface $X(u, v)$.

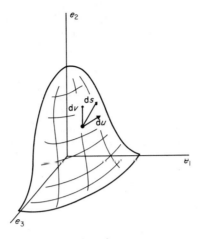

FIG. 5.17. The local metric of a surface ds^2 and its associated fundamental form.

The normal plane

$$N = \frac{X_\theta \times X_\phi}{\| X_\theta \times X_\phi \|}$$

becomes

$$N = (- \sin \phi \cos \theta, - \sin \phi \sin \theta, - \cos \phi).$$

Just as a curve in E^3 is determined uniquely by curvature and torsion vectors, so a surface is determined by two local properties called the first and second fundamental forms. As shown in Fig. 5.17, the quantity

$$dX . dX = (x_u\, du + X_v\, dv)(X_u\, du + X_v\, d_v)$$

determines the local metric

$$ds^2 = E\, du^2 + 2F\, du\, dv + G\, dv^2, \tag{5.20}$$

where

$$E(u, v) = X_u X_u, \quad F(u, v) = X_u X_v, \quad G(u, v) = X_v X_v.$$

The term $EG\text{-}F^2$ is always greater than zero and equal to $\| X_u \times X_v \|^2$. This implies that ds^2 is *positive definite*. This first fundamental form represents a local infinitesimal distance on the surface S from a point p and is the basis for Riemann geometry. It is possible to determine arc lengths, areas, and angle between u- and v-parameter curves as:

arc length is

$$L = \int_a^b \left\| \frac{dX}{ds} \right\| ds = \int_a^b \left[E\left(\frac{du(s)}{ds}\right)^2 + 2F\left(\frac{du}{ds} - \frac{dv}{s}\right) + G\left(\frac{dv(s)}{ds}\right)^2 \right]^{1/2} ds; \tag{5.21}$$

surface area is

$$A = \int\int_W \sqrt{EG - F^2}\, du\, dv, \tag{5.22}$$

where W is the region in the parameter plane which maps onto the region of the surface. Finally, if β is the angle between the u- and v-parameter curves, i.e. the angle between X_u and X_v, then it can be shown that

$$\cos \beta = F/\sqrt{EG}. \qquad (5.23)$$

Consequently, u- and v-parameter curves are perpendicular only if at the point (u, v) on the surface $F(u, v) = 0$.

Whereas the first fundamental form is defined parallel to the tangent plane, the second fundamental form is determined by the unit normal (5.19). The derivative of the unit normal dN is

$$dN = N_u\,du + N_v\,dv,$$

which is parallel to the tangent plane. The quantity $-dX\,dN$ is thus

$$-dX\,dN = -(X_u\,du + X_v\,dv)(N_u\,du + N_v\,dv)$$

or

$$\text{II} = L\,du^2 + 2M\,du\,dv + N\,dv^2, \qquad (5.24)$$

where

$$L(u,v) = -X_u\,N_u, \quad M(u,v) = -\tfrac{1}{2}(X_u\,N_v + X_v\,N_u), \quad N = -X_v\,N_v.$$

II is termed the second fundamental form of the surface S, which stays the same under transformations that preserve the direction of N. Alternate expressions for L, M, N are

$$L = X_{uu}\,N, \quad M = X_{uv}\,N, \quad \text{and} \quad N = X_{vv}\,N,$$

Indicating more directly the orthogonal relationship between the first and second fundamental forms.

The function II (5.24) is called the osculating paraboloid as well as the second fundamental form, since the sign of $LN - M^2$ determines many local properties of the surface. In particular the elliptic $(LN - M^2 > 0)$, hyperbolic $(LN - M^2 < 0)$, and parabolic $(LN - M^2 = 0)$ cases are illustrated in Fig. 5.18. The planar case occurs when $L = M = N = 0$. Of particular interest is the hyperbolic case where the curvature differs at p as a function of whether the u- or v-parameter rulings are employed.

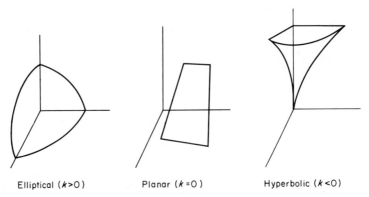

Elliptical $(k > 0)$ Planar $(k = 0)$ Hyperbolic $(k < 0)$

FIG. 5.18. Surfaces—their fundamental forms and (Gaussian) curvatures.

The issue of surface curvature is of great importance in metric geometries, and various curvature measures have been developed over the past two centuries. These we will simply define:

a) Normal curvature

This is the projection of the curvature vector of a curve onto the normal to the surface, or

$$k_n = (kN)N.$$

The actual normal curvature $K_n = kN$.

b) Principal curvature

This refers to the two perpendicular directions for which the values of the normal curvature K_n takes on maximum and minimum values.

c) Gaussian and mean curvature

The principal curvature values are determined from the solutions of

$$(EG - F^2)k^2 - (EN + GL - 2FM)k + (LN - m^2) = 0$$

for (E, F, G) and (L, M, N) as coefficients of the first and second fundamental forms. Now by dividing (5.25) by $(EG - F^2)$ we obtain

$$k^2 - 2HK + k = 0, \tag{5.25}$$

where

$$H_M = \frac{1}{2}(k_1 + k_2) = \frac{EN + GL - 2FM}{2(EG - F^2)}$$

and

$$K_G = k_1 k_2 = \frac{LN - M^2}{EF - G^2}. \tag{5.26}$$

H_M and K_G are termed the mean and Gaussian curvatures at each point of a surface.

It can be shown (Coxeter, 1961) that the surface is: (1) elliptical only if $K_G > 0$, (2) planar only if $K_G = 0$, and (3) hyperbolic only if $K_G < 0$. Whereas the Gaussian curvature determines uniquely the local curvature of a surface, the Gauss–Weingarten equations show that a surface is uniquely determined once the first and second fundamental terms (E, F, G, L, M, N) are known at each point. This is the analogous condition to curvature and torsion determinants of curves as in the Serret–Frenet equations (5.16).

The final concepts we wish to deal with in this section is that of geodesics or arcs of minimum length between two points of a surface. We understand, even define, the geodesic through the fourth curvature vector:

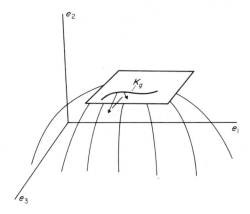

FIG. 5.19. The geodesic curvature vector K_g determined by the curvature vector of the projected curve on the tangent plane.

(d) *Geodesic curvature*

Consider Fig. 5.19. The curvature vector, at point p, of the projection of the curve C onto the tangent plane at p, is called the geodesic curvature vector of C at p (denoted by K_g).

A curve whose geodesic curvature is zero is a geodesic (line). So geodesics are simply the curves between two points whose geodesic curvatures are zero at all positions between the points. This can be alternatively stated by the following equations. For a curve $X(s) = X[u(s), v(s)]$ to be geodesic on a surface it must satisfy

$$\frac{d^2u}{ds^2} + T'_{11}\left(\frac{du}{ds}\right)^2 + 2T'_{12}\frac{du}{ds}\frac{dv}{ds} + T'_{22}\left(\frac{dv}{ds}\right)^2 = 0, \tag{5.27}$$

$$\frac{d^2v}{ds^2} + T^2_{11}\left(\frac{du}{ds}\right)^2 + 2T^2_{12}\frac{du}{ds}\frac{dv}{ds} + T^2_{22}\left(\frac{dv}{ds}\right)^2 = 0,$$

where

$T^i_{jk} \equiv$ Christoffel symbols of the second kind (second-order tensors);

$$T^1_{11} = \frac{GE_u - FF_u + FE_v}{2(EG - F^2)}; \quad T^1_{12} = \frac{GE_v - FG_u}{2(EG - F^2)}; \quad T^1_{22} = \frac{2GF_v - GG_u - FG_v}{2(EG - F^2)};$$

$$T^2_{11} = \frac{2EF_u - EE_v + FE_u}{2(EG - F^2)}; \quad T^2_{12} = \frac{EG_u - FE_v}{2(E.G. - F^2)}; \quad T^2_{22} = \frac{EG_v - 2FF_v + FG_u}{2(EG - F^2)}.$$

So in this section we have reviewed some of the important local properties of curves and surfaces that are used to uniquely define their shapes. We have seen the similarity between curvature and torsion features of curves and the first and second fundamental forms of surfaces. However, we have not considered how these various properties change or are preserved under various transformations. In the following section we shall deal with this problem briefly and introduce the reader to the concept of transformation groups.

We should, finally, point out that the first fundamental form

$$ds^2 = E(x, y)dx^2 + 2F(x, y)dx\,dy + G(x, y)\,dy^2$$

is the local (infinitesimal) metric for a Riemann surface. We readily see that this is Euclidean for $E = G = 1, F = 0$. Secondly, as illustrated in Fig. 5.18 for hyperbolic (negative curvature) Reimann surfaces the sum of the internal angles of a triangle is less than 180°, while in the elliptical case it is greater than 180°. Such properties are important in determining whether a local region of a surface is positive, zero, or negative curvature.

We shall see how such geometric features of surfaces do become quite important when dealing with some of the more complex aspects of binocular vision and colour space in Part II.

5.6. TRANSFORMATIONS OF CURVES AND SURFACES

We have seen that various geometries can be defined axiomatically by critical definitions of parallelism, lengths, angles, etc. For example, we saw that in projective geometry "parallel" lines always intersect, whereas in affine geometry parallel lines occur in the normal accepted sense.

However, there is another approach to the study of geometry and this involves the study of the class of objects invariant under different transformations—at least this was the idea of Felix Klein in 1892. Before studying the Klein approach we shall first note a few of the more well-known transformations. In Euclidean space, for example, on the plane, a linear transformation is defined by

$$x' = ax + by + m, \quad y' = cx + dy + n, \tag{5.28}$$

where $ad - bc \neq 0$. Here point sets $\{x, y\}$ are transformed into $\{x', y'\}$.

When $ad - bc = 1$ (5.28) is called a rigid transformation or rigid motion on the plane composed of a translation component (m, n) and rotation component $(a = \cos\theta, b = \sin\theta, c = -\sin\theta, d = \cos\theta)$ as shown in Fig. 5.20.

For rigid motions (5.28) is uniquely specified by three values: the translation components (m, n) and the rotation component θ. Consequently three points uniquely specify the rigid motion giving the well-known result that rigid motions create congruence relationships between all related triangles.

Another well-known transformation is that of reflections, which involves the motion of a point into its symmetric position with respect to an axis of reflection. It can also be readily seen that every rotation is the resultant of two reflections—in two lines through its centre.

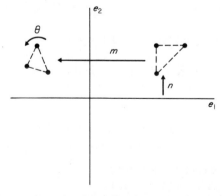

FIG. 5.20. Rigid planar motion uniquely specified by three points: the congruence relation.

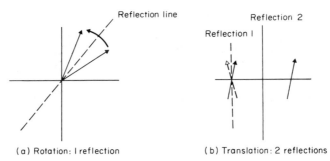

FIG. 5.21. Every rigid motion on the plane can be represented by a series of reflections.

Every translation is the resultant of reflections in two lines perpendicular to its direction (Fig. 5.21). The reflection of a point (x, y) about a line of inclination θ to the -axis, and passing through the origin, is of the form

$$x' = x \cos 2\theta + y \sin 2\theta, \quad y' = x \sin 2\theta - y \cos 2\theta.$$

Whereas the Euclidean transformations are limited to rigid motions, the affine transformations include rotations, translations, reflections, and similarity transforms. These latter transforms refer to dilations

$$x' = \alpha x, \quad y' = \beta y,$$

which do not necessarily preserve lengths, areas and shape. In fact the affine transformations differ from the rigid transformations in so far as they only require $ad - bc \neq 0$ in (5.28). The Euclidean require $ad - bc = 1$. The affine transformations preserve parallels, line intersections, conics, triangles, segments, n-sided polygons, but do not preserve the rigidity of the object. Transformations which are angle preserving are called conformal. The affine transforms are conformal but not isometric (length preserving). However, the projective transformations are not even conformal — only preserving cross-ratios.

We now introduce the concept of a transformation group. If we consider a transformation as an operation T_i, then the following properties hold:

(i) $(T_i T_j) T_k = T_i (T_j T_k)$ (association).
(ii) $T_i T_j = T_k$ (closure).
(iii) for each T_i there exists a T_k such that $T_i T_k = I$, the identity transformation. T_k is the inverse of T_i.
(iv) There exists an I such that for any i, $T_i I = T_i$.

These four properties of closure, association, identity, and inverse endow the transformation T with the properties of a group with respect to the transformation parameter. Consider the rotation group:

$$\left.\begin{array}{l} x' = x \cos \theta + y \sin \theta = \phi(x, y : \theta), \\ y' = -x \sin \theta + y \cos \theta = \psi(x, y : \theta), \end{array}\right\} \tag{5.29}$$

for θ being the rotation angle. Here the identity is $\theta = 0$. The inverse is $-\theta$, and closure and association of rotation angles are guaranteed.

If we observe the behaviour of the rotation group about the identity by means of a Taylor expansion[†] we obtain

$$x' = \phi(x, y : \theta_0) + \sum_{i=1}^{\infty} \frac{(\delta\theta)^i}{i!} \frac{\partial' \phi}{\partial \theta^i}(x, y : \theta_0),$$

$$y' = \psi(x, y : \theta_0) + \sum_{i=1}^{\infty} \frac{(\delta\theta)^i}{i!} \frac{\partial^i \psi}{\partial \theta^i}(x, y : \theta_0). \tag{5.30}$$

By neglecting higher order terms this reduces to

$$\delta x = x' - x = \frac{\partial \phi}{\partial \theta}(x, y : \theta_0)\delta\theta,$$

$$\delta y = y' - y = \frac{\partial \phi}{\partial \theta}(x, y : \theta_0)\delta\theta.$$

By letting

$$\frac{\partial \phi}{\partial \theta} = \xi(x, y), \quad \frac{\partial \phi}{\partial \theta} = \eta(x, y)$$

we get

$$\delta x = \xi(x, y)\delta\theta,$$
$$\delta y = \eta(x, y)\delta\theta.$$

For rotations,

$$\xi = -y, \quad \eta = x,$$

giving

$$\delta x = -y\delta\theta, \quad \delta y = x\delta\theta, \quad \text{or} \quad \frac{\mathrm{d}x}{-y} = \frac{\mathrm{d}y}{x}. \tag{5.31}$$

Cross-multiplying (5.31) results in

$$x\,\mathrm{d}x + y\,\mathrm{d}y = 0, \quad \text{or} \quad x^2 + y^2 = k, \tag{5.32}$$

the equation of a circle.

So the local infinitesimal transformations about the identity ($\theta_0 = 0$) gives us all the information about the locus of points that are invariant under the transformation group—in this case, a circle (5.23). In general the ξ and η define an infinitesimal transformation that, in turn, defines a one-parameter transformation found by solving the system

$$\frac{\mathrm{d}x}{\xi(x, y)} = \frac{\mathrm{d}y}{\eta(x, y)} = \mathrm{d}\theta \tag{5.33}$$

with the initial conditions

$$\theta = 0, \quad x' = x, \quad y' = y.$$

The dot (scalar) product of ξ and η with the gradients of a function $F(x, y)$, with respect

[†] A Taylor expansion of a function $f(x)$ is an approximation to the function within a small neighbourhood of x and is derived as the addition of weighted derivatives:

$$f(x + h) = f(x) + \sum_{i=1}^{\infty} \frac{h^i}{i!} \frac{\mathrm{d}^i f(x)}{\mathrm{d}x^i}.$$

to the coordinate system, is called a differential operator on F or Lie derivative:

$$(\xi, \eta)\left(\frac{\partial F}{\partial x}, \frac{\partial F}{\partial y}\right) = \xi(x, y)\frac{\partial F}{\partial x} + \eta(x, y)\frac{\partial F}{\partial y} = \mathscr{L}(F).$$

When $\mathscr{L}(F) = 0$, then the locus defined by F is invariant under the transformation group (Lie transformation group—after Sophus Lie, 1878) defined locally by (ξ, η). For example:

$$\left(-y\frac{\partial}{\partial x} + x\frac{\partial}{\partial y}\right)(x^2 + y^2) = 0.$$

The Lie group is the group of the parameter space in the rotation case the additive group over the real numbers.

Although we have seen that we can discover the global transformation group (invariant curve—as parameterized) by integration, there is another way, by what is called the exponential map—an analogue to the Taylor expansion, which gave us the local (infinitesimal) description of the transformation. It is defined by

$$x' = x + \sum_{i=1}^{\infty} \frac{\theta^i}{i!}\mathscr{L}^i(x),$$

$$y' = y + \sum_{i=1}^{\infty} \frac{\theta^i}{i!}\mathscr{L}^i(y),$$

(5.34)

For the rotation group, $\mathscr{L} = -y\partial/\partial x + bc\partial/\partial y$,

$$\mathscr{L}(x) = -y \quad \mathscr{L}(y) = x$$
$$\mathscr{L}^2(x) = -x \quad \mathscr{L}^2(y) = -y$$

giving

$$x' = x\left(1 - \frac{\theta^2}{2!} + \frac{\theta^4}{4!} - \frac{\theta^6}{6!} + \cdots\right) - y\left(1 - \frac{\theta^3}{3!} + \frac{\theta^5}{5!} - \frac{\theta^7}{7!} + \cdots\right),$$

$$y' = x\left(1 - \frac{\theta^3}{3!} + \frac{\theta^5}{5!} - \frac{\theta^7}{7!} + \cdots\right) + y\left(1 - \frac{\theta^2}{2!} + \frac{\theta^4}{4!} - \frac{\theta^6}{6!} + \cdots\right).$$

But

$$\cos\theta = 1 - \frac{\theta^2}{2!} + \frac{\theta^4}{4!} - \frac{\theta^6}{6!} + \cdots$$

and

$$\sin\theta = 1 - \frac{\theta^3}{3!} + \frac{\theta^5}{5!} - \frac{\theta^7}{7!} + \cdots$$

resulting in

$$x' = x\cos\theta - y\sin\theta,$$
$$y' = x\sin\theta + y\cos\theta,$$

being the rotation group on the plane. So the exponential map has carried us from a local transformation to the global transformation group. The Lie group is the group associated with the parameter—in this case θ, the addition of rotation angles.

These Lie derivatives may also be combined to form what is called an algebra—an algebra[†] of operators or Lie algebra—as long as a product term is defined. This product term is the commutator, defined by

$$[\mathscr{L}_i, \mathscr{L}_j] = \mathscr{L}_i \mathscr{L}_j - \mathscr{L}_j \mathscr{L}_i. \tag{5.35}$$

There are important properties of the commutator, including

$$[\mathscr{L}_i, \mathscr{L}_j] = -[\mathscr{L}_j, \mathscr{L}_i]$$

and the Jacobi identity

$$[\mathscr{L}_i, [\mathscr{L}_j, \mathscr{L}_k]] + [\mathscr{L}_j, [\mathscr{L}_k, \mathscr{L}_i]] + [\mathscr{L}_k, [\mathscr{L}_i, \mathscr{L}_j]] = 0.$$

One of the great contributions of the Lie groups and algebra is that many transformation groups can be expressed by a few basic operators and their linear combinations. These basic operators, in conjunction with the commutator, are used to generate specific Lie algebras, e.g. the algebra associated with the affine groups of transformations (5.28).

We shall see in Part II that attempts have been made to represent many varied aspects of perception via Lie transformation groups. The language is powerful as non-linear transformations can be reduced to small linear transformations. As to whether this is consistent with how the visual system extracts contours or perceives invariances, will be discussed in the following chapters.

5.7. SPECIAL TOPICS

In this section we shall deal with special geometric structures which do not fit into the traditional geometries discussed so far, but are quite relevant to visual perception. Some of these properties will not be discussed in more detail than presented here. However, references on these issues will be provided.

(a) Metrics

So far we have only discussed two distance metrics: the Euclidean and Riemannian metrics (for curved surfaces). We remember, of course, that metrics—so distances—satisfy the following conditions:

(i) $d_{ij} \geq 0$, where i, j refer to points $\mathbf{x}_i, \mathbf{x}_j$.
(ii) $d_{ij} = d_{ji}$.
(iii) $d_{ij} \leq d_{ik} + d_{kj}$: triangle inequality.

In-n-dimensions the Euclidean metric becomes

$$d_{ij} = \sqrt{\sum_{k=1}^{n} (x_{ik} - x_{jk})^2}$$

and it also satisfies the above conditions. Other metrics, not of the local Riemannian nature

[†] An algebra is a group but also includes a product term in its composition rules.

$(\mathrm{d}s^2 = \ldots)$ exist. For example, the Minkowski r metric, where

$$d_{ij} = \left[\sum_{k=1}^{n} (x_{ik} - x_{jk})^r \right]^{1/r}$$

and the "city-block" metric

$$d_{ij} = \sum_{k=1}^{n} |x_{ik} - x_{jk}|,$$

where $|\cdot|$ refers to the absolute value of $x_{ik} - x_{jk}$.
The Riemann metric

$$\mathrm{d}s^2 = g_{11}\,\mathrm{d}x^2 + 2g_{12}\,\mathrm{d}x\,\mathrm{d}y + g_{22}\,\mathrm{d}y^2$$

generalizes to the local metric of an n-dimensional hypersurface as

$$\mathrm{d}s^2 = \sum_{i=1}^{n} \sum_{i=1}^{n} g_{ij}\,\mathrm{d}x^i\,\mathrm{d}x^j,$$

where g_{ij} refer to the coefficients of the n-dimensional fundamental form. Of course, this surface can be embedded in an $n + 1$-dimensional Euclidean space.

(b) Special transformations

The *Stereographic transform* is a mapping of the points of a globe onto a plane as shown in Fig. 5.22. Here all projections are made from the North Pole, making it a singularity point. In this, mapping angles are preserved—not areas or distances: it is a conformal mapping. If the projection point is moved down to the centre of the sphere then the diameter line c is mapped as a "line at infinity", making the resultant plane a model for the projective plane.

Klein (1928) connected such conformal maps and projective geometry by Fig. 5.22b. A sphere of radius r touches a plane at the point p being the centre of r and s, circles corresponding to the orthogonal projection of the sphere and the projection from the North Pole (N) respectively. Projective lines correspond to vertical circles generated from perpendicular projections of chords of the inner circle. When such vertical circles are stereographically projected back to the plane they are also circles—perpendicular to S—the conformal mapping.

These mappings are related to precise mappings of planar surfaces onto, say, the curved retinal surface. However, with binocular vision the geometry becomes more complex.

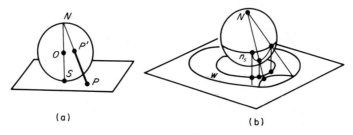

(a)   (b)

FIG. 5.22. (a) Stereographic projection, and (b) the Klein model for projective geometry.

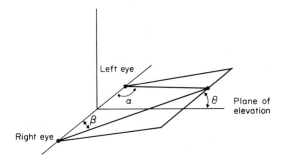

FIG. 5.23. The biopolar coordinate system for binocular vision.

One way to simplify this is to move to biopolar coordinates $\{\alpha, \beta, \theta\}$ as illustrated in Fig. 5.23 having the algebraic form

$$\cot\alpha = \frac{y+1}{\sqrt{x^2+z^2}}, \quad \cot\beta = \frac{1-y}{\sqrt{x^2+z^2}}, \quad \cot\theta = \frac{x}{z}. \tag{5.36}$$

The two eyes perceive the world with horizontal disparity. To encode this we modify the biopolar coordinates by introducing the biopolar latitude

$$\phi = \tfrac{1}{2}(\beta - \alpha) \tag{5.37}$$

and biopolar parallax

$$\gamma = \alpha\pi - (\alpha + \beta).$$

These angles are illustrated in Fig. 5.24, where for $\gamma = $ const. we obtain the Vieth–Müller circles

$$x^2 + y^2 - 2x\cot\gamma = 1.$$

The curves $\phi = $ const. are the hyperbolae of Hillebrand.

$$-x^2 + y^2 + 2xy\cot 2\theta = 1.$$

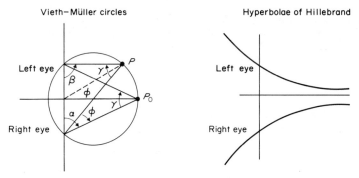

FIG. 5.24. Modified biopolar angles ϕ, γ, and Vieth–Müller circles, hyperbolae of Hillebrand.

So in the horizontal plane (zero elevation),

$$\tan \gamma = \frac{2\sqrt{x^2 + z^2}}{x^2 + y^2 + z^2 - 1},$$

$$\tan 2\phi = \frac{2y\sqrt{x^2 + z^2}}{x^2 + z^2 - y^2 + 1},$$

$$\tan \theta = z/x.$$

Iseikonic transformations are of the form:

$$
\left.
\begin{array}{ll}
\alpha' = \alpha + \delta & \gamma' = \gamma + \tau \\
\beta' = \beta + \varepsilon \quad \text{or} \quad & \phi' = \phi + \sigma \\
\theta' = \theta + \lambda & \theta' = \theta + \lambda
\end{array}
\right\}
\tag{5.38}
$$

for $\{\delta, \varepsilon, \lambda, \tau, \sigma\}$ arbitrary constants. By definition these transforms have the same bipolar, binocular, direction components $\{d\gamma, d\phi, d\theta\}$.

It was Luneburg (1946) who formally developed the bipolar and hyperbolic geometry for binocular vision, and the interested reader is referred to Blank (1978) for a recent review of the investigations of Luneburg's theory (see Chapter 8).

5.8. CONCLUSIONS

In this chapter we have covered, maybe too briefly, the main areas of geometry that seem relevant to issues in perception. We hope to show in Part II that rather than there being a unified geometry for perception, there is diverse application of most areas of geometry to visual perception. After all, geometries represent ways of describing various events— as various as the diverse aspects of visual perception. Finally, it is hoped that the reader no longer assumes that the only important and interesting geometry is the Euclidean geometry.

REFERENCES

AYRES, M. (1967) *Projective Geometry*, Schaum, New York.

BLANK, A. (1978) Metric geometry in human binocular perception: theory and fact. In *Formal Theories of Visual Perception* (E. L. J. Leeuwenberg and H. F. J. M. Buffart, eds.), Wiley, London.

CAELLI, T., HOFFMAN, W., and LINDMAN, H. (1978) Subjective Lorentz transformations and the perception of motion, *J. Opt. Soc. Am.*, 402–417.

COXETER, H. S. M. (1962) *Introduction to Geometry*, Wiley, New York.

KLEIN, F. (1928) *Vorlesungen über Nicht-Euklidische Geometrie*, Springer, Berlin.

LUNEBURG, R. (1946) *Mathematical Analysis of Binocular Vision*, Princeton University Press, Princeton, New Jersey.

PEDOE, D. (1976) *Geometry and the Liberal Arts*, Peregrine, New York.

ROBINSON, J. O. (1972) *The Psychology of Visual Illusions*, Hutchinson, London.

PART II

Applications and Current Approaches to Visual Perception

CONSISTENT with the aim of this book, in Part II we shall investigate how the technologies discussed in Part I are currently applied to problems in vision research. Only a selected group of problems will be examined, mainly to do with spatial vision and motion perception. However, brief notes on colour vision, stereopsis, and binocular vision will be included for completeness. The issues of great interest will be to do with contour, texture, depth, and complex motion perception—so called "central" issues of perception.

Before even commencing this section I wish to emphasise that many other issues and authors are not mentioned—not because their work is not important but simply because the aims of this section are to illustrate just how one may apply the technologies discussed.

CHAPTER 6

Spatial Vision

6.1 INTRODUCTION

Research problems do not arise *in vacuo*. They are usually embedded in the framework of a specific theory or explanation of associated phenomena. The problem context thus carries with it appropriate languages — vocabulary and grammar, which, in fact, even define the types of problems the researcher can ask. For example, the class of research problems, which are generated from assuming that the ear is conducting a Fourier analysis of the auditory signal, are quite different from those generated by assuming that non-linear systems analysis or group theory may be more appropriate a language for auditory perception.

In contrast to the above example, where Fourier analysis does seem singularly important, visual perception has so many quite different facets that a single language (or meta-language) seems highly inappropriate. For example, the geometry of binocular vision involves quite different problems than colour vision or, in turn, motion or contrast perception. For this reason we have covered many different kinds of technology in Part I so that the researcher may be able to study many visual phenomena and not just those relevant to one, or maybe two, technologies acquired previously.

As implicit in the nature of this volume we shall deal with the quantitative or technological approaches to the varied visual phenomena that, in this chapter cover:

6.2. Contrast and intensity perception.
6.3. Texture discrimination.
6.4. Contours and illusions.
6.5. Spatial equivalences and perceptual invariances.

The reader should refer back to the appropriate sections of Part I when in doubt about a specific operation, statement, or whatever.

6.2. CONTRAST AND INTENSITY PERCEPTION

We saw in Chapter 2 how light propagates in waveform as energy packets or quanta (photons). There we also discussed methods for determining the number of quanta radiating from a source and noted that this radiation varied over time. The distribution of photon emissions follows a Poisson law where the number of observed quanta x in a given time

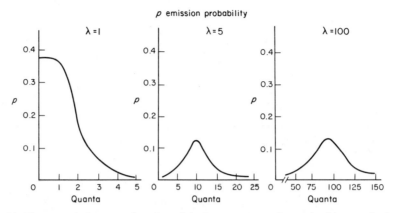

FIG. 6.1. Photon emissions as a function of λ, the average number emitted over a fixed time interval.

interval is defined by

$$p(x) = \frac{\lambda^x}{x!} e^{-\lambda}, \tag{6.1}$$

where λ is the average number of emissions over the same interval. As λ increases the distribution approaches a normal (or gaussian) form as shown in Fig. 6.1.

By measuring intensity in terms of quanta, Hecht *et al.* and (1942) found that the probability of detecting the presence of a signal was directly related to the number of photons emitted (and the variation) in accord with the above Poisson formulation. These curves are called "frequency of seeing" curves and, when fitted to the Poisson cumulative distributions, result in estimates of the mean number of quanta required by the retina to result in signal detection (Fig. 6.2). The major point of the Hecht *et al.* (1942) study was not so much that something like eight quanta (on average) are required to trigger detection, but rather that variations in responses seem consistent with quantal fluctuations in the signal. That is, the human visual system seems directly sensitive to photon emissions.

Needless to say, these response curves vary as a function of retinal location and sampling

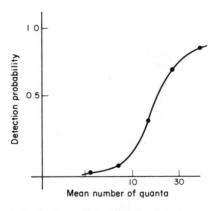

FIG. 6.2. Typical "frequency of seeing" curves for intensity detection as observed by Hecht *et al.* (1942) and compared with cumulative Poissons having random variations about a mean.

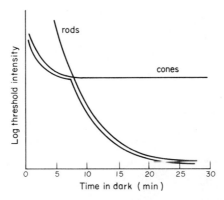

FIG. 6.3. Classical dark adaptation curves indicating the threshold intensity differences between rod and cone systems.

period. For example, we know from classical dark adaptation studies that it is possible to clearly distinguish the photopic (high threshold, cone-driven) and scotopic (low threshold, rod-driven) processes (Fig. 6.3). Here the rod sensitivity increases greatly over time in comparison to the cones (Cornsweet, 1970).

The above results imply that our decisions, even the retinal physiology, are consistent with the physics of light—what many of us would expect. However, there are many important examples of intensity perception where the properties of light do not alone explain what we perceive. The more common examples are to do with edges or relative intensities—simultaneous contrast and Mach bands—where the perceived luminance of a source is dependent on neighbouring luminance values. These contrast effects generally decrease as the spatial contiguity of the two luminance sources decreases. For example simultaneous contrast decreases dramatically even when proximity is slightly changed from the normal case. As will be seen, such results suggest the effect is thus due to edge-detection mechanisms and how they may affect our coding of retinal luminance distributions, say, to optimize the perception of edges.

With Mach bands and simultaneous contrast the neighbouring brighter source induces the darker source to appear even darker, and vice versa. It is also clear that these effects are dependent on the relative sizes and luminance levels of the sources. Heinemann (1955) even demonstrated that the effect can be reversed for low background luminances.

One popular solution to the above differences between contrast and luminance perception is that they address two different systems in the retina. In particular, the contrast mechanisms entail the complex interactive processes between cells as illustrated by lateral inhibition, which is an example of the network for cell interactions discussed in Chapter 4. Specifically lateral inhibition may be modelled by (Bridgeman, 1978):

$$R_i(t) = e_i(t) - \sum_{j=1}^{n} k_{ij}[R_j(t - |i-j|) - R_{ij}^0], \qquad (6.2)$$

where R_i is the firing rate of cell i, $e_i(t)$ is its excitatory input at time t, R_{ij}^0 is the inhibitory threshold for the two cells i and j, and k_{ij} is the inhibitory coefficient or "gain" control. Bridgeman (1978) has considered connections between first-, second-, third- and fourth-order neighbouring cells within such a network, and typical results for varying k_{ij} coefficients are shown in Fig. 6.5. It can be seen that these networks give similar output

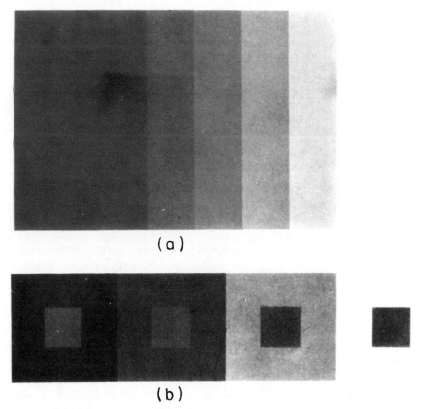

Fig. 6.4. (a) Mach bands and (b) simultaneous contrast effects where perceived luminance profiles do not correspond to the stimulus profile. Note the decrease in the effect due to proximity of intensity distributions.

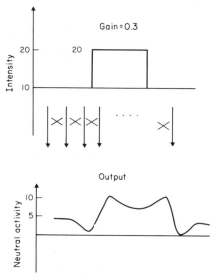

Fig. 6.5. Simulation of lateral inhibition for a gain of 0.3 (see Fig. 4.3).

functions as the type of perceived intensity distributions shown in Fig. 6.4. We shall also see shortly that these luminance profile relationships can be described in terms of band-pass spatial frequency filters. Similar networks have also been used by Weisstein (1968, 1969) and Bridgeman (1978) to explain meta-contrast—the apparent dimming of a briefly exposed source when followed by a mask having common edges with the first source. All such inhibitory networks are repetitive or iterative in nature and developed from the original formulations of lateral inhibition in *Limulus* by Ratliff and Hartline (1957) and Ratliff (1965).

So we see that lateral inhibition is one mechanism proposed to explain some of the anomalies of intensity perception specifically when non-zero contrasts are involved. It assumes spatial contiguity of the sources and, to this stage, no involvement of any cortical activity. Yet it is known that the meta-contrast and other contrast effects do occur under dichoptic presentation conditions (Breitmeyer and Ganz, 1976), so to this end we can conclude that retinal contiguity is not a necessary condition. On the other hand, what seems to be necessary for the effect is that edges—areas of sharp intensity change—exist between the test and masking stimulus. That is, the high contrast information must be contained in the high spatial frequency components of the image—edges are virtually defined by high-frequency components (see Chapter 2 and 3). This connection between spatial frequency and contrast perception has become a central issue in current research— independent of whether one such mechanism for frequency analysis may be lateral inhibition. But before continuing we need to define contrast.

Contrast (or modulation, see Chapter 2) is defined by the difference between maximum and minimum luminances (l_{max} and l_{min} respectively) divided by their sum, or

$$0 \leq c = \frac{l_{max} - l_{min}}{l_{max} + l_{min}} \leq 1.0. \tag{6.3}$$

It is clear that contrast is a necessary condition for the perception of any object, edge, surface, etc., for without contrast the visual field would be simply a uniform luminance distribution to the observer. In addition we know that some objects require more contrast to be perceived than others, e.g. finer or smaller objects, neat edges, etc. Finally, it is also clear that as intensity varies the contrast required to detect an object also varies. So contemporary contrast research has addressed itself largely to the roles of spatial and temporal frequency components of contrast perception—and some remarkable results have been found.

We saw in Chapter 3 that the degree to which the spatial (or temporal) frequencies of an image are modulated in a system is represented by the modulation transfer function (MTF). Over the range of spatial frequencies from 0 to 60 cycles/degree (of visual angle), the typical (ematropic) MTF is shown in Fig. 6.6, where the upper limit of visual acuity is at about 50–60 cycles/degree. This MTF is tabulated using sine-wave gratings and their absolute detection threshold where increased contrast (amplitude) for detection indicates decreased sensitivity.

This requires some further explanation. We saw in Chapter 3 that any reasonably smooth image can be decomposed into spatial frequency and phase components. It was also pointed out that in all optical systems these frequency components are not transferred with equal fidelity. The MTF (Fig. 6.6) is typically dampened at the low- and high-frequency ranges of the image. That is, acuity limitations of the optical system—in this case the visual system—are reflected in the filtering of high-frequency components of the image. With

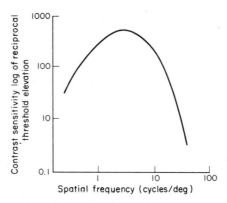

FIG. 6.6. Typical contrast sensitivity function for the human visual system; sine-wave grating stimulus.

images like gratings the amplitude of the sinusoids directly corresponds to contrast and so threshold amplitude values for the detection of such gratings does give us information about the human MTF. At least this was, and is, the working proposition of many research programmes in vision over the last decade or so (Davidson, 1966; Campbell and Robson, 1968). Although, in principle, this seems reasonable, the visual system is not like other optical systems in so far as we have no direct measure of output. So assumptions are made which relate a psychophysical response to the function of the visual system. Before discussing these assumptions we should recall the typical procedure for calculating the contrast sensitivity function.

Subjects observe grating stimuli of a given frequency displayed for a fixed duration on a CRT scope (usually). The task is typically to adjust the contrast until the gratings are just detectable. Psychophysical threshold procedures like random staircases or method of limits are used to ascertain each threshold. Here sensitivity to a given frequency is assumed to be inversely related to its absolute threshold. These reciprocal threshold values are often logarithmically transformed (Fig. 6.6) to result in the sensitivity function. So the assumptions are clear: (a) that increased threshold implies less sensitivity, or amplitude modulation is directly equal to reciprocal threshold—not only for absolute threshold (or low-intensity) vision but, possibly, in general. (b) The visual assumptions involved in making decisions about an image apply: that the detection response is based on the total grating displayed and not on a specific sample or part of the image; that only the visual system is involved; that no higher cognitive functions are invoked, etc.

Such assumptions are made explicit not to dampen (with or without the pun!) the impetus of such MTF-based procedures, but rather to point out that even with all such sources of variation the observed contrast sensitivity functions are highly reliable (see Spikreijse and van der Tweel, 1978, for a recent review on this issue).

As in Chapter 3, if the contrast sensitivity function defined above is representative of a human MTF then it can be used to predict just how an image is perceived—what distortions occur, what is accentuated and lost—as a function of contrast. We shall investigate how this concept has been applied to pattern recognition and visual illusions in the following sections.

However, within contrast perception, as such, strong conjectures have been made about the visual system based on observed contrast sensitivities. Specifically, in their 1968

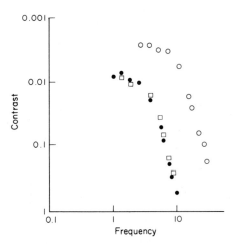

FIG. 6.7. Observed contrast levels for sine/square wave discrimination over frequencies (●) and predicted sensitivity values for third harmonics of square wave (□) based on the normal sensitivity function (○). (From Campbell and Robson, 1968.)

article, Campbell and Robson found that the contrast sensitivity to square waves, saw-tooth waves, could be predicted relative to sine-wave sensitivity through the first (fundamental) term of the Fourier series approximation to the function. For example, a square wave of amplitude m (contrast m) has a first harmonic or fundamental amplitude of $4m/\pi$. So the amplitude ratio between the square and sine wave is 1.273, and Campbell and Robson (1968) report contrast sensitivity increases of this order for square waves of varying spatial frequencies. Similarly, results were found for two luminance levels (500 cd/m^2 and 0.05 cd/m^2) and for saw-tooth waves.

In order to demonstrate just how higher harmonics of the Fourier series may be involved in contrast perception at super threshold intensities, Campbell and Robson (1968) did the following experiment. Since-wave and square-wave gratings were alternatively displayed at fixed contrast ratio ($4/\pi$ to be consistent in the different amplitudes of their fundamentals), and the subject had to increase the contrast of both gratings for each of a series of frequencies so that the two waveforms could be discriminated. The results are shown in Fig. 6.7.

Now, as shown in Fig. 6.7, this contrast range—as a function of spatial frequency— closely corresponds to the normal contrast sensitivity function (Fig. 6.6) but divided by a factor of 3 in spatial frequency and contrast axes. That is, this sensitivity function approximates that of the third harmonic of the square-wave stimulus. These authors argued that the resultant discrimination was due to this harmonic component reaching threshold for the visual system. Secondly, the selective sensitivity to various spatial frequency image components was due to separate frequency channels or band-pass filters in the visual system. Each channel was hypothesized to have a range of about two octaves.

This contrast sensitivity has also been found to occur in individual cortical cells and having similar modulation transfer characteristics as found from psychophysical exponents. Campbell (1976) has directly compared these results (as illustrated in Fig. 6.8).

Yet the responses of individual cortex cells to spatial frequency are far more complex than implied by Fig. 6.8. First, there seems to be different kinds of cells in terms of the frequency response: those that respond particularly to low spatial frequencies (and high temporal frequencies—brisk transient or X-cells), and those that have a preference for high

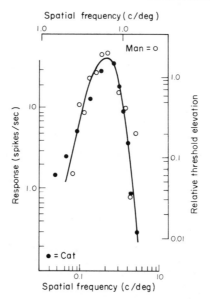

FIG. 6.8. The comparison of responses of individual cortical units of the cat and human contrast
sensitivity to spatial frequency gratings. (From Campbell, 1976.)

spatial frequencies (and low temporal frequencies—sustained or Y-cells). Hoffman (1978) also reports W-cells, which may well constitute 45% of the cat's retinal ganglion cells. They all have low conduction velocities and do have access to the visual cortex. Enroth-Cugell (1978) has reported that the Y-cells are specifically affected by injections of bicuculline or picrotaxin—known GABA antagonists. This may well indicate that the high spatial frequency sensitivity of these cells may be due to considerably greater dendritic and axonal processes, which constitute their receptive fields (see Chapter 4).

Secondly, frequency selectivity and orientation sensitivity are related in specific cortical units. Recently, Maffei (1978) has constructed a two-dimensional map of the primary projection area 17 of the cat's visual cortex and finds a configuration as shown in Fig. 6.9. Here the column orientation sensitivity corresponds to perpendicular penetration to the surface of the cortex, giving the classical Hubel and Weisel (1962, 1965, 1968) orientation selective columns. However, tangential penetrations to the surface give frequency selectivity—the rows of Fig. 6.9.

We saw in Chapters 3 and 4 that the Fourier transform has a phase and amplitude spectrum—the latter measuring frequency components, the former indexing relative position of image elements. That is,

$$F(s,t) = A(s,t)\,e^{i\phi(s,t)}, \tag{6.4}$$

where $A(s,t)$ and $\phi(s,t)$ correspond to amplitude and phase spectra respectively (Chapter 3). Here, oriented line segments in the image domain corresponds to constant "phase lines" in the Fourier transform domain. With this in mind, recent conjectures (for e.g. De Valois, 1978; Andrews and Pollen, 1979) centre around the reinterpretation of Fig. 6.9 as the embodiment of the total Fourier transform in the visual cortex responses.

In a recent experiment Andrews and Pollen (1979) have related receptive field profiles of individual cortical cells to their responses to spatial frequency components of sinusoidal

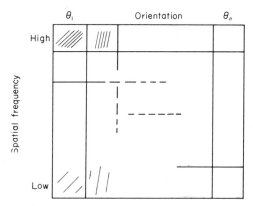

FIG. 6.9. Cortical organization of orientation and frequency selective features of primary projection area cells of the cat's visual cortex (suggested by Maffei, 1978).

gratings. As shown in Chapter 3, a band-pass filter in the Fourier spectrum corresponds to a sinc function in the image domain and vice versa. So a receptive field profile, which is, say, on-centred, off-surround—if regarded as a band-pass filter device—should respond to sinusoidal gratings in accord with the spatial sensitivity profile of the band-pass filter in the Fourier domain. At least this is one of the current conjectures.

Andrews and Pollen (1979) found that the area 17 cells' frequency selectivity was about two to three octaves (to half-maximum amplitude response) and, with moving sinusoidal gratings, was sensitive to the phase angle of the grating with respect to the motion and receptive field profile. These authors found support for relating the excitatory receptive field centre profile to frequency selectivity but could not fully explain the relationship between the "side-lobes" of the fields and frequency sensitivity (Fig. 6.10).

So, to reiterate the conjecture, we see that there is some evidence (ever increasing) which indicates that the orientation, frequency, and phase responses of individual area 17 cells of the cat's visual cortex, can be related to their receptive field profiles by the Fourier transform pair. That is, the receptive field is conjectured to have a specific geometry to simulate the band-pass filters required to build up an image code of frequency, orientation, and phase information. This implies that the receptive field actually reflects the region of the image where the cell performs spatial summation. However, to this stage no direct evidence of linear summation has been found except for the type of summation discussed in Chapter 4.

As shown in Fig. 6.8, one of the amazing aspects of this work on contrast sensitivity is the compatibility between human psychophysical sensitivity functions and the responses of cat's individual cells. The issue of temporal frequency selectivity in such cortical units

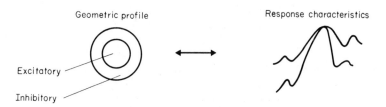

FIG. 6.10. On the conjectured relationship(s) between receptive field profiles and orientation, frequency, and phase responses of individual cortical units, (After Andrews and Pollen, 1979.)

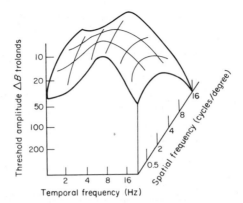

FIG. 6.11. Spatio-temporal contrast sensitivity function examined by Kelly (1978).

has already been mentioned in relation to the X- and Y- cells, the transient and sustained units respectively. A similar "trade-off" between spatial and temporal frequencies has been found in psychophysical functions, as observed by Kelly (1978), for example (Fig. 6.11). In this figure we see the trade-off between spatial and temporal frequencies. That is, as temporal frequency increases spatial frequency sensitivity decreases, and vice versa within the limits of the unimodal temporal frequency sensitivity function (Fig. 6.11).

Spatial frequency specific contrast effects are also dependent on orientation tuning of individual cells, in contradistinction to the suggested independence of these parameters by Maffei (1978). Recently, De Valois (1978) has investigated the responses of single cells in the macaque monkey lateral geniculate and striate cortex to grating and checkerboard patterns. His results are shown in Fig. 6.12, where orientation is represented by polar angle and spatial frequency by increasing from the centre. Here the receptive fields (to half-amplitude response criterion) are shown as darkened areas.

So, all in all, the results of individual cell recordings indicate that receptive field profiles, cells responses to orientation, and spatio-temporal frequency components of the image,

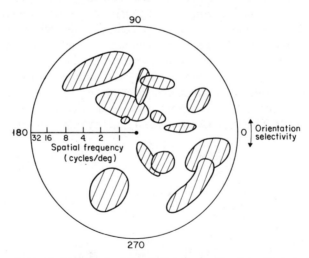

FIG. 6.12. Response range (striped areas) for single cells as a function of orientation and spatial frequency (as proposed by De Valois, 1978).

are all correlated. The evidence, roughly speaking, supports the notion that these profiles correspond to band-pass filters (Chapter 3) whose orientation and temporal response characteristics determine the frequency response range. That is, the specific phase position of each receptive field determine its dynamic range of frequency sensitivity.

The human psychophysical data also indicate similar structures with threshold contrast perception with the added result that the spatio-temporal frequency selectivity, and so the hypothetical receptive field filters, vary as a function of retinal eccentricity (Limb and Rubinstein, 1977). Of particular interest at present in human contrast sensitivity, are the issues dealing with the number of spatial (and temporal) frequency "channels" (or band-pass filter mechanisms), phase-response functions, and their determinants. The so-called "channel hypothesis" is usually tested under the rubric of single or multiple channels defined by:

(i) Space—invariant single channel: the visual field is uniformly covered (not necessarily disjointly) by receptive fields of the same size.

(ii) Space—variant single channel again, only one receptive field is associated with each retinal position, but their size may vary particularly as a function of eccentricity.

(iii) Space—invariant multiple channel: many uniform coverings of the visual field where each covering (as in (i)) consists of a different-sized receptive field.

(iv) Space—variant multiple channel: each retinal position may have a series of varied-sized receptive fields, and this variation itself may vary at different positions.

In a recent experiment, Graham et al. (1978) investigated the single- and multiple-channel models by investigating the detection of compound sinusoidal (Gaussian modulated to avoid edges) gratings of 2 and 6 cycles/degree. Under the assumption of channel independence, the probability of incorrect detection would be (Graham et al., 1978)

$$1 - p_c = (1 - p_2)(1 - p_6)(1 - g), \tag{6.5}$$

where p_2, p_6, and g correspond to probabilities of correctly detecting the 2- and 6-cycle components and g to correctly guessing, respectively. This is called the "probability summation" procedure (Quick, 1974). Quick (1974) derives the probability of a channel (i) detecting a stimulus as

$$p_i = 1 - 2^{-(cS_i)^k}, \tag{6.6}$$

where c is the contrast, S_i is the channel sensitivity to the stimulus, and k is a constant. The results of Graham et al. (1978) are fitted well for $k = 3$ or 4 (Fig. 6.13). When k becomes large the curve approaches the upper and right edges of Fig. 6.13 for the multiple-channel case. In comparison, a single-channel space—invariant model, which also assumes that responses of different receptive fields are perfectly positively correlated—would predict a response curve as the negative diagonal in Fig. 6.13. The authors conclude the results are closer to the multiple-channel model.

So the questions may be asked: How many channels and how are they specified? Various answers have been suggested, and perhaps one of the clearer statements (and characteristic of others) is due to Wilson and Bergen (1979). They contend that there are four channels (mechanisms) corresponding to four receptive field types at each retinal position—two sustained and two transient in nature, and not homogeneous over the visual field. They are illustrated in Fig. 6.14 for two ranges of retinal eccentricity.

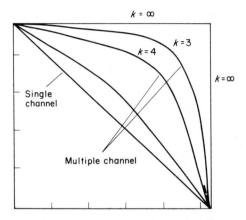

FIG. 6.13. Results of Graham *et al.* (1978) compared to multiple and single-channel models.

Otherwise the area is still open to clear documentation as to just how orientation, temporal and spatial frequencies, and phase information are encoded in the complex two dimensional receptive field structures of the vertebrate retinal and cortical units. Although it is clear that the language of Fourier analysis/linear systems has proved very stimulating in this area, it has not provided us with answers to how the various transforms, filters-receptive fields, actually occur as they do. That is, the Fourier language is a powerful description but not an explanation.

There have been recent attempts to explain just how such mechanisms might occur, particularly in the primary projection areas of the visual cortex. Specifically, the consensus of opinion (e.g. Blavais, 1977; Grossberg, 1978; Sejnowsky, 1977, Chapter 4) would indicate that such receptive fields are formed by the geometric and network properties of the dendritic and axonal processes between cells. As to whether such profiles can be adequately derived simply by a threshold and weighting function, as discussed in Chapter 4, remains to be seen.

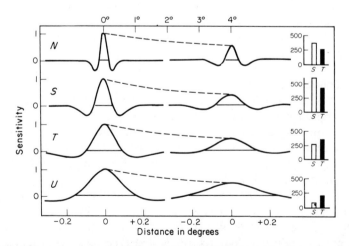

FIG. 6.14. Four channels proposed by Wilson and Bergen (1979) for two retinal positions (0° and 4°) and nomalized for comparisons. Responses on the right indicate sensitivity values, indicating that the two are more sustained *S* while the bottom two are more transient *T* in nature.

So we conclude this introductory section on contrast perception by, again, pointing out that the sensitivity of the visual system to contrast is dependent on orientation, spatio-temporal frequency, eccentricity, and phase components of the image. Much work has addressed the most interesting concept that all such parameters are related and compatible to the receptive field profiles via the Fourier transform pair. Care should be taken about interpreting these conclusions as implying that the Fourier integral or series exists "in the head"—just the contrary. These results simply indicate that some forms of frequency, phase (etc.) analyses are occurring in visual contrast perception, and Fourier *methods* are thus relevant to *describing* such processes.

Although evidence has also been found for chromatic-specific contrast sensitivity (e.g. Stromeyer, 1978, and Mollon, 1978), critical evidence is still lacking for the Fourier series decomposition model. From the earlier Campbell and Robson (1978) results to the current experiments, no clear evidence has been found for the Fourier series past the first two terms or the channel two-octave limit. For such a few number of terms *other* transforms are as possible as the Fourier approximation, from the spherical harmonics of Blavias (1978), the non-linear networks of Grossberg, or even simple Taylor expansions. However, this issue of the compatibility of various descriptive languages will be continued in the following sections, where we shall be dealing largely with supra threshold visual phenomena.

6.3. TEXTURE PERCEPTION

In a way it is possible to classify areas of vision research in terms of those phenomena that are contrast specific and those effects that are largely invariant to great changes in contrast. This is not to imply that many of the principles and models discussed in the previous section are irrelevant but, rather, that phenomena of super threshold vision are not totally explained by contrast-specific mechanisms.

If we regard contrast perception as a more "peripheral" aspect of vision than those phenomena that are not contrast dependent (excluding colour mechanisms, of course), then the problem arises as to when these more "central" processes commence. One historical distinction has been in terms of "figure/ground" relationships—a dichotomy of the perceptual world in terms of what is attended to (in the last analysis) and what is not. Maybe a more useful division is that suggested by Julesz (1970) of *spontaneous* and *scrutinous* perceptual processes, since it implicitly involves the parameters of inspection and fixation times. This impinges on such distinctions as "local/global", "analytic/synthetic"—processes in perception—concepts we hope to make explicit in this chapter.

It is argued that textures, in some way, bridge the gap between specific optical properties of an image (i.e. contrast) and the highly qualitative aspects of pattern and figure perception. Textures are discriminable in terms of their mosaic features, which do not necessarily involve figure perception yet do incorporate visual feature analysis and synthesis. With this in mind a popular question asked of texture pairs is: When are they discriminable given they are matched for contrast, colour, intensity, and the usual peripheral or "optical" conditions?

The answer to this question is, as we shall see, very difficult. However, in 1962 Julesz asked the opposite question: When are two different textures not discriminable? In order to answer this question—in Julesz's terms—we need to introduce the concept of "nth order statistics". Consider an image consisting of a textured region and background. The

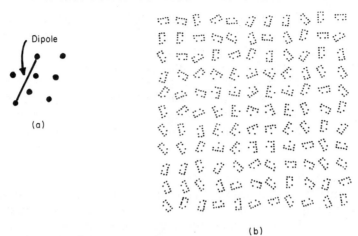

(a)

(b)

FIG. 6.15. (a) Texture dipoles as defined by the second-order statistics for black and white images; and (b) two textures having identical dipole statistics.

nth order statistic of the texture refers to the joint probability distribution that n-points (or texture elements) would fall on the texture and not on the background when thrown, say, randomly onto the image. First-order statistics refer to the spatial density of the texture; the second-order statistics correspond to the joint probability that two random points fall on the textured region etc. For a two-tone (black and white) texture the second-order statistics corresponds to the probability that both end points of an imaginary line, of given length and orientation (dipole of Buffon needle), falls on the black texture elements (Fig. 6.15).

For two-tone textures the third-order statistics correspond to the probability distributions of given sets of three points (triangles) falling on black texture elements. With dipole statistics, if we define the joint probability of points falling on (x, y) and $(x + u, y + u)$ as

$$f(x, y)f(x + u, y + v) = \begin{cases} 1 & \text{if } (x, y) \in T \text{ and } (x + u, y + v) \in T \\ 0 & \text{elsewhere,} \end{cases} \tag{6.7}$$

then the distribution of dipole components (u, v) is derived by

$$A(u, v) = \sum_X \sum_Y f(x, y)f(x + u, y + v) \tag{6.8}$$

or

$$A(u, v) = \int_Y \int_X f(x, y)f(x + u, y + v) \, dx \, dy.$$

We can see that (6.8) constitutes the autocorrelation of the texture (see Chapters 2 and 3).

With these features in mind, Julesz conjectured in 1962 that textures could not be (effortlessly) discriminated that agree in their (first- and) second-order statistics (Julesz, 1962). In turn, this conjecture is equivalent to two textures that are not discriminable if they have identical amplitude spectra or—and a visual system does not detect differences between the phase spectra of two textures—under spontaneous or brief exposure conditions. From 1962 to 1973 (Julesz *et al.*, 1973) no clear counter examples to this conjecture were found nor any competitive models proposed.

Recently, Caelli and Julesz (1978, 1979 a, b, c) have further investigated the conjecture and developed the model extensively for texture discrimination. However, before expanding on the results it is necessary to describe the new methods created to generate critical texture pairs for discrimination experiments. The essence of the method is to generate micropatterns that have the same dipole length distributions and to construct the texture from many duplicates, each having a random rotation to make the dipole orientation distributions uniform over the texture (Fig. 6.15).

These micropatterns were originally restricted to "n-disc" (n-point) configurations and texture discrimination was examined by Caelli and Julesz (1978, 1979a, b, c) for various values of n. The various methods are described below (and Fig. 6.16).

(i) *Original four-disc method*. Here the point A is generated anywhere along the x-axis (Fig. 6.16); points B and C are collinear with the origin (O), equidistant from O; the

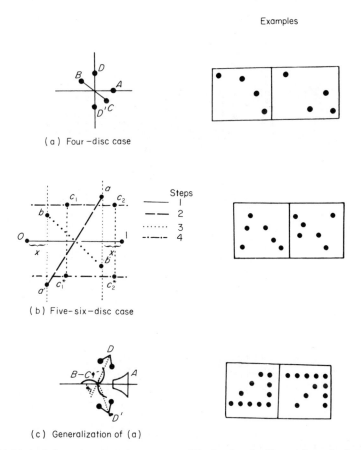

Examples

(a) Four-disc case

Steps
—— 1
—— 2
······ 3
—·—· 4

(b) Five-six-disc case

(c) Generalization of (a)

FIG. 6.16. Methods for generating micropatterns of "n-discs" and arbitrary shapes having identical dipole length distributions. In (a) $AD = AD'$, $BD = D'C$, $BD' = CD$. In (b) $(Oc_i = Oc_i^*$, $1c_i = 1c_i^*$, $i = 1, 2)$, $c_1 c_2 = c_1^* c_2^*$ due to conjugate symmetry, $(Oa = 1a'$, $Ob = 1b'$, $1a = Oa'$, $1b = Ob')$ due to the 180° rotations involved in $a \to 1 - a$, $b \to 1 - b$, where $a' = 1 - a$ and $b' = 1 - b$. Finally, $(ac_1 = b'c_1^*, ac_2 = b'c_2^*, bc_1 - d'c_1^*, bc_2 = a'c_2^*)$. In (c) A is any bilaterally symmetric shape, $B-C$: any 180°/n rotation invariant object; D, D': symmetric with respect to axes determined by 360°/n rotations.

points D and D' are on the y-axis equivalent from O. The sets $\{A,B,C,D\}$ and $\{A,B,C,D'\}$ have equal interpoint (dipole) distance distributions.

  (ii) Five- and six-disc method. Here the two sets of numbers have identical dipole lengths: $\{0,1,a,b,c_1,c_2\}$, $\{0,1,a,1-b,c_1^*,c_2^*\}$, for all being complex numbers: $x+iy$; and $Re(a+b)=1$, $Im(a+b-2c_i)=0$, $i=1,2$; c_i^* being the complex conjugate $(x-iy)$ of c_i the five-disc case occurs for $c_1=c_2$ (Fig. 6.16).

 (iii) *Generalization to n-discs or objects.* It can be shown (Caelli *et al.*, 1979) that there is a generalization of the four-disc method which leads to iso-dipole textures whose micropatterns are not restricted to discs. The conditions are (Fig. 6.16):

    (a) disk A in (i) can be replaced by any bilaterally symmetric shape;

    (b) B and C in (i) replaced by any $180°$ rotation invariant shape;

    (c) D and D' in (i) replaced by two shapes where each shape is invariant under reflections on the y-axis and D' is the x-axis reflection of D.

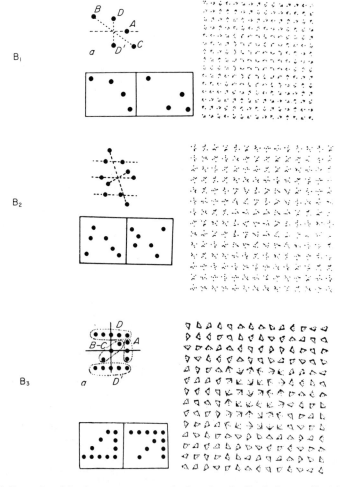

FIG. 6.17. Examples of the three counter-examples found to the dipole (*iso*-amplitude) texture conjecture as discovered by Caelli and Julesz.

Finally (B, C) can be rotation invariant for $180°/n$ rotations, while D and D' would be, accordingly, symmetric with respect to axes determined by $360°/n$ rotations (Fig. 6.16).

As already mentioned, the *iso*-dipole conjecture is equivalent to that of two textures not being discriminable if they have identical amplitude spectra. From the previous section on contrast perception, this conjecture seems reasonable. However, the very point of the above methods is that we (Caelli and Julesz) have found clear exceptions to this conjecture based on specific geometric configurations of the micropatterns.

In order, the first counter-example was discovered with the four-disc method when (and only when) four discs in one micropattern formed a clear rectangular structure — "quasi-collinear" — as illustrated in Fig. 6.17. Two other counter-examples occurred with the six-disc method and the generalized method, using disc objects. These corresponded to the "corner" and "closure" micropatterns respectively, as shown in Fig. 6.17.

We showed (Caelli and Julesz, 1979a) that each of the collinearity, corner, and closure features were independent of each other and so postulated the existence of three detector mechanisms in the visual system, which would act in conjunction with the dipole extraction process to result in texture discrimination. We even proposed that the dipole, or amplitude, sensitivity is a "ground-like" process while these local (retinal-location specific) feature detectors were the primitive elements of the "figure-perception" process. This seemed reasonable in the light of the importance of precisely these geometric properties for figure identification. Any attempt to represent these features in terms of phase spectra (see Chapter 3) has proved ineffective due to the highly non-linear nature of phase spectra filtering and the global similarity between the spectra for these clearly discriminable textures — as shown in Fig. 6.18 (Julesz and Caelli, 1979).

Although these above detectors are independent of dipole differences or similarities, it should be remembered that they are exceptions rather than the rule. More often iso-dipole textures (texture pairs with identical dipole distributions) are not discriminable, as shown

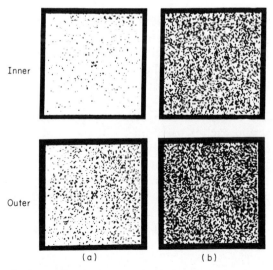

FIG. 6.18. (a) Amplitude, and (b) phase spectra for the inner and outer textures in Fig. 6.17(c).

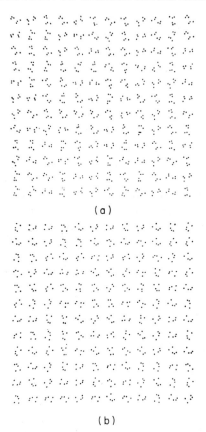

(a)

(b)

FIG. 6.19. Two typical cases of non-discrimination of textures with (a) four- and (b) six-disc micro-patterns having *iso*-dipole statistics while B class detectors are in equilibrium.

in Fig. 6.19. For this reason we concluded that there are two processes involved in figure/ground perception. The first—pertaining more to "ground" or textures as such—relies on dipole statistics and global texture properties involving integration over the total region (class A detectors, Fig. 6.20). The class B detectors refer to the specific feature detectors illustrated in Fig. 6.18—local in definition, as if the visual system is tuned to detect these specific geometric features of an image.

Attempts have recently been made to develop a psychophysics for dipole-detection mechanisms. The first approach is based on the known result (Julesz, 1970; Caelli and Julesz, 1978) that short dipoles are more salient to the visual system than those greater than 3° of visual angle. Fox and Mayhew (1979) have recently argued that texture dis-crimination may be based on the analyses of "*p*-graphs" or nearest-neighbour connectivity graphs and that their symmetry matches between and within textures. This is an example of the *n*-gram analyses suggested by Julesz (1970), and would seem most profitable since such *p*-graphs may be related to cortical receptive field features.

A slightly different approach to dipole statistic differences has also been developed by Caelli and Julesz (1979). The approach is based directly on the dipole length and orientation distributions for simple textures. The two textures shown in Fig. 6.21 have identical dipole

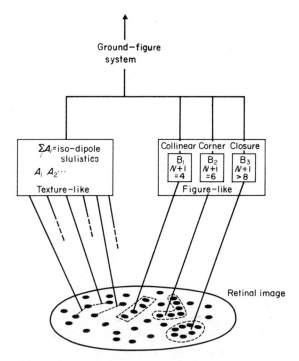

FIG. 6.20. Class A and B analysers in the figure/ground system.

length R but different orientation θ distributions. Both θ distributions are uniform, differing only in their range or variance and having identical means. Now if each texture has n micropatterns, then the amplitude difference $A_\theta(n)$ (Fig. 6.21) between the two textures becomes

$$A_0(n) = n\left[\frac{1}{\theta_2} - \frac{1}{\theta_1}\right], \tag{6.7}$$

where θ_1 and θ_2 correspond to the right and left orientation ranges respectively.

Considering another texture pair having orientation ranges θ'_1 and θ'_2 with n' micropatterns per texture, and if we assume a constant difference for texture discrimination,

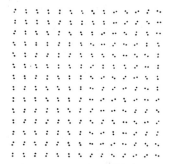

FIG. 6.21. Two textures having uniform micropattern dipole orientation distributions. The left varies between 70–100°; right: 0–180°

then we obtain

$$n' \left[\frac{1}{\theta'_2} - \frac{1}{\theta'_1} \right] = n \left[\frac{1}{\theta_2} - \frac{1}{\theta_1} \right]. \tag{6.8}$$

For $n' = n + \mathrm{d}n, \theta'_i = \theta_i + \mathrm{d}\theta'_i$, we obtain from (6.8)

$$\theta + \mathrm{d}\theta = \frac{(n + \mathrm{d}n)c\theta}{nc + \theta \mathrm{d}n} \tag{6.9}$$

for $c = \theta_1 = \theta'_1$ (constant orientation range) and $\theta = \theta_2$.

Thus (6.9) yields $\theta = c/[1 + (\alpha/n)]$ for α-integration constant. So for k-constant (6.9) reduces to

$$\log n = \log \theta - \log (c - \theta) + k, \tag{6.10}$$

which is the texture discrimination psychophysical function relating dipole orientation range to the number of texture micropatterns. In the following experiment, which we shall describe in some detail (the interested reader is referred to Caelli and Julesz, 1979b, for more details), we investigated the predictive power of this formulation for texture discrimination since it *directly* investigates the integrative (or summation) feature of the class A detector types.

The texture displays consisted of texture pairs presented on a Hewlett–Packard CRO (P_4 phosphor) for a 50 msec duration. As in previous studies, each display subtended a visual angle of 8.62° to the observer. A stimulus item consisted of two textures (except for catch trials—comprising 10% of the presentations) placed side by side having an $n \times n$ grid organization. These displays were generated by a PDP 11/20 computer which also recorded responses and generated stimuli orderings for presentation.

Stimuli varied in their θ ranges (Fig. 6.21), and for a given number of micropatterns and dipole length an experimental trial consisted of the S fixating on a centre fixation point for 2 sec, after which the texture pair was displayed for 50 msec. The S simply responded as to whether the textures appeared the same or different. Four ascending and four descending series were employed for each texture micropattern number, and a random staircase procedure was adopted about threshold (for further details see Caelli and Julesz, 1978a). From these eight thresholds mean and standard deviations were tabulated for each resolution n over each subject. This procedure was used with both θ and R distributions, where one θ range was always between $0 - 180°$, uniform and constant R. The other texture always had a smaller range, constant R-values, as well as identical 90° means (Fig. 6.21).

This whole procedure was repeated for two R-values (dipole lengths of 6 and 10 units corresponding to 12 and 20 of visual angle respectively). All textures were restricted to a constant visual angle of 8.62° and so increasing or decreasing the number of two-point micropatterns directly increased or decreased the image spatial density. Finally, as always the case in these textures, the dipole length and orientation parameters were systematically varied within each micropattern (in this case only one dipole between each two-point pair; see Caelli and Julesz, 1978 a, b).

Figure 6.22 illustrates mean orientation θ thresholds as a function of the number of micropatterns for each S over the two R-values. The 45° lines represent predicted thresholds according to the psychophysical law proposed (6.10), involving simple summation and amplitude difference detection. Standard deviations are also noted in degrees, and illustrate the stability of the threshold judgements.

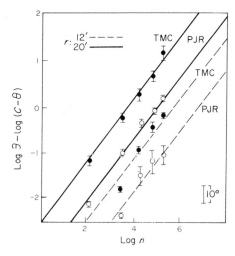

FIG. 6.22. Orientation θ discrimination thresholds as a function of number of dipole elements. Lines correspond to theoretical predictions (n is the number of micropatterns, $c = 180°$ range, θ = threshold range for discrimination (degrees); bars represent standard deviations in degrees; log is of base e).

Perhaps the more important aspect of these results is that decreasing dipole lengths from 20 to 12 of arc simply *translates* the psychophysical function to the right for each S in Fig. 6.22. This decline in orientation sensitivity as a function of length was found earlier by Caelli and Julesz (1978a), but, with respect to (6.10), the result implies that length is indexed by the integration constant k.

We should also mention a most interesting result. When we tried to do the identical experiment with the dipole length R as the variable — θ always fixed as either having identical uniform distributions or a constant angle — Ss could not discriminate between textures even for very large R-variance differences. One case is shown in Fig. 6.23, where the left texture has even constant (zero variance) R-values — the right having a range from 4 to 24 of arc. Both textures have the same mean R-values and identical θ distributions.

The correlation between θ thresholds and the number of texture dipoles (sample size), found in the present task, indicate the existence of at least a simple form of summation given that the observer compares the amplitude differences between texture distributions. What is surprising is that this formulation does not work with the dipole R parameter. This is clearly illustrated in Fig. 6.23, indicating the blindness of the visual system (under brief exposure conditions) to dipole length variance differences. As to whether the already determined dipole mean length sensitivity (Caelli and Julesz, 1978a) represents the limits of dipole length difference detection or not, remains to be seen.

One alternative explanation to this θ versus R (dipole) sensitivity may lie in existence of a "global" receptive field, rectangular or ellipsoidal in nature, which extracts orientation-specific information from the whole image by summation. Each region of the image would contribute θ information and the resultant composite rectangles would be compared in terms of aspect ratios. This would explain why the R-variance differences do not yield discrimination under the fixed or random dipole distributions. Needless to say, such "rectangular" (or slit-type) detectors would be to a major extent size-invariant as only relative aspect ratios would be of interest to the visual system.

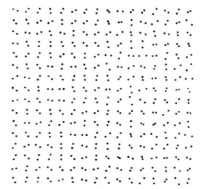

FIG. 6.23. Left and right textures differ in dipole length variances (left is zero) and no discrimination occurs.

A rectangular-shaped receptive field was recently found by Julesz *et al.* (1978), and might be regarded as a class B "granularity" or B_4 detector (Fig. 6.20). Texture discrimination, in these cases, would be due to local granularity differences, which globally do not manifest themselves, since these textures are iso-trigon, thus by definition also iso-dipole, and therefore have identical power spectra.

Although various perceptual aspects of textures have been investigated over the years, grouping of micropatterns by Beck (1966), perspective and texture gradients (Gibson, 1956), etc., perhaps the other more recent approach to texture perception *per se* involves the Fourier methods described in the previous section. Richards (1978) and Harvey and Gervais (1977) have conducted some initial investigations along these lines. Specifically, the latter authors have investigated groupings of textures in terms of similarities in their spatial frequencies in the range of 0.3 to 25.6 cycles/degree. The subjects then arranged thirty such textures into a total of five groups, based on the attempts of minimizing within group differences and maximizing between group differences.

These authors compared groupings to a four frequency channel model having different types of filter characteristics: the exponential

$$H(f_r) = \exp\left[-\frac{1}{2}\left(\frac{f_r - f_0}{w}\right)^2 \right]$$

and, Butterworth,

$$H(f_r) = \left[1 + \left(\frac{f_r - f_0}{w}\right)^2 \right]^{-1/2},$$

where f_r, f_0, and w correspond to frequency, peak frequency, and frequency bandwidth respectively. This, in conjunction with similarity scaling conducted by the authors, indicates that with grating-type textures, spatial frequency correlations (as expected) do predict perceived similarity. Secondly, that the thirty textures appeared to cluster into four perceptual categories—consistent with the four-channel model of Richards and Polit (1974)—is subject to debate, the reasons being that the channel filter characteristics are crucial to deciding the actual number, and also that regression or discriminant analysis uses the linear combination of frequency weights to predict performance-making the filter limits somewhat transparent.

So, in conclusion, it is clear that both frequency (amplitude) and phase components of textures are detected by the visual system in texture discrimination and similarity judgements. As to whether it is better to investigate amplitude spectra differences in terms of filter models or dipole statistic differences, is probably a matter of preference. However, the results from both approaches seem to indicate that there are very specific frequency and phase features that the visual system is strongly sensitive to—from our class B detectors to specific frequency bandwidths not dissimilar from some of the results on contrast perception. Of course, what is amazing is that the texture results are largely independent of contrast since our texture discrimination results still occur when contrast is markedly changed from just above threshold to clearly detectable presentations.

As to whether the very complex tasks of judging the complexity, groupings, and degrees of symmetry between textures (studied by Beck, 1966, and others) will ever be reduced to the types of processes discussed already, also remains to be seen.

6.4. CONTOURS AND ILLUSIONS (MECHANISMS)

I have deliberately used the word "contour" instead of figure pattern in order to avoid the historical connotations of these words in psychology and other related disciplines. In this section we wish to cover recent concepts as to how the visual system may extract line, orientation, edge, curvature, and other types of information relevant to the perception of contours—even shapes. In this vein current research in "pattern perception" is no longer concerned with the "nature" of form, as was of interest even to the late 1960s (see Zusne, 1970), but rather, the psychophysics of various geometric properties of shapes and boundaries, which are clear delimiters of patterns.

This is not mean to imply that the great philosophical problems of the "image in the brain" are to be disregarded. On the contrary, recent neurophysiological evidence of feature extraction indicates a pressing need for modern vision research to ask the right question as to how the brain may fuse such features (if it ever does) into a contiguous unified image. Some would argue that such a synthetic process is not the domain of visual perception but is the role of the interpreter of sensory information—the cognitive processes. With all this in mind we shall deal with the modern technologies and phenomena of interest in visual perception—relevant to such issues.

There are two types of approaches made to the problems of contour and illusion perception—not contradictory and, as we shall see, probably complementary. The first approach, dealt with in this section, considers aspects of these phenomena in terms of neurophysiological and psychophysical mechanisms, which may represent how we encode the stimulus. The second approach, more the domain of sections 6.4 and Chapter 7, deals with how we may interpret such encoding and so, in turn, how our interpretations may feed back on our encoding processes. In those sections a very central concept is that of invariance structures. In this section the central concepts are "co-operativity" and filtering.

The word "co-operativity" has recently been associated with the concept of elements, say, image points, having influences on each other in the process of primitive encoding. For example, lateral inhibition is co-operative since one stimulus element inhibits the perception of luminance (contrast) in another. This concept turns up in stereopsis, texture perception, and in recent models for contour and illusion perception in a very common way. That is, elements (and they require definition) are argued to be processed in such a way that we can represent perceptual interactions by some connectivity matrix ("weighting" matrix) between element pairs of the image. Such a weighting function (filter) is so argued to deliver perceptions of contours, extract edges, etc., and, by nature, result in illusory perceptions of the world.

There are two theoretical stances on this, for want of a better word, "mechanisms" approach. The simplest position, called the "feature-coding" strategy, states that the visual system, in perceiving contours, encodes specific features of the stimulus, and the unitary shape is a collective statement about how the features are configured in the stimulus. Specifically, visual illusions are seen to evolve from interactions between feature coding channels involving processes of adaptation, inhibition, and facilitation. Here orientation, size, motion, colour, etc., are seen as specific features to be encoded. The second position, more complex, assumes very little about what are "features" and argues that the feature lists, assumed by many investigators to be primary, are relative to the total configuration. In this latter approach such effects as orientation tuning curves are to be derived from more basic interacting networks, which lay underneath the receptive field structure.

An exemplar of the feature-coding strategy is the orientation-specific feature encoding literature. Representative assumptions include:

(i) the visual system has a finite number of orientation sensitivities over a full 360°, where
(ii) each orientation "channel" applies to all areas of the visual field but not necessarily in a homogeneous fashion;
(iii) the orientation selectivity has a response function with one optimum orientation, and usually endowed with monotonically decreasing sensitivity either side. Sometimes this function is endowed with inhibitory and post-inhibitory excitation flanks as shown in Fig. 6.24.

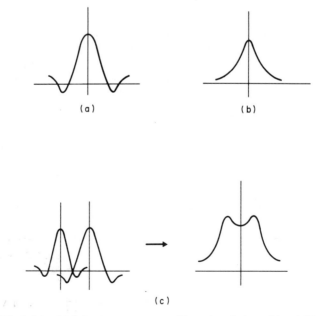

Fig. 6.24. Orientation selectivity curves as proposed in various feature: (a) and (b), encoding models, (c) illustrates simple forms of interaction.

Similar "feature-specific tuning curves", as illustrated, have been proposed for other simple geometric and optical properties of an image (Uttal, 1973). Of course, the initial discoveries of feature specific cortical cell responses dealt with the fly detector of Lettvin *et al.* (1959) in the frog and the orientation, motion, and size-detecting mechanisms of Hubel and Wiesel (1962, 1968). In all such instances the feature specific receptive fields were delineated by probing cortical areas of convergent ganglion cell activity in the hope of finding preferred responses to stimuli that seemed important to the animal. Flies are important for frogs as orientation seems important to cats and monkeys. However, as recently demonstrated by Creutzfeldt *et al.* (1973) and Frost (1978), the extent of the receptive fields are far wider than previously thought, and the actual stimulus parameter of importance is not always absolute. For example, Frost (1978) has found that it is the relative motion of a source that is of interest for some cells in the pigeons' cortex—not absolute motion components alone.

Withstanding such complexities, a series of psychophysical experiments have been made based on these basic neurophysiological observations. For example, McCullough (1965) found orientation/direction specific colour-adaptation effects; Carpenter and Blakemore (1973) related orientation angle differences on the orientation illusion (and so tilt illusion and tilt aftereffect) to the tuning of orientation cells in the vertebrate visual cortex. In all cases the argument is simple—even objectively stated by Weisstein (1969): that human psychophysical results are consistent with results of microelectrode studies of individual vertebrate cortex cells since both represent the same sources of brain function.

The assumptions behind such an argument are quite strong or restrictive—the visual system is totally homogeneous and linear, that a multiple-channel space-invariant model would apply—as we saw in section 6.1. The problems with this feature specific approach are numerous when used to "explain" the processes of contour perception. A sample of these problems are:

(a) What are the criteria for deciding the number of features necessary to describe the stimulus and their associated tuning characteristics? Are there infinite features?
(b) How does the visual system piece together such coded features to perceive contours? Does feature encoding help solve the problem of contour perception?
(c) How do we define specific features such as oriented line segment, motion, velocity, etc?

A number of projects over the past decade have attempted to bridge the gap between this simple encoding model and the second "mechanisms" strategy mentioned above. Perhaps the simplest example lies in the spatial-frequency results. Here, as shown by many experiments (Sekuler, 1974), adaptation effects can be induced with grating stimuli in such a way to support the concept of spatial frequency tuning curves where frequency channels are envisaged to interact as a function of frequency proximities. We have already reviewed this literature in section 6.1, but here point out that frequency is not simply an image property or feature like orientation, velocity, etc. To conjecture that the visual system has spatial frequency specific feature detectors is to argue for detectors that are tuned to global features of an image.

Besides the evidence from the contrast experiments it is still not known whether contour extraction or encoding clearly involves specific spatial frequency channels. A number of projects have examined the concept. However, it should be noted, before expanding on these types of mechanism, that frequency encoding is not sufficient to define a shape; phase is also equally important, as already observed in the previous results on texture discrimination. The problem with the feature detector strategy for contour extraction is that the integration aspect is not tackled, an aspect which was and still is *the* problem of pattern perception (whether it be viable or not). So before dealing with the filtering or "co-operative" network approaches to these problems and their relationship to the feature specific models, a few points need clarifying. Firstly, the definition of pattern is relative to the context. For example, an oriented line segment—a candidate for feature detectors—is itself a pattern. So either a contour extraction process has to be able to derive such features as detector tuning curves or be capable of coping with the relativities of definition with contours or patterns. Secondly, the issues as to which regions of the image amplitude spectra the human visual system may be specifically tuned for—which orientations are preferred—are all issues relevant to *what* we perceive, but not *how* we perceive contours or shapes.

The process of contour perception involves, at least, the grouping and ordering of some portions of the visual input on the basis of relative position. The portions or elements of the input, which are grouped, may be dots, stars, line elements (as in the case of continuous curves), or any other elements which are "similar". In general, these elements are distinguished on the basis of luminance and chromatic contrast across the visual manifold. Any theory of contour extraction must provide a process for how such groupings and orderings of elements occur within the visual system. One of the consequences of these operations is that a connectivity measure (probability) can be associated between any image element pair. The various models should be at least assessed in these terms so that psychophysical predictions about contour formations may be compared from the basis of each theoretical position.

As mentioned earlier, it is the relative position of similar elements that forms the primitive input code for the extraction and integration of features that permit contour perception. Consequently, the visual input can be described by delta functions—a representation which encodes position only. In this way the forms of the "elements", which constitute the input, are ignored since their similarity and relative position are the only relevant parameters in a general contour extraction process.

The delta function $\delta(x)$ on a vector manifold is a function which is zero everywhere except at the origin, where its value is so large that

$$\int_{-\infty}^{\infty} \delta(x)\,dx = 1.$$

Hence a pattern which is non-zero only at points $x_1 \ldots x_k$ can be defined by

$$p(x) = \sum_{i=1}^{k} \delta(x - x_i). \tag{6.11}$$

Most discussions of pattern perception consider the input to the visual system to be real (or possibly vector) valued functions on a two-dimensional retinal surface. The δ-function representation is different in that it allows "infinite" valued functions as inputs—hypothetically at least. The difference, however, is only one of mathematical convenience. Any visual input, such as a pattern of dots or stars, may be derived from the δ-function representation by convolution. For example, consider a pattern $h(x)$ having elements located at $x_1 \ldots x_k$. If $g(x)$ is a function positioned at the origin, which describes the shape of the individual pattern elements, then the pattern is given by

$$h(x) = (g \times p)(x) = \int \int g(u) p(x - u) du.$$

That is,

$$h(x) = \sum_{i=1}^{k} \int \int g(u) \, \delta(u - x_i) du.$$

In this way $h(x)$ can be obtained from $p(x)$ by a simple integration process. Provided that the elements of $h(x)$ are small there is little mathematical difference between $h(x)$ and $p(x)$. The function $h(x)$ is essentially a "smudging" of $p(x)$ and, as such, when used in place of $p(x)$, results in a slight smoothing of each element—a quantitative rather than qualitative change.

It is not contended that the δ-function representation encodes the entire retinal signal for each pattern element. It does, however, represent the essential properties of input elements to the cortical contour extraction process. In this way even intrinsically complex local features can still be considered as having a unitary contribution to the pattern extraction process although such features may well be products of previous pattern or feature detection processes.

With this in mind we now review the current approaches to contour extraction of the "co-operative" or global nature, noting that we have cited flaws in the trigger feature approach centring around the problems of infinite feature lists and integration.

6.4.1. Fourier and low-pass filter approaches

Another approach to the packaging of information in the visual system is that developed by Campbell and Robson (1968). In the experiments on the threshold detection of sinusoidal and square-wave grating they contend that the visual system is selectively sensitive to various frequency bands of the gratings' Fourier spectra. These authors (and others, see Breitmeyer and Ganz, 1976) have concluded that the visual system has spatial "channels" and that shape may be analysed via the frequency components of the image.

Kabrisky (1966) and Ginsberg (1973) also use the Fourier approach in their band-pass filter model for pattern perception and contend that the perception of contour is a result of the ability of the visual system to low-pass frequency filter the image. The filtering out of high-frequency components is contended to result in perceived connectivity ("smudging") between elements in various regions of the stimulus.

The Fourier transform $F(s, t)$ of a two-dimensional function $f(x, y)$ is a complex-valued function given by (Chapter 3):

$$F(s, t) = \int_{-\infty}^{\infty} \int f(x, y) \exp\left[-i(sx + ty)\right] dx \, dy.$$

Filtering is a linear operation which has the effect of modifying $F(s, t)$. For instance, low-pass filtering removes (sets to zero) the values of F for large (in absolute value) $S = (s, t)$, and effectively smudges the function $f(x, y)$. In fact, any filtering operation can be performed by a convolution. Low-pass filtering with a bandwidth α is equivalent to convoluting with the weighting function (Chapter 3).

$$g_\alpha(x) = \frac{\sin(\alpha \| x \|)}{\alpha \| x \|} \tag{6.12}$$

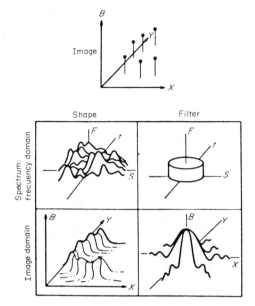

FIG. 6.25. Image and frequency spectrum profiles of a pattern and low pass filter (F, amplitude; B, luminance).

if $p(x)$ is represented by (6.11) (a sum of δ-functions) then, low-pass filtering produces the function $p_L(x)$ given by

$$p_L(x) = \sum_{i=1}^{k} \frac{\sin(\alpha \| x - x_i \|)}{\alpha \| x - x_i \|}. \tag{6.13}$$

The smoothing effect of the filter is illustrated in Fig. 6.25.

The weighting function (6.12) provides a local connectivity measure between image elements as a function of their separation. However, the Fourier approach does not provide a means of patching together (ordering) the local connectivities (derived by the weighting function) to obtain global contour paths.

Pribram *et al.* (1974) also contended that the visual system, by encoding the spectral and phase components of the image, constructs a holographic representation—the basis of visual memory—according to these authors.

6.4.2. Autocorrelation approaches

The low-pass filter and trigger feature models imply that position is preserved and that local connectivities are perceived by means of local weighting processes. The question as to how such connections are patched together to extract global contours or structures, remains unsolved.

Other approaches have been proposed in terms of global configuration properties of the image. The exemplar of such approaches is the autocorrelation theory proposed by Uttal (1975). This model has been used in computer pattern recognition (Clowes, 1962, Moore and Parker, 1974) and human pattern perception for weil over a decade (Licklider,

1959; Dodwell, 1970). The essential proposition is that the visual system encodes structure via the distribution of inter-element distances based on the autocorrelation function

$$A(u,v) = \int_Y \int_X f(x,y)f(x+u, y+v)\,dx\,dy. \qquad (6.14)$$

The autocorrelogram $A(u,v)$ is contended to represent the "neural interactions" (Uttal, 1975) between cortical cells and pattern elements.

Geometrically, $A(u,v)$ represents the frequency distribution of all pairs of discrete image elements. Such pairs are also the "dipoles" (Julesz, 1971), and we have already shown how these second-order statistics are correlated with texture perception. However, their usefulness in pattern perception is restricted to situations where periodicities, linearities, repetitions, etc., are important and consequently are not applicable to curvature detection (Caelli and Umansky, 1976).

As autocorrelation is a global process, and since particular (u,v) statistics do not remain associated with particular points, it is not possible to use it alone to obtain groupings and orderings of image elements. Furthermore, the model does not solve the problem of contour recognition since the autocorrelogram, in its own right, is a pattern requiring recognition.

6.4.3. Network models

Grossberg (1976a), Leake and Anninos (1976), and Sejnowski (1976) have developed models for interactive neural processes based on the following type of network equation (see Chapter 4):

$$\phi_i = \eta_i + \sum_j C_{ij} g(\phi_j) \qquad (6.15)$$

The terms of (6.15) are generally interpreted as: η_i is the external input to cell i (afferent volley including the resting potential), ϕ_i is the output of cell i (e.g. average membrane potential), $g(\phi_j)$ is some function of the input or output of cell i relevant as input to other cells, and c_{ij} is the connectivity between cells i and j reflecting complex dendritic processes (C_{ii} would correspond to recurrent collaterals).

Equation (6.15) implies that the response of a cortical cell has two components—a retinotopic component η_i and a component resulting from a weighing of other cell responses. These authors have analysed the retinal ganglion receptive fields, cortical trigger features, and spatial frequency channels as examples of such "mass action" network processes (6.15).

This model raises the question as to the optimum form of the weighting function, C_{ij}, which relates relative position to the extraction of contour information. The low-pass filter model suggests a sinc function (6.13). Leake and Anninos (1976) have shown that exponential decay functions, derived from Poisson dendritic arborization processes, are consistent with properties of cortical receptive fields. Coleman and Renninger (1975) have also demonstrated the applicability of exponential decay processes in determining the retinal ganglion cell profiles of *Limulus*. These processes suggest the use of an exponential decay function for encoding spatial interactions as being more likely than other weighting functions (e.g. sinc functions).

Grossberg (1976b) introduced the concept of adaptive resonance between two fields of cell populations to demonstrate how even simple network devices may provide a basis for the extraction of global codes necessary for contour perception. In this system feedback signals oscillate between the two fields until amplitude increases become stabilized or go into resonance. Given a geometric interpretation of (6.15), such as the formation of contour specific orientation, then these feedback conditions may well be a basis for the extraction of invariant paths between local tangential orientations.

Each of the above approaches to contour perception have proposed that the neuro-physiological structure of the cortex enables the observer to locally connect elements of the image. The most common mechanism is a weighting function C_{ij} (6.15), which is subject to spatial summation. In this sense these approaches are "co-operative" since contours are argued to be processed via the interactions between coding elements, reflected in a weighting function (or filter) in the image domain (see Chapter 3 for more details). From a series of experimental results ideal weighting functions are centred about a monotonically decreasing function having half-amplitude at $2°$ of visual angle (see Caelli *et al.*, 1978).

Although such filtering mechanisms are capable of predicting local perceptual contour directions, "contour" or shape is merely collectively defined. No mechanisms are proposed for how we may combine each locally filtered region. In other words these mechanisms require implanting into another process, which would integrate the filter outputs to register the total contour (presuming such a concept is meaningful). One such process is illustrated in Fig. 6.26 where local filtering contributes directional information, which, in turn, signals curvature and more distant contour information.

An alternative framework in which to discuss problems of contour and pattern perception has been proposed by Hoffman (1966, 1978). He contends that the visual system, in perceiving contour, employs local differential operations (Lie derivatives) to "drag the flow" of a contour along its perceived path. This is equivalent to establishing a direction component (tangent vector) at each contour position which is tangential to the contour paths at the point. Points are then grouped and ordered in such a way that contour is perceived as an interpolation between elements consistent with the tangent directions. That is, contour is perceived as an invariant vector field (Fig. 6.26; Chapter 5).

This language seems applicable to describing phenomena such as apparent motion (Foster, 1973) and restricted cases of contour perception (Caelli, 1976). For example, the results of Glass and Switkes (1976) indicate that global moiré patterns can be perceived in random dot configurations when pair-wise (dipole) dot elements form tangential orientations to the perceived paths—isocline solutions for invariant vector fields. However, to that stage the geometric approach only supplies a language for contour perception and not a quantitative process. A formulation is required that can predict a contour direction at each location as a function of the general cortical network process and the geometry of the stimulus input.

Tangent vectors may be determined at each element position by a summation process involving a weighting function. Given such a function $[C_{ij}, (6.15)]$, which weights points as a (decaying) function of distance, a constellation of direction components is obtained at each image point (stage II, Fig. 6.26). Tangent vectors are then determined by an averaging of each constellation (stage III, Fig. 6.26).

Curvature vectors—the rate of change of tangent vectors with respect to position—may be formed by a similar weighting process on the tangent vectors (stage IV, Fig. 6.26). These tangent and curvature vectors would enable the visual system to patch (group and

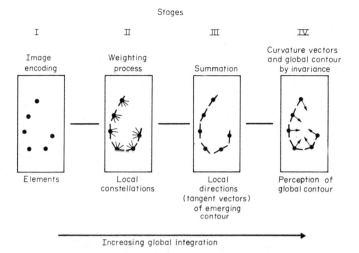

Stages

I   II   III   IV

Image encoding   Weighting process   Summation   Curvature vectors and global contour by invariance

Elements   Local constellations   Local directions (tangent vectors) of emerging contour   Perception of global contour

Increasing global integration

FIG. 6.26. Proposed stages in the emergence of contour: I, encoding of relative position of similar elements in the visual input; II, association of image element pairs weighed for distance; III, summation of direction components of II to form weighted tangent at end point; IV, the extraction of contour via tangent and curvature vector operators.

order) image elements into contour paths by means of the inherent invariance properties of vector fields (see Caelli *et al.*, 1978, for more details).

The essence of this approach is that weighting functions are associated with the formation of geometric operators that generate local tangent and curvature vectors whose invariance properties lead to the perception of contour. That is, we can describe the network processes in terms of the formation of various geometric operators.

Various attempts have been made to apply these processes to the prediction of human contour perception from visual illusions to the perception of contours from simple dot configurations. For example, observers invariably perceive contour paths through the points in Fig. 6.27a as shown in Fig. 6.27b, where the line thickness is representative of contour strength or connection frequency (Caelli *et al.*, 1978).

As shown in (6.13) and (6.15), such perceptual connectivities can be modelled by the low-pass filtering and general network formulations respectively. Both models have a single decay parameter α (the latter having $C_{ij} = \exp(-\alpha d_{ij})$, d_{ij} being the interpoint distance). Correlating the filter (FLPF) and exponential decay filter (EDP) with observed connectivities over various α-values results in the curves shown in Fig. 6.27c. Results indicated that best fitting decay rates of $\alpha = 16$ for EDP and $\alpha = 25$ for FLPF models corresponded to half-amplitude values of $2°$ of visual angle. Such connectivities correspond to the primitive filtering process described as stage II in Fig. 6.26.

The outcome of stage III type processes is illustrated in Fig. 6.27d where a vector can be associated with each point, representative of the predicted predominant contour path, to the observer, at the point. For convenience the length of the line corresponds to the contour strength $\alpha = 16$ for the EDP process.

The summation process predicts a perceived direction component at each point of the image due to weighted interactions between elements. One consequence of this is that when the observer is presented two contours in close proximity a form of contour interaction should be perceived. In particular, when the contours are intersecting line segments

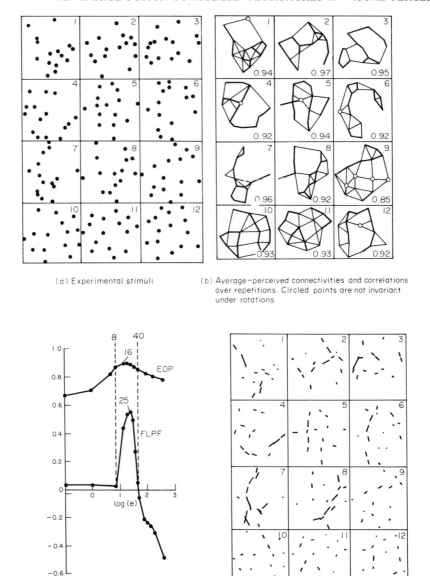

(a) Experimental stimuli

(b) Average–perceived connectivities and correlations over repetitions. Circled points are not invariant under rotations

(c) Comparison of EDP and FLPF filters with experimental data (average correlation r)

(d) Computed tangent vectors using EDP with $\alpha = 16.0$

FIG. 6.27. (a)–(c) Experimental results on perceived contours in random not displays, and (d) predicted contour directions at each point.

(Fig. 6.28b) the process predicts a perceived distortion of the intersection angle and curvature of the lines. In psychophysical studies on orientation interactions (Weisstein, 1969) it has been found that the degree of contour interaction is a function of the intersection angle. Typical data from Levine and Grossberg (1976) has been replotted in Fig. 6.28a to illustrate this effect. Summation vectors were again calculated (EDP, $\alpha = 16$) for discretized

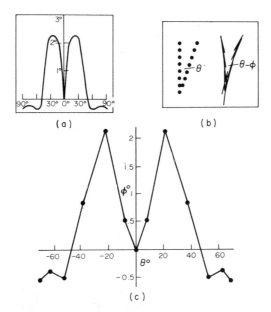

(a)   (b)

(c)

FIG. 6.28. Orientation interaction curves: (a) typical orientation interaction curve, (b) discretized intersecting line segments and resultant tangent vectors, and (c) orientation interaction curve from summation process.

intersecting line segments (Fig. 6.28b) over a range of intersection angles. A new intersection angle was calculated as the average of vector orientations and a "tuning curve" resulted (Fig. 6.28c), which is compatible with known orientation illusion magnitudes (Fig. 6.28a).

The EDP summation process also predicts distortions in the perceptions of length as a function of intersecting contours (Caelli, 1977). To illustrate these distortions tangent vectors were calculated for discretized Müller–Lyer and Poggendorff stimuli. The results are shown in Fig. 6.29a, b with the observed illusory effects (Robinson, 1972). Other illu-

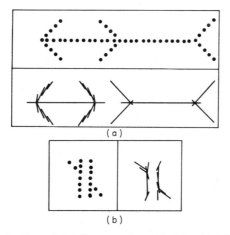

(a)

(b)

FIG. 6.29. Discretized stimuli predicted illusory paths and lengths, (a) Müller–Lyer illusion, and (b) Poggendorff illusion.

sions, such as the Zollner Herring, are also predicted from this model having illusory orientations and lengths due to the generation of vectors affected by elements from both contours.

The results of the random dot display experiment and the illusion analyses may be summarized as follows:

(1) In the process of extracting contours from discrete displays the human observer weights elements as an inverse function of distance.
(2) The preferred contour path is a result of the vector orientations formed by summation. This contour formation process would seem to predict some facets of orientation and length illusions.
(3) Points which are unstable under rotations are those that have small direction vectors, a result of being bifurcation or distant points in a configuration (Fig. 6.27b).

These results indicate that local groupings, connectivities, and global contour perception are not products of simple nearest-neighbour rules but that the "mass action" (Grossberg, 1976a) of the configuration determines local contour paths. Similarly, global contour perception is a product of ordering and invariance properties of the local processes; local and global processes are highly interactive in the extraction of structure from the image.

It was suggested in Chapter 4 that the EDP process may be representative of the complex axo-dendritic and axo-somatic processes in the visual cortex. Recent evidence indicates that individual cortex cells are excited by essentially one retinal ganglion cell but that many other cortical cells, anisotropically related to this receptive field, are also excited. This implies that the cortex preserves retinotopic gradients and that the cortical axon collaterals and dendritic processes, related to a particular retinal ganglion receptive field, are randomly (uniformly) distributed over the visual manifold (Leake and Anninos, 1976).

Using intracellular recordings, Creutzfeldt et al. (1974) found that, with direction specific oriented line segments, inhibition of cortical neurons reached over distances larger than the orientation columns of Hubel and Wiesel (1962, 1968). Similarly, Valverde (1976) has found anatomical axonal processes that are not limited to these orientation specific structural units. Consequently, these far-reaching anatomical and functional processes, being randomly distributed with respect to the retinotopic map of the visual image, suggest a network interconnectivity matrix having Poisson or exponentially distributed transmissions of excitatory and inhibitory post-synaptic potentials (IPSOs) (Grossberg, 1976a; Leake and Anninos, 1976). This suggests that the visual system summates information inversely with eccentricity when forming local profiles of spatial interactions.

However, to our knowledge no neurophysiological process has been found which could account for the summation stage in the formation of direction vectors. The initial stage (stage II) of determining the weighted direction vectors between image elements may well be consistent with the orientation selective cells described by Hubel and Wiesel (1962). However, the receptive fields of such cells would spread to far greater areas than originally suggested. Since these vectors were highly correlated with the preferred contour paths and illusions of length and orientation, they remain powerful psychophysical operators.

These concepts and processes are not new although often expressed in different terms (see Watson, 1978, for a Riemann surface interpretation; Chiang, 1968). The point of what has been offered above is that it is possible to cover both feature detector profile models and filtering processes by the same conceptual framework, probably best exemplified by

(6.15). We shall see in the following section that there are other approaches to visual illusions and other demonstrations that indicate that past experience and expected transformation properties of images—all affect our perceptions of events. However, it seems clear that the issues of feature detectors, filtering, and integration all have a singular basis in contour perception and visual illusion processes. Coren and Girgus (1978) discuss the multiple factors involved in visual illusions (optical, retinal, cortical, and cognitive), concluding that all play a clear role in the net effect of a specific illusion. In this chapter we have concentrated on the neuronal or cortical components due to the current interest in this aspect of spatial vision

This is not to imply that specific filter parameters, even filter types (ex-FLPF compared to EDP), will always adequately predict various aspects of pattern recognition or discrimination. For example, in a recent paper Coffin (1978) has had little success in predicting alphabetic discrimination in terms of the correlation between each character pair amplitude spectra. Rather, these mechanisms are attempts at bridging the gap between individual cell function and visual psychophysics. To this stage critical experiments have not been conducted that would confirm or deny the role of specific filters in visual image processing. For example, it is not clear whether we can predict many illusory effects by observing the MTF (see section 6.1) of an individual observer; it is also not clear whether nonlinear systems as Wiener expansions are more salient representations of neural integration activity than the more simple linear filters involved in, say, than frequency encoding models (Palm and Poggio, 1977).

Maybe it is reasonable to use the "channel" model for contour perception as proposed by Breitmeyer and Ganz (1976), where sustained and transient channels and their interactions are allocated for specific spatio-temporal event encoding. Yet, to this stage, more categorical proof is needed for such processes being at the basis of many spatial phenomena than those demonstrations given by Ginsberg (1975), where illusions are simply regarded as examples of band-pass filtering (in many ways).

Space prohibits more detailed analyses of precious models for contour extraction and illusions. The reader is referred to texts like Dodwell (1970), on visual pattern perception, and Uttal's (1973, 1975) books on sensory coding and pattern perception. Finally, the author is referred to Julesz's (1971) book on spatial (cyclopean) vision and Leeuwenberg and Buffart (1978) for complementary reading to this section.

6.5. SPATIAL EQUIVALENCES AND PERCEPTUAL INVARIANTS

One major problem with investigations into the processes of contour or pattern perception is that other processes than the visual psychophysics play a role. For example, our memories for shape, experiences, and environmental conditions all determine the types of shapes and perceptual organizations we experience. As to whether we have developed such networks as described in Section 6.3 to interpret these factors, or whether the reverse dependence applies, is open to debate. However, it is clear that there are two ways of looking at the topic and, in this section, we will briefly review the so-called "invariance" or "transformations" perspective to shape perception.

There are a few basic insights that are fundamental to this approach and that should be stated. Although obvious, they reveal very strong properties of the human visual system. The first is that although our optical retinal image of the world is in continuous flux and its projections are non-uniform, we believe and interpret the perceptual world as a stable and contiguous phenomenon. This implies a second quality for perception—that we can spontaneously extract the image properties that are invariant under these continuous transformations. For example, the vertebrate optical system centrally projects the image, and hence the relationships between the object and image are governed by projective geometry (see Chapter 5; Johansson, 1978), particularly when depth perception is of concern.

The preservation of image properties such as angle, size, distance, etc., are termed "constancy" structures in the psychological literature since they do refer to the invariance of image properties while the image is undergoing transformations. What is often missed is that it is really our perceptions of the image properties which are constant. For example, when we perceive the kinetic depth effect—the perception of a three-dimensional rotating object from two-dimensional projections of it (see Chapter 7 for more details)—it is our visual system that is reconstructing the image as three-dimensional. Now if the rotating object is changed or the projection surface bent and we perceive the identical three-dimensional object, the "constancy" lies in the interpretation process itself and not in the image.

With this in mind the so-called "constancy explanation" of visual illusions suffers from the problem of endowing the stimulus with the mechanisms of constancy. Here the argument is simple, yet equivocal. We expect geometrical properties of objects and their relationships to satisfy common (ecologically viable—presumably) transformations. For example, that the image appears smaller as it increases in distance from the observer, the image of a slanted circle is an ellipse, etc. So when we create the circumstances, which dispose one to interpret events under such conditions but do not present the "vertical" (corresponding) environment, an illusion is reported. In Day's (1972) terms: "Illusions occur when stimuli that normally preserve constancy are operative but with the image of the object not varied."

Some typical examples of this approach are shown in Fig. 6.30.

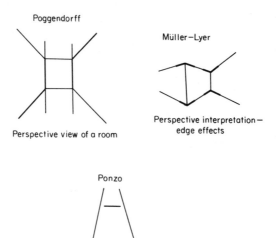

FIG. 6.30 Some examples of illusions used to illustrate the constancy explanation.

One problem with the above statements about the "constancy explanation" is that it is circular. Specifically, stimuli that preserve constancy are not defined in any strict fashion. Rather they are defined by exactly those stimuli that give us illusions. No *a priori* unequivocal conditions have been defined that could locate the source of such illusory stimuli to such an extent that critics of this "explanation" may well conclude that the position simply states that illusions occur when stimuli that normally give illusions give illusions! However, what is generally meant is that, besides "constancies" as "shape", colour, brightness, the visual system only preserves the *affine* properties of an image and may interpret the Euclidean features at will (see Chapter 5)—at least when a depth component is involved.

In order to overcome such equivocation and tautology, yet preserve the profound nature of the constancy concept, some recent attempts have been made to restrict the invariances to simple aspects of spatial contour perception which involve definable transformations. Perhaps the clearest examples of this position are seen in the works of Hoffman (1966, 1978) and Johannson (1978) and various specific applications of Foster (1978), the author (Caelli, 1976, 1978), and Shepard (1978).

The Johannson work (1977, 1978) is concerned with how we perceptually decompose and integrate relative motions of small numbers of dots on the surface of a CRT. The results (to be discussed further in Chapter 7) indicate three strong properties of visual image processing:

(1) That we have a disposition to interpret the motion of objects as preserving projective relationships.
(2) That we perceptually decompose relative motions in terms of relative and common motion components—a form of vector analysis.
(3) That (2) occurs when motions or images are adjacent. These observations are consistent with the previous observations regarding illusions and constancy. For example, the projective invariance "constancy" would result in relative vector components (1) and (2) compatible with illusory effects.

The Johannson work is an extension of the earlier Gibson (1950) work where the very concepts of preservation of image properties with respect to the optical transforms were exposed. Figure 6.31 illustrates some of the Johannson results.

The Hoffman (1966, 1978) LTG formation (Lie transformation groups) is quite a deal more extensive (and controversial in content) than the Johannson formulation and specifically provides a "metalanguage" for perceptual processes, where individual mechanisms may be interpreted to have specific roles in extracting invariance properties of the image.

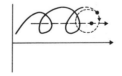

(a) Rotation in depth from two sources   (b) Epicyclic motion breaks down into
                                                    its rotation and translation components

FIG. 6.31. Specific effects with dot configurations observed by Johannson (1977, 1978).

The assumptions made about the visual system for this formulation are as follows. The first important condition is that the visual field (the "perceived world") is a manifold in so far as it has no "holes" (it has complete covering) and has a covering by locally Euclidean neighbourhoods (Guggenheimer, 1963). The covering properties of this manifold M are determined, in the first instance, by the complex receptive field structure of the retina at the retinal cells. The receptive fields overlap (are not disjoint) at this stage and vary in size. Such receptive fields seem tuned to extract contrast, spatial frequency (in a limited way) and position (Rodieck, 1973).

The next assumption is that the visual cortex has a hierarchy of cells that are driven by retinal ganglion cells and affected by the functions of neighbouring cortical cells. The input signals to these cells would seem to be differential in form. That is, orientation, spatial and temporal frequencies, direction, motion, and relevant coordinations of these parameters all represent spatio-temporal information that encodes (rates of) change of particular parameters (Caelli and Umansky, 1976). That is, the visual cortex adds to the visual manifold small spatio-temporal "arrows" representing direction fields at each point on M.

Recent experiments at the neurophysiological and psychophysical levels (Breitmeyer and Ganz, 1976) indicate that these parameters may be adapted, masked in a similar way to retinal contrast parameters (Cornsweet, 1970). That is, they are "local" or peripheral to the pattern recognition process that integrates and forms contour from such information. Geometrically these cortical parameters are defined with respect to an arbitrary contour f on M where at each point $P \in M$, there is a local coordinate system. That is, it is impossible to contend that orientation is perceived with respect to an absolute uniform visual coordinate system because it does not exist (Luneburg, 1950). In particular, when contours appear on the manifold the perception of distance, angle, and the other above mentioned parameters would seem to change with respect to the contour.

Consequently, such differential parameters must be represented as collections of vector fields $X(p)$, $Y(p)$ defined as follows (see Chapter 5):

(1) $Xf(p) = k \in R$, the real line, representing a tangent vector at p.

(2) $[X(p) + Y(p)]f(p) = X(p)f(p) + Y(p)f(p)$ (6.16)

(3) For $\alpha \in R, (\alpha X)(p)f(p) = \alpha[X(p)f(p)]$.

(4) $[X(p), Y(p)] = (X, Y)(p) = XY(p) - YX(p)$.   (6.17)

These conditions assert that the differential parameters form a vector space (and the basis for a Lie algebra) and, it is argued, psychophysical studies support this conjecture since the various adaptation and masking studies indicate that the parameter is closed (e.g. orientation simply assumes another value) and additive.

The assumption that the cortical cells extract differential information from retinal and geniculate cells suggests an alternative mechanism for their function to that originally proposed by Hubel and Wiesel (1965) in the spatial orientation domain. In their model orientation specificity is determined by the union of overlapping retinal ganglion cell receptive fields, assuming a threshold model. That cortical cells extract differential information implies that orientation specificity comes from the ability of the cortical cell to respond differentially to impulses from the retinal ganglion cells.

The LTG theory contends that such contours are precisely determined by these vector field features and that the perceived contour (shape) is the geometric trajectory of the

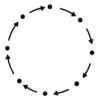

Fig. 6.32. Position and direction determinants of the rotation path.

resultant invariant vector field. That is, the visual system searches for the function that satisfied the condition that, at each point $p \in M$,

$$X_1 \frac{\partial f}{\partial x}\bigg|_p + X_2 \frac{\partial f}{\partial y}\bigg|_p = 0. \tag{6.18}$$

This invariance condition can be seen to hold in a variety of stimulus situations. For example, Fig. 6.32 illustrates the case where position and direction fields consistently determine the invariant trajectories of a circle. That is, at each point (x, y) there is a direction component

$$\mathrm{d}y/\mathrm{d}x = x/y. \tag{6.19}$$

The perceived contour (circular path) is determined (Guggenheimer, 1963) by

$$\mathscr{L}_R = -y \frac{\partial f}{\partial x} + x \frac{\partial f}{\partial y} \tag{6.20}$$

or $$x^2 + y^2 = c.$$

This perceived circular path is defined by transformation, which carries (in an ordered fashion) one oriented line segment into another while preserving the relationship (6.18). This preservation (invariance) operation is perceived in Fig. 6.32 b where:

(1) the visual system ignores orientation and solely constructs the circular path on position; or
(2) orientation is accommodated by projecting the circle in depth to obtain invariance; or
(3) the circular path is replaced by the perception of a series of linear paths.

All three possibilities indicate that the visual system spontaneously perceives contours from position and/or direction fields and that the path curve is essentially a 1-parameter curve that preserves (makes invariant) the local pattern features. Figure 6.32 also illustrates this process and indicates how the visual system combines both position and assigned directions to establish a "bent" circular path. These demonstration, from the Hoffman formulation, simply indicate that the visual system extracts contour through its annulment by the differential operator

$$f(x, y) \frac{\partial F}{\partial x} + g(x, y) \frac{\partial F}{\partial y} = 0, \tag{6.21}$$

where $F(x, y)$ corresponds to the contour, (x, y) (in two-dimensions) corresponds to the local coordinate system of the visual manifold, and $(\mathrm{d}y/\mathrm{d}x) = [g(x, y)/f(x, y)]$ represents the differential code (primary cortical projections) of the local pattern feature information.

Lie proved (Guggenheimer, 1963) that this solution (6.21) can be accomplished by appropriate "Lie transformation groups". That is, at each point $p \varepsilon M$, a Lie operator (generalized directional derivative) "drags the flow" of the direction field along the contour $F(x, y)$. This correspondence between the global transformation groups and the (local) Lie transformation group about each point is illustrated for the case of rotations. The rotation group on the plane about the origin is

$$x' = x \cos \theta - y \sin \theta, \quad y' = x \sin \theta + y \cos \theta.$$

The bases of the associated vector fields $(f(x, y), g(x, y); 6.21)$ are determined by taking a Taylor expansion of the transformation $X(x, y; \theta)$, $Y(x, y; \theta)$ about the identity element θ_0 (Chapter 5).

For $\theta = \theta_0$, the identity element of the transformation group, it can be seen that for rotations $f(x, y) = -y$ and $g(x, y) = x$.

As a consequence it can be shown that these Lie operators concatonate by linear addition, as with the formation of spiral trajectories from local rotations $(\mathscr{L}_R)$ and dilations $[\mathscr{L}_s = x(\partial/\partial x) + y(\partial/\partial y)]$:

$$\mathscr{L}_{sp} = \alpha \mathscr{L}_R + \beta \mathscr{L}_s.$$

Such operators may be orthogonal, where $\mathscr{L}_A \perp \mathscr{L}_B$ if

$$\mathscr{L}_A = f \frac{\partial}{\partial x} + g \frac{\partial}{\partial y}$$

and

$$\mathscr{L}_B = -g \frac{\partial}{\partial x} + f \frac{\partial}{\partial y}.$$

A Lie Algebra is formed when the commutator (product term, 6.17)

$$[\mathscr{L}_A, \mathscr{L}_B] = \mathscr{L}_A \mathscr{L}_B - \mathscr{L}_B \mathscr{L}_A$$

of the Lie operators spans the linear manifold of these operators.

Hoffman (1966, 1967, 1970) restricts the Lie algebra to those listed in Table 6.1. However, the more fundamental propositions of the model are that:

P_1 : Pattern features constitute position and direction fields on the visual manifold.

P_2 : The contours perceived from such features are those which are invariant under the action of the Lie derivatives.

P_3 : The combination rules of addition, products of Lie operators, have some perceptual interpretation.

P_4 : The mechanisms for such pattern formation processes reside in the ability of the visual system to apply a series of difference operators that act until invariance is attained.

Some evidence has been presented by the author (Caelli, 1976, 1978) for the direct application of this approach to pattern or contour extraction. Similarly, Foster (1973, 1978a, b) has shown how the affine invariant transformation groups are representative of permissible apparent motions and identities between dot configurations. Certainly the demonstrations of "flow" patterns by McKay (1961) and moiré patterns of Glass and Switkes (1976) are

Table 6.1. Visual constancies versus the corresponding transformation groups

Perceptual invariance	Lie transformation group	Lie derivative(s)[a]
A. *Shape constancy* (a) Location in the field of view	A. *Affine group* Horizontal and vertical translation groups	$L_X = \dfrac{\partial}{\partial x}, L_Y = \dfrac{\partial}{\partial y}$
(b) (Form memory, "object constancy")	Time translations	$L_t = \dfrac{\partial}{\partial t}$
(c) Orientation	Rotation group	$L_R = -y\dfrac{\partial}{\partial x} + x\dfrac{\partial}{\partial y}$
(d) Binocular vision	Pseudo-Euclidean (hyperbolic) rotations	$L_b = y\dfrac{\partial}{\partial x} + x\dfrac{\partial}{\partial y}$
B. (Efferent binocular perception)	B. (Hyperbolic rotations in plane-time)	$L_B = x\dfrac{\partial}{\partial x} - y\dfrac{\partial}{\partial y}$ $L_{Bi} = t\dfrac{\partial}{\partial t} - x\dfrac{\partial}{\partial x}$ $L_{B_2} = t\dfrac{\partial}{\partial t} - y\dfrac{\partial}{\partial y}$
C. Size constancy	C. Dilation group	$L_S = x\dfrac{\partial}{\partial x} + y\dfrac{y}{\partial y}$
D. Motion invariance	D. Lorentz group of order 2	$L_m = -L_R$ $L_m = ct\dfrac{\partial}{\partial y} + x\dfrac{\partial}{\partial(ct)}$ $L_{m_2} = ct\dfrac{\partial}{\partial y} + y\dfrac{\partial}{\partial(ct)}$
E. (Cyclopean, or egocentred perception)	E. Rotation group in plane-time	$L_m = -L_{0'}$ $L_m = x\dfrac{\partial}{\partial(ct)} - ct\dfrac{\partial}{\partial x}$ $L_{m_2} = y\dfrac{\partial}{\partial(ct)} - ct\dfrac{\partial}{\partial y}$

[a] x = horizontal distance from the perceptual centre;
y = vertical distance from the centre of perception;
t = time measured from observer's present in cortical (neuropsychological) units:
c = maximum flow velocity of cortical signals.
(From Hoffman, 1971.)

examples of invariant vector fields. However, it is the view of the author that the Hoffman formation is a meta-language, a most convenient way of conveying concepts of perceptual invariances. Just like the Gibson (1966) formulation, it requires detailed lower level models to provide the necessary psychophysical validity before it can be satisfactorily used in a predictive way. All the "constancy models" suffer from this problem—that of providing unequivocal mechanisms for how we extract the invariant properties of an object while it is undergoing continuous change.

In this and the previous section we have briefly reviewed the essential concepts behind filtering and constancy approaches to shape perception and have noted inadequacies in both perspectives. The filtering mechanisms do not encompass the highly interpretive aspects of the constancies, while the constancies themselves do not provide mechanisms or unequivocal predictions about perceptual behaviour. Clearly both aspects are important in our normal perceptual experiences, and since they are not opposed it is false to set them up as two contradictory approaches—as some do. For example, there would seem to be both context effects and filtering (weighting function) mechanisms in illusions and, as suggested earlier, rather than be in contradiction, maybe the filtering approach and perceptual invariances are two sides of the same process—that of processing the geometry of the environment from a limited optical perspective. A clear example of this type of position is contained in the recent finding of Schwartz (1977) that the cortical retinotopic map is conformal in nature (see Chapter 5).

Maybe the greatest problem in spatial vision today is to piece together the various known results and conjectured mechanisms into a unified visual field theory that can represent contrast, networks, filtering, and invariances in a truly psychophysical way. Possibly the type of cooperative filtering network—and its associated geometric properties—discussed in this chapter is a precurser to the type of solution required. For now we move into motion perception—and its problems—leaving other spatial vision issues like stereopsis and depth perception to Chapter 8.

REFERENCES

ANDREWS, B. and POLLEN, D. (1979) Relationship between spatial frequency selectivity and receptive field profile of simple cells, *J. Physiol.* **287**, 163–176.

BECK, J. (1966) Perceptual grouping produced by changes in orientation and shape, *Science* **154**, 538–540.

BLAVAIS, A. S. (1975) Theory of Lie group representations, *Math. Biosci.* **28**, 45–67.

BREITMEYER, B. G. and GANZ, L. (1976) Implications of sustained and transient channels for theories of visual pattern masking, saccadic suppression, and information processing, *Psychol. Rev.* **83**, 1–36.

BRIDGEMAN, B. (1978) Distributed sensory coding applied to sinulations of iconic storage and metacontrast, *Math. Biol.* **40**, 605–620.

CAELLI, T. M. (1976) The prediction of interactions between visual forms by products of Lie operations, *Math. Biosci.* **30**, 191–205.

CAELLI, T. M. (1977a) Is perceived length affected by interactions between orientation detectors?, *Vision Res.* **17**, 837–841.

CAELLI, T. M. (1977b) Psychophysical interpretations and experimental evidence for the Hoffman LTG/NP theory of perception, *Cashiers de Psychol.* **20**, 107–134

CAELLI, T. M. and JULESZ, B. (1978) On perceptual analyzers underlying visual texture discrimination: Part 1, *Biol Cybernetics* **28**, 167–175.

CAELLI, T. M. and JULESZ, B. (1979) Psychophysical evidence for global feature processing in visual texture discrimination, *J. Opt. Soc. Am.* **69** (5) 675–677.

CAELLI, T. M. and UMANSKY, J. (1976) Interpolation in the visual system, *Vision Res.* **16**, 1055–1060.

CAELLI, T. M. JULESZ, B., and GILBERT, E. N. (1978) On perceptual analyzers underlying visual texture discrimination: Part II, *Biol. Cybernetics* **39**, 201–214.

CAELLI, T. M., PRESTON, G., and HOWELL, E. (1978) Implication of spatial summation models for processes of contour perception: a geometric perspective, *Vision Res.* **18**, 723–734.

CAMPBELL, F. (1976) The Transmission of spatial information through the visual system, *Scient. Am.* 95–103.

CAMPBELL, F. W., and ROBSON, J. G. (1968) Application of Fourier analysis to the visibility of gratings, *J. Physiol.* (*Lond*) **197**, 551–566.

CARPENTER, R. H. S. and BLAKEMORE, C. (1973) Interactions between orientations in human vision, *Expl. Brain Res.* **18**, 287–303.

CHIANG, C. (1968) A new theory to explain geometric illusions produced by crossing lines, *Percept Psychophys.* **3**, 174–176.

CLOWES, M. B. (1962) The use of multiple autocorrelation in character recognition, in *Optical Character Recognition* (Fisher, G. L. *et al.*,) eds., Spartan Books (Macmillan), New Yotk.

COFFIN, S. (1978) Spatial frequency analysis of block letters does not predict experimental confusions, *Percept. Psychophys.* **23** (1) 69–74.

COLEMAN, B. D. and RENNINGER, G. H. (1975) Consequences of delayed lateral inhibition in the retina of limulus: I, Elementary theory of spatially uniform fields, *J. Theoret. Biol.* **51**, 243–266.

COREN, S. and GIRGUS, J. (1978) *Visual Illusions* In *Handbook of Sensory Physiology: Perception* (Held, R., Leibowitz, H., and Teuber, H., eds), Vol. VIII, pp. 540–567. Springer-Verlag, New York,,

CORNSWEET, T. (1970) *Visual Perception*, Academic Press, New York.

CREUTZFELDT, O. D., KUHNT, U., and BENEVENTO, L. A. (1974) An intracellular analysis of visual cortical neurones to moving stimuli: responses in a co-operative neuronal network. *Expl. Brain Res.* **21**, 251–274.

DAVIDSON, M. L. (1966) A perturbation analysis of spatial brightness interaction in flashed visual fields, PhD thesis, University of California, Berkeley.

DAY, R. H. (1969) *Human Perception*, N.Y. Wiley, New York.

DAY, R. H. (1972) Visual spatial illusions: a general explanation, *Science*, **175**, 1335–1340.

DE VALOIS, R. (1978) Spatial tuning of LGN and cortical cells in monkey visual system. In *Spatial Contrast*. (Spikreijse, H. and van der Tweel, L., eds.), Akademie van Wetenschapern, Konuiklijke Nederlandse, 60–64.

DODWELL, P. C. (1970) *Visual Pattern Recognition*, Holt, Rhinehart & Winston, New York.

ENROTH-CUGELL, C. (1978) Center-surround receptive field organisation. In *Spatial Contrast* (Speikreijse, H. and van der Tweel, L., eds.), Akademie van Wetenschapern, Koninklijke Nederlandse, pp. 50–53.

FOSTER, D. H. (1972) A method for the investigation for those transformations under which the visual recognition of a given object in invariant, *Kybernetik* **11**, 217–222.

FOSTER, D. H. (1978) Visual apparent motion and the calculus of variations. In *Formal Theories of Visual Perception*. (Leeuwenberg, E. and Buffart, H., eds.), Wiley, New York, pp. 231–246.

FOSTER, D. M. (1973) An experimental examination of a hypothesis connecting visual pattern recognition and apparent motion, *Kybernetik* **14**, 63–70.

FROST, B. DIANE DI FRANCO (1978) Motion characteristics of single units in the pidgeon optic tectum, *Vision Res.* **16**, 1229–1234.

FOX, J. and MAYHEW, J. (1978) Texture discrimination and the analysis of proximity, *Perception* **18**, 75–91.

GIBSON, J. J. (1950) *The Perception of the Visual World*, Houghton Mifflin, New York.

GIBSON, J. J. (1966) *The Senses Considered as Perceptual System*, Houghton Mifflin, New York.

GINSBURG, A. P. (1975) Pattern recognition techniques suggested from psychological correlates of a model of the human visual system, *IEEE Trans. Aerospace Electron.* **9**, 625.

GLASS, L. and SWITKES, E. (1976) Pattern recognition in humans: correlations which cannot be perceived, *Perception* **5**, 67–72.

GRAHAM, N., ROBSON, J., and NACHMIAS, J. (1978) Grating summation in fovea and periphery, *Vision Res.* **18**, (7) 815–826.

GROSSBERG S, (1976a) Adaptive pattern classification and universal recoding: 1, Parallel development and coding of neural feature detectors, *Biol. Cybernetics* **23**, 121–134.

GROSSBERG, S. (1976b) Adaptive pattern classification and universal recording: 2, Feedback, expectation, olfaction, illusions, *Biol. Cybernetics* **23**, 187–202

GROSSBERG, S. (1978) A theory of visual coding, memory and development. In *Formal Theories of Visual Perception*. (Leeuwenberg, E. and Buffart, H., eds.), Wiley, New York, pp. 7–26.

GUGGENHEIMER, H. W. (1963) *Differential Geometry*, McGraw-Hill, New York.

HARVEY, L. O. and GERVAIS, M. J. (1977) Fourier analyses and the perceptual similarity of texture. Paper presented at the meeting of the Association of Research in Vision and Ophthalmology, Sarasota, Florida, April 1977.

HECHT, S., SCHALAER, S., and PIRENNE, M. H. (1942) Energy, quanta, and vision, *J. Gen. Physiol.* **25**, 819–840.

HEINEMANN, E. G. (1955) Simultaneous brightness induction as a function of inducing and test-field luminance. *Jl Expl. Psychol.* **50**, 89–96.

HOFFMAN, K. P. (1978) The projection of X-, Y- and W-cells. In *Spatial Contrast*, (Spikerijse, H. and van der Tweel, L., eds.), Akademie van Wetenschapern, Koninklijke Nederlandse, pp. 55–60.

HOFFMAN, W. C. (1966) The Lie algebra of visual perception, *J. Math. Psychol.* **3**, 65–98.

HOFFMAN, W. C. (1978) The Lie transformation group approach to visual neuropsychology. In *Formal Theories of Visual Perception*. (Leeuwenberg, E. and Buffart, H., eds.) Wiley, New York. pp. 27–66.

HUBEL, D. M. and WIESEL, T. N. (1962) Receptive fields, binocular interaction and functional architecture in the cats' visual cortex, *J. Physiol.* **160**, 106–154.

HUBEL, D. M. and WIESEL, T. N. (1965) Receptive fields and functional architecture in two nostriate visual areas (18 and 19) of the cat, *J. Neurophysiol.* **28**, 229–289.

HUBEL, D. M. and WIESEL, T. N. (1968) Receptive fields and functional architecture of monkey striate cortex, *J. Physiol.* **195**, 215–243.

JOHANNSON, G. (1978) About the geometry underlying spontaneous visual decoding of the optical message. In *Formal Theories of Visual Perception*. (Leeuwenberg, E. and Buffart, H., eds.), Wiley, New York, pp. 265–276.

JULESZ, B. (1962) Visual texture discrimination, *IRE Trans. Inf. Theory IT-***8**, 84–92.

JULESZ, B. (1971) *Foundations of Cyclopean Perception*, University of Chicago Press, Chicago.

JULESZ, B and CAELLI, T. M. (1979) On the limits of Fourier decompositions in visual texture perception, *Perception* **8**, 69–73.

JULESZ, B. GILBERT, E. N., SHEPP, L. A., and FRISCH, H. (1973) Inability of humans to discriminate between visual textures that agree in second-order statistics revisited, *Perception* **2**, 391–405.

JULESZ, B., GILBERT, E.N., and VICTOR, J. D. (1978) Visual texture discrimination of textures with identical third-order statistics, *Biol. Cybernetics* **31**, 137–140.

KABRISKY, M. (1966) *A Proposed Model for Visual Information Processing in the Human Brain*, University of Illinois Press, Urbana, Illinois.

KELLY, D. (1978) Spatial, temporal and chromatic relations. In *Spatial Contrast* (Spikreijse, H. and van der Tweel, L., eds.), Akademie Van Wetenschapern, Koninklijke Nederlandse, pp. 29–33.

LEAKE, B., and ANNINOS, P. A. (1976) Effects of connectivity on the activity of neuronal net models, *J. Theoret. Biol.* **58**, 337–363.

LEEUWENBERG, E. and BUFFART, H. (ed.) (1978) *Formal Theories of Visual Perception*, Wiley, New York

LETTVIN, J. MATURANA, H., MCCOLLOCH, W., and PITTS, W. (1959) What the frog's eye tells the frog's brain, *Proc. IRE*, **47**, 1940–1951.

LEVINE, D. S. and GROSSBERG, S. (1976) Visual illusions in neural networks: line neutralization, tilt after effect, and angle expansion, *J. Theoret. Biol.* **61**, 477–504.

LICKLIDER, J. C. R. (1959) Three auditory theories. In *Psychology: A Study of Science* (Koch, S., ed.)., Study 1, *Conceptual and Systematic*, Vol. 1, *Sensory, Perceptual and Physiological Formulations*, McGraw-Hill, New York, pp. 41–144.

LIMB, J. and RUBINSTEIN, C. (1977) A model of threshold vision incorporating inhomogeneity of the visual field, *Vision Res.* **17**, 571–585.

LUNEBURG, R. K. (1950) The metric of binocular visual space, *J. Opt. Soc. of Am.* **40**, 627–642.

MACKAY, D. M. (1961) Moving visual images produced by regular stationary patterns, *Nature* **180**, 849–850.

MCCULLOUGH, C. (1965) Color adaptation of edge-detectors in the human visual system, *Science* **149**, 1115–1116.

MAFFEI, L. (1978) Properties and architectural organization of spatial frequency detectors. In *Spatial Contrast*. (Spikreijse, H. and van der Tweel, L., eds.), Akademie Van Wetenschapern, Koninklijke Nederlands, 64–66.

MOLLON, J. D. (1978) Contrast and collor perception, In *Spatial Contrast* (Spikreijse, H. and van der Tweel, L., eds.), Akademie van Wetenschapern Koninklijke Nederlandse, pp. 40–42.

MOORE, D. J. H. and PARKER, D. J. (1974) Analysis of global pattern features, *Pattern Recognition* **6**, 149–164.

PALM, G. and POGGIO, T. (1977) Wiener-like system identification in physiology. *J. Math. Biol.* **4**, 375–381.

PRIBRAM, K. H., NUWER, M., and BARON, R. J. (1974) The holographic hypothesis of memory structure in brain function and .perception. In *Contemporary Developments in Mathematical Psychology* (Krantz, D. H., Atkinson, R. C., Luce, R. D. and Suppes, P., eds.), Freeman, San Francisco.

QUICK, R. F. (1974) A vector-magnitude model of contrast detection, *Kybernetik* **16**, 65–67.

RATLIFF, (1965) *Mach Bands: Quantitative Studies on Neural Networks in the Petina*, Holden Day, San Fransisco.

RATLIFF, F. and HARTLINE, H. K. (1959) The responses of *Limulus* optic nerve fibres to patterns of illumination on the retinal mosaic, *J. Gen. Physiol.* **42**, 1241–1355.

RICHARDS, W. and POLIT, A. (1974) Texture matching, *Kybernetik* **16**, 155–162.

RICHARDS, W. and PURKS, S. (1978) On random-dot texture discrimination, MIT report, Uo. 02189.

ROBINSON, J. O. (1972) *The Psychology of Visual Illusions*, Hutchinson, London.

RODIECK, R. W. (1973) *The Vertebrate Retina*, San Fransisco, Freeman.

SCHWARTZ, E. (1977) Spatial mapping in the primate sensory projection: analytic structure and relevance to perception, *Biol. Cybernetics* **25**, 181–194.

SEKULAR, R. (1974) Spatial vision. *Ann. Rev. Psychol.* **25**, 292–232.

SEJNOWSKI, T. J. (1976) On global properties of neuronal interaction, *Biol. Cybernetics* **22**, 85–95.

SHEPARD, R. (1978) The circumplex and related topological manifolds in the study of perception. In *Theory Construction and Data Analysis in the Behavioral Sciences* (Shye, S., ed.), Ossey-Bass, San Fransisco.

SPIKREIJSE, H. and VAN DER TWEEL, L. (1978) *Spatial Contrast*, Akademie Van Wetenschapern, Koninklijke Nederlandse.

STROMEYER, C., KRANDA, K. and STERNHEIM, C. (1978) Selective chromatic adaptation of different spatial frequencies, *Vision Res.* **18** (4) 427–438.

UTTAL, W. (1973) *The Psychobiology of Sensory Coding*, Harper & Row, New York.

UTTAL, W. R. (1975) *An Autocorrelation Theory of Form Detection*, Lawrence Eribaum Associates, New Jersey,

VALVERDE, F. (1976) Aspects of cortical organisation related to the geometry of neurons with intra-cortical axons, *J. Neurocytol.* **5**, 509–529.

WATSON, A. S. (1978) A Rieman geometric explanation of the visual illusions and figural after-effects. In *Formal Theories of Visual Perception*. (Leeuwenberg, E. and Buffar, H., eds.), Wiley, New York, pp. 139–170.

WEISSTEIN, N. (1968) A Rashevsky-Landahl neural net: stimulation of matacontrast. *Psych. Rev.* **75**, 494–521.

WEISSTEIN, N. (1969) What the frog's eye tells the human brain: single cell analysers in the human visual system, *Psychol. Bull* **72**, 157–176.

WILSON, H. and BERGEN, J. (1979) A four mechanism model for threshold spatial vision, *Vision Res.* **19**, 19–32.

ZUSNE, L. (1970) *Visual Perception of Form*, Academic Press, New York.

CHAPTER 7

The Perception of Motion

7.1. INTRODUCTION

Whereas contrast, intensity, or colour are relatively easy to define for perception, motion does not have such an unequivocal position. Although we simply define motion as the rate of change of distance with respect to time, we shall see that the definition does not adequately represent many facets of how we perceive motion, and in some instances is just not consistent with the perceptual effects. In this chapter we shall endeavour to present current approaches as to how motion is coded by the visual system in a way consistent with many such anomalous results.

For Helmholtz motion was registered by tracking eye movement information and was so allocated to the efferent side of visual information processing (see Southal, 1962). It was already noted by von Kries (ibid., p. 270), in response to the Helmholtz claim, that motion perception does occur under fixation and even retinal stabilization conditions. This indicates an afferent property of motion perception and so raises the questions (as we have seen in Chapter 6 with spatial parameters) as to the appropriate code for perceived velocities. For example, do we directly respond to motion, *per se*, or do we perceptually derive it from our objective definition (velocity = distance/time)? Perceptionists have observed consistently that these three components (velocity, distance, and time (v, s, t) are all perceptually related. That is, velocity affects our perception of time and distance travelled, and vice-versa. So it is not clear which of the three parameters are the "natural" independent ones for motion perception or, rather, spatio-temporal vision. It will be argued in section 7.2 that motion perception and the perception of spatio-temporal events is highly relativistic and that we have to investigate alternate ways of viewing the inherent geometrics to the simple fixed system employed by most.

As in the previous chapter, we shall endeavor to compare the various networks proposed for motion perception mechanisms with the apparent geometries present in visual space–time. Specifically we shall deal with the perception of object motion in depth, apparent motion, and relative motion effects. These phenomena are critical for our understanding of motion and even some aspects of spatial vision. Again, the concept of filtering, and its geometric interpretations, is of central importance to understanding current approaches to motion perception—whether it be real or apparent.

Accumulated microelectrode recording results indicate that motion sensitivity occurs in retinal ganglion cells (Barlow *et al.*, 1964) and cortical units (Breitmeyer and Ganz, 1976). The issues as to whether these cells have directional sensitivity, in general, or whether they simply differentially respond to spatio-temporal change is not clear. However, one general principle does seem to be agreed upon—that there is a trade-off between spatial and

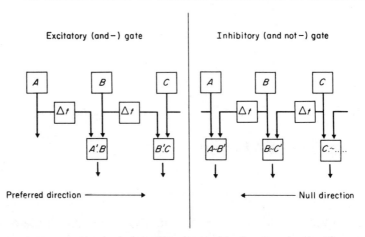

FIG. 7.1. Two logical units proposed by Barlow and Levick (1965) to represent directional sensitivity of ganglion cells in the rabbit's retina.

temporal frequency sensitivities. If a cell is highly sensitive to spatial frequency information then it typically is "sluggish" in its response to temporal frequency and vice versa. This principle will become very important when dealing with apparent motion perception.

Perhaps the most popular example of how motion, more properly directional sensitivity, may be encoded in the rabbit retina, is that of Barlow *et al.* (1964) and Barlow and Levick (1965). They observed that the retinal ganglion cells responded to specific directions and velocities of spots moving across the receptive fields of the rabbit, and modelled this by the process shown in Fig. 7.1. Here logic networks are attributed to calculate the directional sensitivity through excitatory or inhibitory mechanisms.

Two specific problems with this model are that varying velocity sensitivities would require the Δt (time lag) variable to assume a very large range of values, and that the model does not code relative motion components (recently observed by Frost, 1976). Otherwise the model was seminal to many explanations of perceptual phenomena from motion aftereffects to the very encoding of motion in human motion perception.

However, the areas of motion perception are far more rich in structures and observations than models for the retinal coding of motion. The following section will deal with some aspects of the psychophysics of real motion perception—in particular its relativity.

7.2. PSYCHOPHYSICS OF REAL MOTION PERCEPTION—RELATIVISTIC PERSPECTIVE

As already mentioned, such factors as distance, size, homogeneity and structure of background, orientation of the direction of movement, brightness, and mode of observation affect the perception of velocity. Similarly, the velocity of a moving stimulus is known to have specific effects on the static parameters of the perceived shape. For example, it is known that the apparent length of a moving object decreases as its velocity increases both in linear and rotary directions of motion (Ansbacher, 1944; Bhatia and Verghese, 1964; Brown, 1931).

One puzzling observation, which has intrigued many investigators, is that perceived velocity is not proportional to physical velocity in terms of the (Galilean) distance-to-time ratio (Mashhour, 1964). These results indicate that subjective estimates of visual spatio-temporal events undergoing motion are inconsistent with a Galilean perspective of the visual space–time geometry: a perspective that does not consider the relative nature of such estimates.

It is clear that motion itself can induce the perception of extra motions even when the source may be stationary—as we see in induced motion and motion aftereffects. Secondly, motion perception is limited, having a lower bound of about 0.2 cm/sec for a 7.5 × 2.5 cm source at 2 m to the observer—and can vary markedly for various displays (Bonnet, 1977). The upper bound also varies, but reports are from 30° to about 100° of visual angle per second (Kolers, 1972). In order to encompass the limits of real motion perception and its clear relativity, we have developed an application of the Lorentz transformations to represent the perception of motion (Caelli *et al.*, 1978a, b).

To distinguish between what we term the physical and perceptual frames of reference, consider a light source translating horizontally at velocity v with respect to a stationary observer. Here there are two physical frames: one moving (P_1, Fig. 7.2a) at velocity v with respect to the stationary (observer) frame (P_2). In this system signals propagate at the speed of light, c, and no distortions would occur in the detection of velocities within the range of human velocity perception. This system assumes that the detector can process velocities at the speed of light. However, the perceptual frames of reference are more limited. If we regard P_2, the physical stationary frame, as having a human observer centred at its origin (S_2, Fig. 7.2b), then the observer's processing of the velocity of the moving object (S_1) is

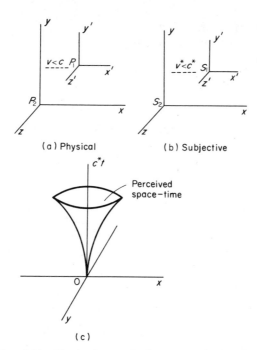

(a) Physical   (b) Subjective

(c)

FIG. 7.2. (a) Physical, and (b) subjective frames of reference: standard configurations; (c) the geometrical structure of visual space–time according to the relativistic formulation of motion perception.

limited by the maximum velocity of perceived movement c^*. This maximum velocity is considerably lower than the physical propagation rate of light ($c^* \ll c$) and is a measure of the finite propagation rate of signals in the human visual system. The similarity between c and c^* is solely in terms of the limiting information transmission rates between the various reference frames. In the physical situation distortions in the measurement of physical events are due to the finite speed of light, which governs information transmission between the frames. In the perceptual application the visual system has also a limited information transmission rate c^*. However, the only requirement we make within this context is that the perception of spatio-temporal events be invariant with respect to the reference frames whose relative velocities cannot exceed c^* to be discriminated. These perceptual events constitute the basis for subjective estimates of visual spatio-temporal magnitudes. Such limitations are possibly due to a variety of phenomena from retinal persistence to more general finite neural propagation rates along the visual pathways.

Past treatments of the problem of movement perception have invariably assumed that the subjective frames S_1 and S_2 are Galilean, related as simple translations at relative velocity v^*. However, the motion system has stronger conditions or restrictions than this. We (Caelli et al., 1978a) proposed that the following four postulates apply· to the visual system.

(1) *The perceived motion from one space–time frame to another should be symmetrical.*
(2) *Perceived spatio-temporal events of one frame should remain finite when the observer changes frames.*
(3) *If there is no perceived motion between two frames, the frames are equivalent to the observer.*
(4) *The addition laws of perceived velocities must be such that the maximum velocity of signal processing c^* remains invariant ($c^* = c'^*$).*

If these postulates hold in the perception of motion, then the Lorentz factor (Rindler, 1969)

$$\gamma^* = \gamma(v^*) = 1/\sqrt{1 - (v^*/c^*)^2} \tag{7.1}$$

plays a crucial role in predicting perceptual effects due to the relativity of the moving frames (see Rindler, 1969, for the derivation of the Lorentz transforms from these assumptions). The following properties of γ^* are notable:

(i) γ^* is ≥ 1 and $\gamma^* \to \infty$ as $v^* \to c^*$.
(ii) γ^* becomes imaginary for $v^* > c^*$.
(iii) $\gamma^* v^* = c^*(\gamma^{*2} - 1)^{1/2}$.
(iv) $d(\gamma^* v^*) = \gamma^{*3}\, dv^*$.

In terms of γ^* the direct and inverse Lorentz transformations from S_2 to S_1 assume a particularly symmetric form:

$$x^* = \gamma^*(x - v^*t), \quad y^* = y,$$
$$z^* = z, \quad t^* = \gamma^*[t - (v^*x/c^{*2})], \tag{7.2}$$

and

$$x = \gamma^*(x^* + v^*t), \quad y = y^*,$$
$$z = z^*, \quad t = \gamma^*[t^* + (v^*x^*/c^{*2})]. \tag{7.3}$$

In effect, (7.3) follows from (7.2) by interchanging coordinates and replacing v^* by $-v^*$ (representing the symmetry of the two frames).

The point of this formulation is that the relationships between perceived moving and stationary frames are governed by the Lorentz transformations

$$x^* = \frac{x - v^*t}{(1 - \beta^{*2})^{1/2}}, \quad y^* = y,$$

$$z^* = z, \quad t^* = \frac{t - (x/c^*)\beta^*}{(1 - \beta^{*2})^{1/2}}, \tag{7.4}$$

where $\beta^* = v^*/c^*$ and c^* is the maximum velocity of perceived movement. This limit c^* is reached at velocities of a moving light source where the observer no longer perceives motion. For example, with repetitively presented motions the observer perceives a stationary sheet of light. This limiting velocity has been found to lie in the range of 30–100 degrees of visual angle per second, depending on the properties of the light source employed (Brown, 1931; Kaufman et al., 1971).

The Lorentz transformations preserves are lengths between fixed and moving frames $ds^2 = ds^{*2}$, where the local metrics (see Chapter 5) are

$$ds^2 = dx^2 + dy^2 + dz^2 - (c^* \, dt)^2,$$
$$ds^{*2} = dx^{*2} + dy^{*2} + dz^{*2} - (c^* \, dt^*)^2,$$

resulting in the Riemann space–time surface (as shown in Fig. (7.2c)) for motion perception. This results in the prediction of length contractions (1), time dilations (2), and velocity comparisons (3) as shown below for horizontally moving sources (see Caelli et al., 1978a, b for more details):

(1) Perceived length l' is related to physical length l by

$$l' = l\sqrt{1 - (v/c^*)^2} \tag{7.5}$$

for physical velocity v and maximum velocity of perceived motion c^*.

(2) Perceived time dilation t' as a function of velocity and physical time interval t would so be

$$t' = t/\sqrt{1 - (v/c^*)^2}. \tag{7.6}$$

(3) Since each psychophysical technique employs different numbers of moving frames, the present theory has to be applied individually to each technique. For example, in a fractionation task, where subjects are asked to make half-velocity judgements by comparing the relative velocities of two moving sources, the following formulation would apply.

Consider the velocity of the fixed (criterion) source as v with respect to the observer's fixed frame. The subject is then required to adjust the velocity of another moving source, of velocity u with respect to his fixed frame, such that it is perceived (with respect to his fixed frame) to be half the velocity of v. In the Galilean formulation this is equivalent to $u = v - u$ or $2u = v$. However, in the Lorentzian formulation the perceived half-velocity u^* in the physical frame is related to the velocities u and v in the fixed frame by

$$u^* = u = \frac{v - u}{1 - (uv/c^{*2})}. \tag{7.7}$$

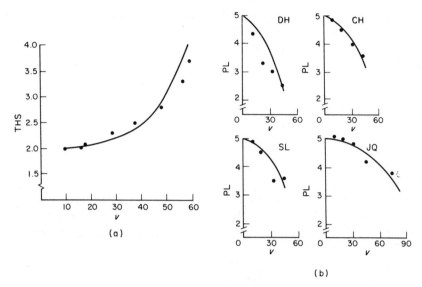

FIG. 7.3. (a) Threshold size (THS) as a function of velocity (Bhatia and Verghese, 1964). Continuous line is the predicted increase in THS due to the Lorentz formulation with $c^* = 54.74$ deg/s. (b) Perceived lengths (PL) from experimental data (dotted line) and predicted contractions (continuous line) over each subject.

The equality between u^*, the velocity of u in the moving frame, and v in the fixed frame, is due to the fact that estimates of u, the perceived half-velocities, are equated with the (physical) adjusted velocity u^*. Equation (7.7) results in the solution

$$u = c^{*2} \frac{\{1 - [1 - (v/c^*)^2]^{1/2}\}}{v}, \tag{7.8}$$

which indicates that half-velocities are overestimated, particularly as v approaches c^*.

Fortunately there already exists results on these three facets of motion perception perceived extent, time, and velocity of moving sources, and some of these results are shown in Figs. 7.3–7.5 in conjunction with results reported in our initial study of this approach (Caelli et al., 1978a). Figure 7.3a illustrates results from Bhatia and Verghese (1964) indicating how the size of a moving source has to be increased to appear the same size as a stationary one. Here the maximum velocity factor c^* was (least-squares) estimated at 54.75° per sec. Figure 7.3b shows results on perceived contractions by subjects who adjusted the length of the stationary source to correspond to the perceived length of the moving. c^* measures were made on each subject, hence the plot of data to predicted contraction curve is deterministic, specified by (7.5). The data seemed consistent with the formulation.

We then examined time estimation as a function of velocity given by (7.6). Subjects were asked to adjust the flicker frequency of a moving source such that it appeared to have the same frequency as the stationary source. Three different frequencies were employed and in all cases subjects increased the frequency as motion increased (Fig. 7.4). Again, individual c^* values were calculated and so (7.6) could be directly plotted and compared with results (Fig. 7.4).

Finally, perceived half-velocity judgements were tabulated by a method identical to Ekman and Dahlback (1965) where subjects adjusted the speed of one source with respect

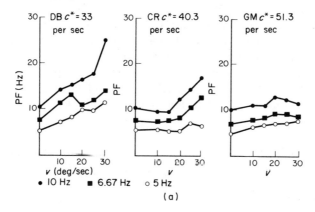

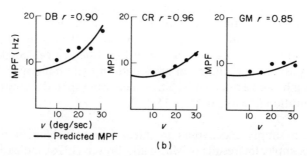

FIG. 7.4. (a) Points of perceived equality (PF) between moving flicker rate and stationary source for 10, 6.67, and 5 cps. Hz (b) Average PF (MBF) values correlated with predicted time dilations.

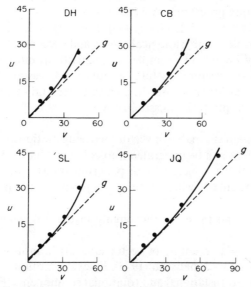

FIG. 7.5. Half-velocity estimation data (*U*) (•), predicted Lorentz function (continuous line), and Galilean velocity (dashed line) for each subject.

to another criterion moving stimulus. Results are shown in Fig. 7.5 (over many trials), and this figure also shows the predicted half-velocity values determined by (7.8) alone (see Caelli *et al.*, 1978a, b, for more procedural details).

The point of these three studies is that they indicate how perceived time, length, and velocity are all interdependent, and so any definition of velocity perception based on a fixed concept of distance–time is bound to fail. Similar results have already been found on velocity estimation by:

(a) Mashhour (1964), who related perceived velocity v^* to physical by

$$v^* = kv^p, \quad 0.63 \leq p0.94;$$

(b) Ekman and Dahlback (1965), where even at low velocities some overestimation occurred as a function of velocity.

(c) Henderson (1973) has demonstrated that motion thresholds are triggered (but not necessarily encoded) by a critical separation in space and time of at least two events. He also concludes that there is an inverse relationship between the two parameters, which implies that the motion threshold for points further apart is higher than for points that are close together. By regarding this critical condition for motion threshold as attaining a minimum arc length in hyperbolic space–time (Fig. 7.2b), then this length can be attained by either increasing spatial separation or decreasing temporal duration (see ds^2, ds^{*2}, p. 151).

This formulation simply endeavours to integrate many different results on motion perception. For example, the results of Matin and Bowen (1976), indicating that perceived simultaneity of events is determined by attentional and spatial relationships between events, are compatible with the relativistic approach. The model is geometric and mainly descriptive. The only term (although fundamental) which could be related to a process would be the c^* or limiting processing rate factor. However, when compared to the earlier formulations of, say, Barlow and Levick (1965) (Fig. 7.1), it is easy to see how there is still quite a gap between electrophysiological results and perceptual performance.

There are other very important examples of relativity in motion perception that are more representative of the vectorial nature of motion processing. These examples come mainly from the Gogel and Johansson studies. These latter studies indicate three important properties of motion perception (Johansson, 1978):

(1) that the visual system is capable of vector analysing motions;
(2) that relative motions can be integrated into coherent shapes by the visual system;
(3) that there seems to be a hierarchy of preferred transformational invariants in (2) and (1) above, particularly when motion in depth is a consequent perception.

We shall examine (2) and (3) more thoroughly in the following section, and, for the moment, consider (1).

Perhaps the most popular example of vector analysis in motion perception is that of epicyclic motion, reported by Johansson (1973). Epicyclic motion is the motion of a point on a rolling wheel having translational and rotational components (Fig. 7.6). This motion is easily perceived with one point source. However, when a second translating source is introduced (Fig. 7.6b) the residual rotary motion is only perceived in the other source,

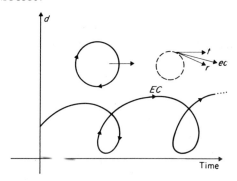

FIG. 7.6. The perceptual breakdown of epicyclic (EC) motion. Here $EC = r$(rotation + t(transla-tion). When translations are simultaneously presented one perceived $EC - t = r$: only rotations.

demonstrating that the visual system is sensitized to the vectorial composition of motions.

Many other demonstrations have been presented by Johansson and his associates regarding the vectorial analysis of motion stimuli. For example, Borjesson and von Hofsten (1972, 1973) have analysed the relative and common vector components of two- and three-point planar motions for the conditions which result in strong depth components to the perceived motion. Some examples are shown in Fig. 7.7a. Similarly, Johansson and Jansson (1968) and Jansson and Johansson (1973) have investigated conditions under which changes in a planar line and the sides of polygons result in motion in depth (Fig. 7.7b).

Johansson (1978) concludes from these experiments that the visual motion system is primarily tuned to interpret motions as projective transformations and not Euclidean motions (see Chapter 5 for definitions). That is to say we perceive object motions, which do not preserve congruence relationships, areas, angles of the object, as we see in Fig. 7.7b, where the depth component of the motions are concurrent with our perceptions of a perspective view of a three-dimensional object in motion. Yet Johansson and his associates

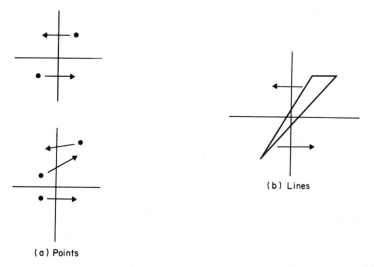

(b) Lines

(a) Points

FIG. 7.7. Relative and common vector components of two and three point motions and line elements which result in the perception of depth.

have also shown that such depth components require non-zero relative motion components between the stimulus motion sources and that such motions be relatively proximate in the visual field.

Interesting enough, Gogel (1978) and Gogel and Tietz (1973), while studying the "adjacency principle" and induced motion effects due to such things as head movements, the specific distance tendency, and motion parallax, have observed similar phenomena as Johansson and his associates. They analysed the perception of rotations of a rigid rod due to head movements and developed the following equations for Fig. 7.8:

$$m' = A(D - D')/D,$$

$$m'_j - m'_k = A(D'_k/D_k - D'_j/D_j),$$

where m' denotes the apparent motion, with m'_j being the apparent motion of the bottom of the stimulus object and m'_k that of the top. A is the distance through which the head moves. It is assumed here that the observer correctly judges this head movement or that $A = A'$. D is the physical distance of the object from the observer, with D_j being the physical distance of the bottom of the object and being that of the top. D' is the perceived distance of the object from the observer, with D'_j being the perceived distance from the bottom of the object and D'_k that from the top.

In their experiments the perceived slant of the stimulus object was varied with respect to its physical slant by means of perspective cues. It was expected that apparent relative motion would occur when $D'_k/D_k = D'_j/D_j$ or $m'_j \lessgtr m'_k$ whenever $D'_k/D_k \lessgtr D'_j/D_j$. Apparent common motion was expected to occur when m'_j and m'_k were both different from zero and had the same sign. The results were consistent for apparent relative motion, but not for apparent common motion. This apparent relative motion led to apparent rotations.

In a second experiment they let $D_k = D_j$, i.e. the object was always physically in the fronto-parallel plane. So

$$m'_j - m'_k = A(D'_k - D'_j)/D.$$

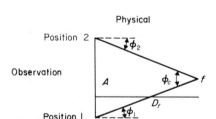

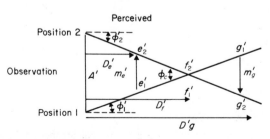

FIG. 7.8. The Gogel formulation for the analysis of perceived depth rotations of a physically station-ary point f as a result of laterally moving the head from position 1 to position 2.

Perspective cues were introduced to give illusions of depth. It was found that when the top end of the object appeared more distant than the bottom end, the object appeared to rotate clockwise as the head moved from right to left. When the top end of the object appeared less distant than the bottom end, the direction of apparent rotation relative to to the direction of the head movement was reversed.

Therefore, from Gogel and Tietz (1974) it could be concluded that a necessary condition for the perception of rotation is the perception of a difference in depth cues between the endpoints of the object.

So both the Gogel and Johansson results (including those not mentioned here) support (1) and (2) on page 154 that the vector decompositions of motion into relative and common vectors supplies information to the integration of motions into coherent motions of shapes, particularly having a depth component. In conjunction with the work reported directly on relativity effects in motion perception, it seems clear that the real motion processing system does not encode motions as isolated events but rather treats motions as relative to each other and the spatio-temporal parameters of such events as contingent on such perceived motions.

7.3. TRANSFORMATIONS AND ANALYSIS IN MOTION PERCEPTION— DEPTH EFFECTS

As already noted above, the visual system often interprets planar motions of individual dotted elements as signalling the motion of an object in depth. Johansson (1978) concludes that this tendency is also governed by the visual system's priority in perceiving such motions as invariant under projective transformations, not necessarily rigid motions. So dynamically changing the eccentricity of elliptical planar motions of, say, two dots, results in the perception of a changing tilt in depth of a rotating circle, supporting, as Johansson (1978) argues, the equivalence of all conics to the visual system, or projective interpretations of the image (see Chapter 5). The point is that there seems to be two aspects of stimulus processing in motion perception. One, involving vector analysis, the other incorporating some form of integration where the perceived image is reconstructed from its optical projections in such a way that we observe three-dimensional motions from what is really a two-dimensional spatial image on the retinal surface. We shall now consider this reconstruction process in more detail with particular reference to the kinetic depth effect.

When observing planar projections of three-dimensional rotating objects or configurations it is often possible to perceive the original three-dimensional object rotating in depth—the kinetic depth effect (Wallach and O'Connell, 1953). It has been known for at least 80 years (Kenyon, 1898) that the relative motions of objects in depth is equivocally interpreted. In particular, with rotating wire objects (trapezoids, cubes, etc.) or solid objects it is almost impossible, at slow velocities, to decide whether the motion is clockwise, anti-clockwise, or just oscillating (alternating). As shown by Graham (1966; Fig. 7.9), this result is consistent with the visual system perceiving such objects as projections. That is, by reconstructing the three-dimensional rotating object as a projected stimulus (with respect to the point of projection and the projection plane, Fig. 7.9) relative motion cues are equivocal. Table 7.1 summarizes most of the conditions known to date which induce the perception of three-dimensional motions from two-dimensional moving objects.

What are the geometric implications of these results? From definitions of direction,

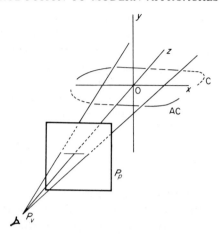

FIG. 7.9. The projected vectors (on the projection plane: P_p) for clockwise (C) and anticlockwise (AC) 3D motions can be identical with respect to the viewing position. (P_t).

TABLE 7.1. Known determinants of fronto-parallel motion which are sufficient conditions for inducing 3D motion perception

Stimulus	Presentation	Conditions for 3D	Perception	Principles for 3D
Solid or skeletal rotating 3D object[a]	Projection at slow rotation speed	Change in lengths and orientations: possibly acceleration	Vertical objects either rotating or alternating	Priority of central projections: need two-parameter change
At least two dots on the screen of a CRT. lines as well[b],[d]	Slow translations: non-zero relative motion cues	Parallel motions with non-zero relative motion vector at slow speed	Elements seen to have elliptical motion in depth	Priority of projective transforms. Vector analysis
Two static images (projections) of one 3D object[c],[d]	Under conditions for apparent motion	Affine transform between the 2 images in 3D	Solid 3D object rotating from one image to the other	Affine equivalence and priority of perspective transforms

[a] See Braunstein (1976) for review. [c] See Shepard (1978) for review.
[b] See Johansson (1978) for review. [d] Involving spatial contiguity, see Gogel (1978).

curvature, and torsion parameters of a curve (Chapter 5) we can see that:

(1) In reconstructing a 3D (three-dimensional) object from 2D (two-dimensional) information we endow the image with torsion (or screw action; Coxeter, 1961).
(2) We often cannot decide the sign of the curvature vector—perceptual oscillations corresponding to a constant sign curvature vector (positive or negative); direction being similarly affected.

(3) If the perceptual reconstruction process involves reinterpretations of these basic geometric features of shapes, then it is sequential, having a tangent → curvature → torsion information extraction order.

So two expectations are obvious: firstly, that the process is time dependent, even sequential in nature; and, secondly, that information loss occurs from torsion downwards to tangential or directional features.

Consider the case of three-dimensional rotating objects projected onto a screen in front of an observer. The observer under these conditions may perceive 3D motion. Now as rotation velocity increases the above conclusions predict that torsion information should attenuate more rapidly than curvature information. A zero torsion condition is equivalent to loss of 3D motion, while the constant sign on the curvature vector implies the perception of an oscillating as opposed to a rotating source. The author (Caelli, 1979) has investigated these conclusions with three types of rotating objects (sets 1 to 3; Fig. 7.10). In each case the stimulus was projected onto a screen and the observer responded as to whether rotations (directions included clockwise or anticlockwise), oscillations in depth, or planar motions were perceived—as velocity was changed (Fig. 7.10).

Set 1 stimuli were chosen to test whether the perceived 3D motion would be due to velocity as opposed to temporal frequency limits; set 2 were chosen to investigate whether we could discriminate torsion sign as left-handed right-handed helices only differ in their torsion sign; set 3 were chosen to investigate the role of adjacency or spatial contiguity in this reconstruction process.

Results for sets 1 and 2 are shown in Fig. 7.11 (for details of the procedure, see Caelli, 1979). In both cases reports to 3D rotations decreased to 50% at about 2 Hz. With set 1 subjects reported oscillations instead of rotations, i.e. loss of curvature sign change information; while with set 2 loss of 3D screw motion resulted in planar sinusoidal motion—a complete loss of torsion information. Set 1 results also indicated no effect due to the horizon-

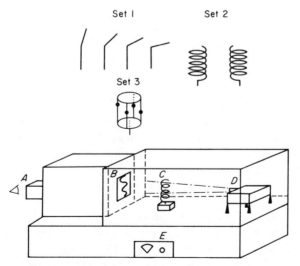

FIG. 7.10. Sets 1, 2, and 3 refer to stimulus sets positioned on the apparatus at position C such that central (polar) projections could be made of each object onto the surface B equidistant from light source D and observation position A. Rotation speed was controlled at position E.

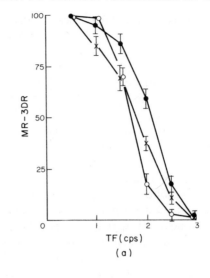

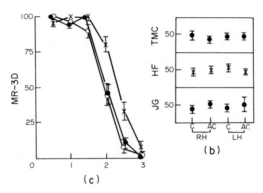

FIG. 7.11. (a) Percentage reports of 3D rotations (MR–3DR) as a function of revolutions per second (TF, in Hz) for each subject: TMC, xHF, °JG. (b) Percentage of clockwise motion reports as a function of the helix type (right—RH, left—LH) and physical rotation direction (clockwise, C; anticlockwise, AC) for each subject.(c) Perceived 3D rotations (MR–3D) percentages as a function of velocities for each subject TMC, xHF, °JG.

tal displacement (or velocity) differences, leaving the conclusion that the effect is due to the temporal sampling rate alone. Set 2 stimuli did not differ in clockwise/anticlockwise motion reports, indicating that we can not discriminate between motions which *only* differ in their torsion signs.

The results from sets 1 and 2 stimuli indicate that curvature and torsion information is attenuated as a function of temporal frequency; and that, at about the 2 Hz frequency, curvature assumes a constant sign, and torsion information is lost. This applies to contiguous objects—rigid objects where proximity factors are disguised in the continuous nature of the stimulus. With set 3 stimuli the question as to the geometric nature of the perceptual reconstruction with discrete disc elements was asked.

With this set only informal observations were made, due to their highly consistent nature, over subjects. With two discs rotating such that their projected horizontal displacement on the observer's screen was constant at 5 cm, all subjects perceived rotations up to

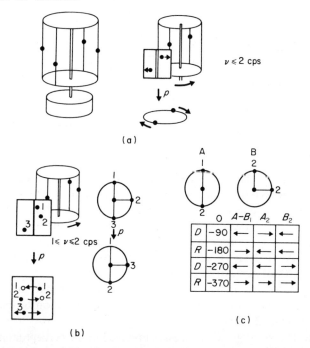

FIG. 7.12. (a) Two-disc case showing perceived elliptical rotations in depth, (b) three-disc case showing perceptual rotations of adjacent discs 1 and 2 perceived as collinear with the centre pole, (c) shows how rotations going to symmetric transform (90–180, 270–360) of the original configurations result in identical relative motion directions of numbers 2 and 3 with respect to the first disc ($S \equiv$ same, $D \equiv$ different directions).

about 2 cps as found with set 1 stimuli. When shown three discs (Fig. 7.12) numbered in decending projection order 1, 2, and 3, the observer consistently perceives that disc pairs which are closer together subtend an angle of 180° with respect to the centre pole—even if physically it is only 90°. Hence, if the projected distance between 1 and 2 is shorter that 2 to 3 or 1 to 3, the 1–2 angle of 90° will be perceived as 180° while the disc 3 motion is adjusted accordingly. This also applied to four disc cases. Figure 7.12 illustrates how relative motion components for each perceptual interpretation (1 collinear with 2 or 3, through the centre pole) are equivocal.

Results with these disc configurations illustrate two principles:

(1) that proximate motions are interpreted as central projections of collinearities, which
(2) form the bases for interpreting the residual motion components of more distant elements (Fig. 7.12).

What is most interesting is that these effects occurred consistently between 1 and 2 Hz. Below 1 cps the observers could readily perceive the 3D fixed configuration. For example, with three discs a rigid triangle rotating about the centre pole is perceived, while above 1 cps the unity of the three discs gives way to the types of effect mentioned. Above 2 Hz, motion typically became planar—as found already.

The results of these experiments indicate that in perceiving 3D transformations (or curves) from 2D dynamic information the visual system would seem to reinterpret curvature

TABLE 7.2.

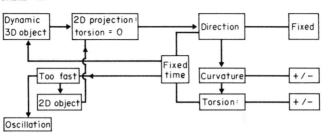

and torsion information equivocally with respect to the signs ± of these vectors. Secondly, the reconstruction process requires a low temporal frequency of less than 2 Hz to be attained reliably. The results lead one to conjecture that the visual system cannot discriminate between two curves in 3D solely on the basis of torsion information. This constitutes an exact analogy to the second-order statistics limit conjecture with textures (Julesz, 1971; Caelli and Julesz, 1978). That is, since torsion involves third-order differences between successive elements (third derivatives), this conjecture means that in perceiving 3D curves the visual system cannot discriminate between two curves that differ only in their torsion. For example, Ss could not discriminate between the screw action of the left- and right-handed helices used in set 2 elements.

Table 7.2 illustrates the proposed processes involved in the perceptual reconstruction of 3D objects from their 2D projections. The reversion of 90–180° separations found in set 3 stimuli and the previous results on ambiguities in perceived rotations and oscillations (Table 7.1) are all consistent with the present conjecture which effectively contends that one cannot discriminate between curves having symmetric right-handed triples (Chapter 5). The issue of adjacency would seem to be involved in so far as these fundamental geometric features are local in nature. Consequently the more distant elements become, the less likely they are to be involved in forming a unit that would produce direction, curvature, or torsion information.

What is envisaged in Table 7.2 is that:

(1) The visual system extracts, in the first instance, the geometric properties of small regions of a configuration: more distant elements are not related during this phase.
(2) This process involves the adjacency principle and an interpretation of the projection values (or perspective) of each region to the observer with respect to the object.
(3) Direction, curvature, and torsion information is then extracted up to sign ambiguities. Here orientations (e.g. what elements are 90° and what are 180° apart) and distances are established in the perceived 3D space.
(4) The relative motions of more distant elements are determined with respect to these local properties—as evidenced with set 3 stimuli.

This process implies that more complex geometric properties take more time to extract. Shepard (1978) has observed that the visual system tends to connect two perspective presentations by rotations in 3D which are affine invariant and rigid transforms. Yet these perceptual transformations are not necessarily "shortest" in spatial path or perceptual geodesics. That is, by a series of different transformations, the spatial path between the two images could be shorter than the smooth rotations in depth or on the picture plane described in the Shepard and Metzler (1971) experiment. However, the point is clear—the rotations (as perceived) are more simple than planar motions since the rotations limit the dynamics to constant curvatures in motion paths. Finally, it should be noted that Braunstein's (1976) conclusion that acceleration in the vertical–horizontal projection plane are important for 2D motion perception is consistent with the notion of curvature extraction in Table 7.2.

It seems clear from these experiments and results of previous studies that the visual system has a priority for interpreting projected 2D images as central projections and that there is a tendency (consistency) to preserve the rigidity of the (rotating) reconstructed 3D object. This implies that the visual system is capable of floating between affine (projective) and Euclidean interpretations of the visual environment. The model proposed in Table 7.2 suggests that this situation results in the local ambiguities in curvature and torsion perception which, in turn, is due to a limited (temporal frequency) sampling rate in spatio-temporal vision. The implications to perceptual geodesics are consequently predictable from just how much curvature or torsion information has been extracted within the limited interval.

7.4. APPARENT MOTION

We have already presented perspectives of motion perception that indicate that physical motion is not necessarily perceived as it "is". Rather, motion parameters and paths are determined by subjective factors as limiting processing rates, analytic extraction limits, and geometric transformations, which are claimed to be "natural" to the visual system. Apparent motion (phi-, beta-, stroboscopic motion) is also an example of motion determined by subjective factors and therefore has been of great interest to perceptionists over the ages. In this section we wish to cover two aspects of apparent motion (AM)—its existence conditions and geometric paths in visual space–time.

Although AM occurs in many visual phenomena, including movies, most attention has been paid to the simple configuration of two light sources presented sequentially such that, at the correct intensities and spatio-temporal separations, motion is perceived between them (Fig. 7.13). Over the past 50 years various attempts have been made to explain certain aspects of these limits for AM, specifically those limits conjectured by Korte (1915) and investigated by Neuhaus (1930), as illustrated in Fig. 7.13b.

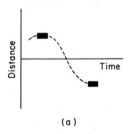

(a)

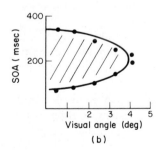

(b)

FIG. 7.13. (a) Apparent motion (AM) stimulus configuration indicating motion path (dotted), and (b) typical spatio-temporal limits for AM.

The Korte's "laws" stated that to preserve AM:

(1) for a fixed interstimulus interval *ISI*, spatial separation *S*, and intensity *I* were directly related: $I \propto S$;
(2) for fixed *S*, intensity and *ISI* varied inversely: $I \propto 1/ISI$;
(3) for fixed *I*, *ISI* varied directly with *S*: $ISI \propto S$.

"Intensity" for Korte meant anything which improved the figures perceptibility, not just luminance (Kolers, 1972).

It can be seen from Fig. 7.13 that these laws are too simple—in fact even incorrect. For example, as separation increases it is more the case that the temporal bandwidth decreases (stimulus onset asynchrony) (SOA) rather than law (3), which relates only to the bottom side (higher temporal frequencies) of the curves in Fig. 7.13b. More traditional attempts to explain mechanisms for AM have never quantitatively connected the parameters *S*, *I*, and *ISI* above (Kolers, 1972) as evidenced, say, by the excitation theories where AM was vaguely seen as motion registered in the brain by temporal behaviour of electrical fields (Kolers, 1972). Even the more recent (relatively speaking) memory models (e.g. Kinchla and Allan, 1969) do not produce the exact relationships—as observed. The reader is so referred to Kolers (1972) for extensive reviews on these previous models.

As in spatial vision the concept of filtering channels has been extensively applied to motion perception. For example, Breitmeyer and Ganz (1976) note that some brightness suppression has been observed in the first of the two stimuli in AM—a masking effect, which they attribute to the inhibitory action of transient on sustained channels. In a similar way Bonnet (1977) argues for two systems in motion perception—one for velocity and amplitude, the other for spatio-temporal frequencies; the latter being governed by the apparently accepted proposition that there is a "trade-off" between spatial and temporal frequency responses (see Chapter 6).

This concept of filtering has been extended recently by the author (Caelli *et al.*, 1978b; Caelli and Finlay, 1979; Finlay and Caelli, 1979). This particular application was based on the simple relationship between the spatio-temporal loci (noted in Fig. 7.12b) for AM, and the conjectured sinusoidal nature of the motion (Fig. 7.13a). The typically elliptical loci can be reconverted back to a circular path by a constant (conjectured to be c^*—the maximum velocity of perceivable motion of the source). Given this resultant compatibility between distance and time (now converted to a distance by c^*), then the relationship between the loci and motion was argued to be exactly that of phase plane to sinusoidal motion (Fig. 7.14a).

Alternatively, this model suggests that AM is conveyed to the visual system by the fundamental temporal frequency component of the spatio-temporal profile (Fig. 7.14a, b). In a series of experiments the authors (ibid.) have investigated consequences of such a model:

(a) that perceived spatial displacement would be consistent with the sinusoidal motion;
(b) that the spatio-temporal limits for AM are elliptical;
(c) that the interactions between various AM sources are a function of their phase relationships.

To illustrate this model (as shown in Fig. 7.14b) we observed (ibid.) AM reports with

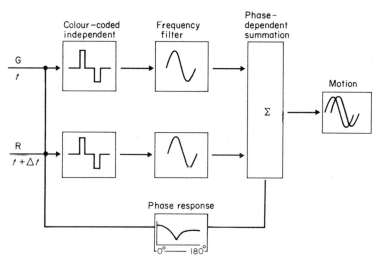

FIG. 7.14. Proposed role of colour, frequency, and phase coding in the perception of apparent motion. Colour is associated with the formulation of individual motion paths. Frequency filtering determines its sinusoidal nature and, finally, the various motions combine, or add, as a function of their phase relationships.

two types of sources. The initial source consisted of red–red and surrounding green–green lights (Fig. 7.15a), the second being horizontally parallel pairs of lights. The temporal phase between light pairs was increased from zero to 160° (almost a half-cycle). AM reports were calculated at each phase position for various spatial separation parameters (Fig. 7.15). Here we observe a phase-specific effect — different from the frequency determinants already noted (ibid.). The effect is optimum in the 90 ± 30° phase angle range, and was more symmetric about 90° for the horizontal–vertical configuration than the red–green sources.

The reason for using red–green coloured sources was due to the finding of Kolers and von Grünan (1976), indicating that AM does not occur as continuous motion on the colour dimension between red and green. The transition is abrupt. With this in mind we thought

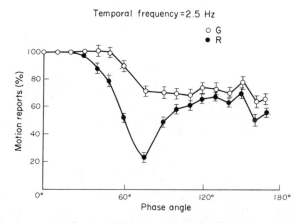

FIG. 7.15. Percentage reports of red–red (R) and green–green (G) motions as a function of phase angle between the two sources (standard deviations included): the phase modulation function. More symmetrical curves have recently been found by Finlay and Caelli (1979).

it possible to induce two independent AM conditions: red–red and green–green, so that we could then study the relative phase component between the AMs. The resultant AM report curves are somewhat akin to a "phase modulation function"—the analogue to the frequency modulation function discussed in Chapters 3 and 6.

In both experiments it was also consistently found that optimum reports of AM occurred around the 2 Hz temporal frequency range. So, to summarize, we have discussed existence conditions for AM in terms of a filter model based on the conjecture that AM is perceived via the extraction of low-frequency sinusoidal components of the image that, in turn, is indicative of simple harmonic motion. It would seem difficult to relate these low temporal frequency components to, say, sustained mechanisms in the visual system since the motion occurs over a large range of temporal frequencies (typically between 20 and 500 msec SOA), not simply the low-frequency range response usually attributed to these channels

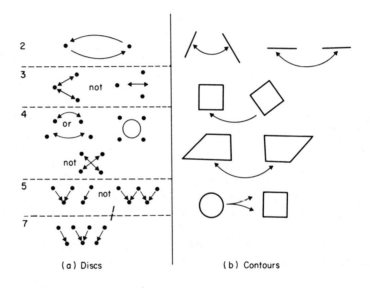

(a) Discs   (b) Contours

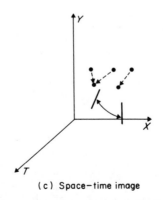

(c) Space–time image

Fig. 7.16. The effects of stimulus configurations on perceived paths of apparent motion (AM).

(Chapter 6). As for now we move on to consider the perceived paths of AM as a function of configurational properties of the stimuli.

Due to the association of AM with such Gestalt psychologists as Wertheimer (1912) it has more often than not been studied in the context of shape perception and its affect on the quality of AM. Three of the more interesting aspects of the motion are:

(1) the motion can occur as a smooth motion between two quite different shapes;
(2) that AM occurs between two or more points such that the associations are not made purely on a near-neighbour basis;
(3) the dimensionality of the perceived motion is contingent on figural properties of the stimuli.

Examples of these conditions are shown in Fig. 7.16.

One of the earlier concepts was that AM would be more readily perceived between two shapes, which were regarded as similar or equivalent to the visual system, a variation on the attraction/repulsion model of Brown and Voth (1937). However, as pointed out by Kolers (1972) and recently by Navon (1976), there seems to be little evidence for this—even given very simple measures of shape similarities.

An alternative to the stimulus equivalence concept was the transformation invariance motion recently observed by Foster (1975, 1978) and Shepard (1978). Here AM may be induced between two configurations (not necessarily "shapes", e.g. Foster employer dotted configurations) if the motion path constitute a valid affine transformation between the two images. Although some evidence for this occurs with dot configurations where no obvious figures are detectable, the conjecture does not apply in general since AM can be induced between objects that are not even topologically equivalent.

One aspect of AM does seem clear—that the path is smooth and, in some way, is the simplest such continuous path between the image pair (Fig. 7.16). Various attempts have been made to model such AM contours via filtering mechanisms. For example, Foster (1978) has proposed a vector field model based on the concept that the path minimizes "energy", where at a point $\mathbf{r}$ the vector field induced by two points $\mathbf{p}, \mathbf{q}$ is defined by

$$F(\mathbf{r}) = \int_{S_1} \frac{\mathbf{r} - \mathbf{p}}{|\mathbf{r} - \mathbf{p}|^3} \, ds(\mathbf{p}) - \int_{S_2} \frac{\mathbf{r} - \mathbf{q}}{|\mathbf{r} - \mathbf{q}|^3} \, ds(q)$$

for $p \in S_1, q \in S_2$: stimulus S_1 and S_2 respectively. This is also a variation of the weighting and summation process discussed in Chapter 6 where the weighting function consists of an inverse square distance $[1/(r - p)^2]$ between elements.

The network discussed in Chapter 6 may be applied to AM by including feedback (forward-iterative) conditions. The output vector at $\mathbf{x}_i$ moves the predicted AM path to $\mathbf{x}_{i+1}$ where the process starts again until the total contour moves between the two stimulus configurations (Fig. 7.17).

The spatio-temporal filter (Fig. 7.17) would be an extension of the spatial filter w_{ij} discussed in Chapter 6. One form of it's decay components could be:

$$w_{ij} = \alpha \exp\left[-\alpha d_{ij}\right], \quad d_{ij} = \alpha\sqrt{r_{ij}^2 + \beta t_{ij}^2}$$

for r_{ij} being the spatial in degrees, and t_{ij} the temporal in milliseconds distances between points $\mathbf{x}_i$ and $\mathbf{x}_j$. In a rather informal experiment we (Caelli and Dodwell, 1979) investigated how such a process may predict the AM paths perceived with dotted stimuli as shown in

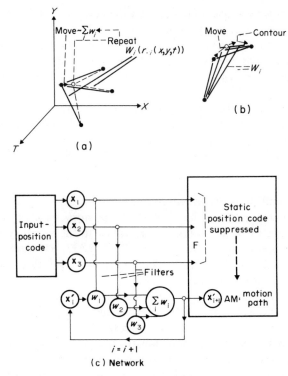

FIG. 7.17. Spatio-temporal network for the extraction of AM contour paths (From Caelli and Dodwell, 1980.)

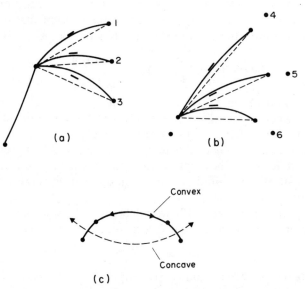

FIG. 7.18. Average observed probe positions and orientations and paths predicted by network for $\alpha = 0.20$.

Fig. 7.18. The task consisted of the observer adjusting the position and orientation of a vector probe to correspond to the perceived AM motion path between stimulus elements (Fig. 7.18).

Average probe positions and orientations are shown in Fig. 7.18 for each configuration used. In addition the continuous lines represent interpolated AM contour paths for $\beta = 22.5$ and $\alpha = 0.20$ in w_{ij} above. We have also noted that when applied to some illusions both the network and our observations support an augmentation in the illusion when shown in AM. For example, by displaying the left, then right, portions of the standard Poggendorff illusion under AM conditions, the illusion is almost doubled.

So we conclude that, by virtue of the spatio-temporal separation component to AM, the visual system must, in some ways, filter the image in order to produce a continuous motion effect. As to whether the types of filters discussed all fit a common purpose or not, is uncertain. Similarly, the geometry of perceived AM paths, as predicted by any of the above considerations, has not been fully determined—just as in the case of spatial contour extraction. Yet it can be seen that the mechanisms discussed are suitable for studying these processes and do quantify many of the phenomenal aspects of the effects. Maybe the connections between perceived geometric motion properties are determined by the network mechanisms discussed!

7.5. CONCLUSIONS

In this chapter we have reviewed some recent approaches to motion perception involving concepts of the geometry of visual space–time, priority structures with respect to interpretations of motions in depth, and, finally, filtering and network processes in AM perception. It is clear from the results discussed that it is not adequate to conceive of motion—as perceived—in terms of the visual distance–time derived quantity, nor solely in terms of possible simple gating processes situated in the ganglion cells of the retina. As discussed already, cortical units are selectively sensitive to motion direction in conjunction with spatial profiles of orientation and frequency components. Maybe motion encoding follows a similar line to the encoding of other image parameters in humans, i.e. a fixed retinal process in the lower vertebrate seems to generalize to the cortical units in humans where retinal inhibitory activity is also generalized to interacortical inhibition and possibly excitatory interneural activity (Uttal, 1973).

REFERENCES

ANSBACHER, H. L. (1944) Distortion in the perception of real movement. *J. Exp. Psychol.* **34**, 1–23.

BARLOW, H. B. and LEVICK, W. R. (1965) The mechanism of directionally selective units in rabbits retina, *J. Physiol.* **178**, 477–504.

BARLOW, H. B., HILL, R. M., and LEVICK, W. R. (1964) Retinal ganglion cells responding selectively to direction and speed of image in the rabbit, *J. Physol.* **173**, 377–407.

BHATIA, B. and VERGHESE, C. A. (1964) Threshold size of a moving object as a function of its speed, *J. Opt. Soc. Am.* **54**, 948–950.

BONNET, C. (1977) Visual motion detection models: features and frequency filters, *Perception* **6**, 491–500.

BORJESSON, E. and VON HOFSTEN, C. (1972) Spatial determinants of depth perception in two-dot motion patterns, *Percept. Psychophys.* **11**, 263–268.

BORJESSON, E. and VON HOFSTEN, C. (1973) Visual perception of motion in depth: application of a vector model to three-dot motion patterns, *Percept. Psychophys.* **13**, (2) 169–179.

BRAUNSTEIN, M. (1976) *Depth Perception Through Motion*, Academic Press, New York.

BREITMEYER, B. and GANZ, L. (1976) Implications of sustained and transient channels for theories of visual pattern Masking, Saccadic suppression, and information processing, *Psychol. Rev.* **83**, (1) 1–36.

BROWN, J. F. (1931) The thresholds of visual movement, *Psycholog, Forsch.* **14**, 249–268.

BROWN, J. F. and VOTH, A. C. (1937) The path of seen movement as a function of the vector-field, *Am. J. Psychol.* **49**, 543–563.

CAELLI, T. M. (1979) On the perception of some geometric properties of rotating three-dimensional objects. *Biol. Cybernetics* **33**, 29–37.

CAELLI, T. M. and DODWELL, P. C. (1979) On the contours of apparent motion: a new perspective on visual space-time, *Biol. Cybernetics.* (in Press).

CAELLI, T. M. and FINLAY, D. C. (1979) Frequency, phase, and colour coding in apparent motion, *Perception* **8**, 59–68.

CAELLI, T. M. and JULESZ, B. (1978) On perceptual analyzers underlying visual extreme discrimination: Part II. *Biol. Cybernetics* **29**, 201–214.

CAELLI, T. M., HOFFMAN, W. C., and LINDMAN, H. (1978a) Apparent motion: self-excited oscillations induced by retarded neuronal flows. *In Formal Theories of Visual Perception* (Leeuwenberg and Buffart, eds.), Wiley, New York, pp. 103–116.

CAELLI, T. M., HOFFMAN, W. C. and LINDMAN, H. (1978b) Subjective Lorentz transformations and the perception of motion. *J. Opt. Soc. Am.* **68**, 402–417.

COXETER, H. (1961) *Introduction to Geometry*, Wiley, New York.

EKMAN, G. and DAHLBACK, B. (1965) A subjective scale of velocity. In *Readings in the Study of Visually Perceived Movement* (I.M. Spigel, ed.), Harper & Row, New York.

FINLAY, D. C. and CAELLI, T. M. (1979) Frequency, phase, and colour coding in apparent motion: II, *Perception* **8**, 595–602.

FOSTER, D. H. (1972) A method for the investigation for those transformations under which the visual recognition of a given object in invariant, *Kybernetik* **11**, 217–222.

FOSTER, D. H. (1975) Visual apparent motion and some preferred paths in the rotation group SO (3), *Biol. Kybernetics* **18**, 81–89.

FOSTER, D. H. and MASON, R. J. (1978) Transformation and relational–structure scheme for visual pattern recognition, *Biol. Cybernetics* **32**, 85–93.

FROST, B. and Diane DiFRANCO (1976) Motion characteristics of single units in the pidgeon optic tectum, *Vision Res.* **16**, 1229–1234.

GOGEL, W. (1974) Relative motion and the adjacency principle, *J. Exp. Psychol.* **26**, 425–437.

GOGEL, W. C. (1976) The metric of visual space. In *Stability and Consistency in Visual Perception.* (Epstein, W., ed.), Wiley, New York.

GOGEL, W. C. (1978) The adjacency principle in visual perception, *Scient. Am.* **238** (5) 126–139.

GOGEL, W. and TIETZ, J. (1973) Absolute motion parallax and the specific distance tendency, *Percept. Psychophys.* **13**, (2) 284–292.

GRAHAM, C. (1966) The perception of motion, In *Vision and Visual Perception* (Graham, C. ed.), Academic Press, New York.

HELMHOLTZ, H. VON. (1924–25) *Handbuch der Physioligischen Optik*, 1st edn., Voss, Hamburg and Leipzig, 1866; 3rd edn. Voss, Leipzig, 1911; English edn., J. P. C. Southall, (trans.), *Treatise on Physiological Optics,* Optical Society of American, Rodester, N. Y. 3 vols.

HENDERSON, D. C. (1973) Visual discrimination of motion: stimulus relationships at threshold and the question of luminance-time reciprocity *Percept. Psychophys.* **1**, 121–130.

JANSSON, G. and JOHANSSON, G. (1973) Visual perception of bending motion, *Perception* **2**, 321–326.

JOHANSSON, G. (1973) Visual perception of biological motion and a model for its analysis, *Percept. Psychophys.* **14**, 201–211.

JOHANSSON, G. (1978) About the geometry underlying spontaneous visual decoding of the optical message. In *Formal Theories of Visual Perception*, (Leeuwenberg, E. and Buffart, H., ed.), Wiley, New York.

JOHANNSON, G. and JANSSON, G. (1968) Perceived rotary motion from changes in a straight line, *Percept. Psychophys.* **4**, 165–170.

KAUFMAN, L., CYRULNICK, I., KAPLOWITZ, J., MELNICK, G., and STOTT, D. (1971) The complementarity of apparent and real motion., *Psychol. Forsch.* **34**, 343–348.

KENYON, F. C. (1898) A curious optical illusion connected with an electric fan, *Science* **8**, 371–372.

KINCHLA, R. and ALLAN, L. (1969) A theory of visual movement perception, *Psychol. Rev.* **76**, 537–558.

KOLERS, P. A. (1972) *Aspects of Motion Perception*, Pergamon Press, New York.

KOLERS, P. A. and PORNERANTZ, J. R. (1971) Figural change in apparent motion, *J. Exp. Psychol.* **87**, 99–108.

KOLERS, P. A. and VON GRUNAN, M. (1976) Shape and color in apparent motion, *Vision Res.* **16**, 329–335.

KORTE, A. (1915) Kinamatoskopische Untersuchungen, *Z. Psychol.* **72**, 194–296.

MASHHOUR, M. (1964) *Psychophysical Relations in the Perception of Velocity.* Almquist & Wiksell, Stockholm.

MATIN, L. and BOWEN, R. (1976) Measuring the duration of perception, *Percept. Psychophys.* **20**, 66–76.

NAVON, D. (1976) Irrelevance of figural identity for resolving ambiguities in apparent motion, *J. Exp. Psychol. Human Perception and Performance*, **2**, 130–138.

NEUHAUS, W. (1930) Experimentelle Untersuchung der Scheinbewegung, *Arch. Ges. Psychol.*, **75**, 315–458.

RINDLER, W. (1969) *Essential Relativity*, van Nostrand, Reinhold, New York.

SHEPARD, R. (1978) The circumflex and related topological manifolds in the study of perception, In *Theory Construction and Data Analysis in the Behavioral Sciences* (S. Shye, ed.), Ossey-Bass, San Francisco.

SHEPARD, R., METZLER, J. (1971) Mental rotations of three-dimensional objects, *Science* **171**, 701–703.

TYLER, C. W. (1973) Temporal characteristics in apparent movement: omega movement vs. phi movement, *Q. J. Exp. Psychol.* **25**, 182–192.

UTTAL, W. (1973) *The Psychobiology of Sensory Coding*, Harper? Row, New York.

WALLACH, H. and O'CONNELL, D. N. (1953) The kinetic depth effect, *J. Exp. Psychol.* **45**, (4) 205–217.

WERTHEIMER, M. (1912) Experimentelle Studien uber das Schen von Bewgung, *Z. Psychol.* **61**, 161–265. Translated in part in *Classics in Psychology*. (T. Shipley, ed), New York. Philosophical History, New York.

CHAPTER 8

Specific Issues in Vision

IN THIS chapter we wish to briefly cover some remaining issues in visual perception that employ to a marked extent the technologies discussed in Part I. These areas are: colour perception, binocular vision, and steriopsis. In one sense these issues should have been discussed at the beginning of Part II since they present clear examples of where filtering mechanisms, networks, and geometry are important tools for understanding perceptual processes. These areas share the common goal of relating specific neurophysiological functions to psychophysical responses and the modelling of such relationships via the mechanisms discussed in Part I.

8.1. COLOUR VISION

Of all areas of vision research, colour perception has received the most rigorous treatment to the extent that it remains a "paradigm" system for most other aspects of perception. This is mainly due to the discovery (of old) that most colours could be generated by combinations of three basic hues, suggesting that only three types of receptor mechanisms or colour channels may exist in normal colour vision such that chromatic sensitivity can be expressed as a function of the various states of each channel response. In the following section we shall briefly review the retinal encoding and spectral sensitivity aspects of such processes.

8.1.1. Retinal encoding and spectral sensitivity

The molecule known to be responsible for encoding light quanta in the retinal rod and cone systems is rhodopsin (visual purple). This molecule is a composite of protein and retinal molecules where the amount of binding constitutes the amount of rhodopsin pigment. Light quanta separates these two molecules (via isomerization) in the adsorption process that, in turn, acts to bleach the pigment. Full rebinding of the molecules restores the pigment, giving a rod receptor the ability to respond again to light quanta. Isomerization has a time course such that a molecule has a 0.5 regeneration probability in any 5 min period. For example, 5 min after a brief flash of light 50% of the molecules have regenerated their pigment (Cornsweet, 1970). However, it is not possible to predict visual light quanta sensitivity from such rhodopsin response characteristics of receptors since there are other pigments in the retina besides those in the rods and cones, e.g. in the choroidal pigment layer.

As pointed out in Chapter 2, the visual system has a preferred sensitivity to light in the

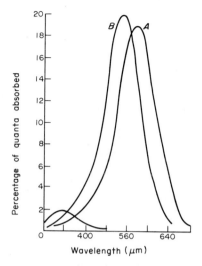

FIG. 8.1. Scotopic spectral sensitivity curves *A* with ocular media and *B* with the absorption spectrum of the ocular media removed.

middle range of the visible spectrum. Both photopic and scotopic spectral sensitivity curves (Fig. 2.5) (Wald, 1955) indicate peak sensitivity ranges in the 450–600 nm bandwidth, with ocular media or choroidal pigment responses included (Fig. 8.1a) or excluded (Fig. 8.1b).

Yet it is clear that visual sensitivity to light is not simply proportional to the fraction of regenerated pigment molecules. For example, Rushton (1962) found that bleaching 25% of the pigment molecules increases light detection threshold by a factor of 100,000. He concluded that it was the logarithm of the threshold that is proportional to the bleached pigment fraction, or

$$\log \frac{\Delta I}{\Delta I_0} = aB, \tag{8.1}$$

where ΔI is the threshold intensity, ΔI_0 is the threshold after complete dark adaptation, $a \approx 20$, and B is the fraction of rod pigment in a bleached state (Fig. 8.2). Results would

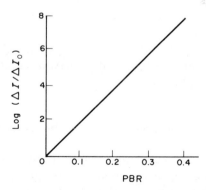

FIG. 8.2. Threshold intensity $\log (\Delta I / \Delta I_0)$ and its relation to the proportion of rod pigments in a bleached state (*PBR*). (Adapted from Rushton, 1965.)

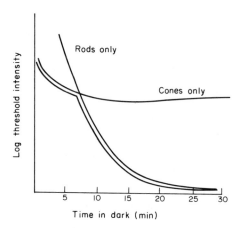

Fig. 8.3. Classical dark adaptation curves indicating the different time course for rods and cones.

seem to indicate that about nine visual pigment molecules need to be isomerized (bleached) before a dark adapted observer would perceive a flash of light. This non-linear relationship (8.1) would seem to reflect the, as yet not fully understood, neural encoding of the bleaching signal (Wyszecki and Stiles, 1967).

Of course, we now remind ourselves that the above characteristics are subject to the fact that there are two receptors, each exhibiting different spectral response curves. The rods converge to a much greater degree onto ganglion cells than do the cones, and this heightened sensitivity difference is illustrated over time in the classical dark adaptation curves (Fig. 8.3). The adaptation effect on cones does not change much after 5 min, while the rod adaptation can take up to 30 min—the joint curve being the composite adaptation curve for the totally exposed eye.

There are other differences between rods and cones, which include the 50 nm shift in the sensitivity curves, with rods being more sensitive than cones (Fig. 2.5)—the Purkinje shift. Wald (1955) argued that this difference was due to differences in the protein molecules, while Rushton (1962) found that the relationship between threshold elevation and bleaching fraction for cones was similar to the rods (8.1) where $a \approx 3$. Here the cones recover more quickly than rods. There would seem to be sufficient evidence to indicate the existence of three types of cone receptors specified by their spectral absorption curves. Coupled with the rod receptors, this results in a tetrachromatic system of retinal spectral encoding. Yet we shall see how a "three-colour" system would seem sufficient to describe most aspects of colour perception. Finally, it should be noted that an implicit assumption of the above discussion is that once a quantum is absorbed it will have an effect on the molecule, independent of the quantum wavelength.

8.1.2. Colour mechanisms and line elements

We saw in Chapter 2 that objects produce different absorption spectra and so radiate different colours—so named. These absorption spectra indicate that intensity and wavelength bond together so that a person even without cone vision can often discriminate colours on the basis of luminance differences. In this situation two different wavelengths

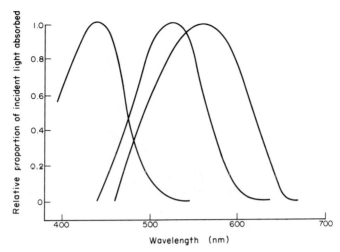

FIG. 8.4. Estimated absorption curves for the three colour channels. (Adapted from Wald, 1964.)

can be adjusted in intensities to have the same effect on the visual system, resulting in no discrimination. So if all our receptors had identical absorption spectra we would be mono-chromats under the assumption (as stated above) that all absorbed quanta produce the same effect on the pigment molecules independent of wavelength. Two different absorption spectra would result in dichromacy: three different spectra and trichromacy or normal colour vision. The estimated absorption curves for these colour "channels" (red, green, blue) are shown in Fig. 8.4.

   Like the monochromat, the dichromat and trichromat can match patches of various wavelengths. Two patches, consisting of three wavelengths, can be matched by the dichro-mat with varying only two sources, and similar results occur in trichromats with four wavelengths and three variable sources. Consider the dichromat. For q_{ij} = number of quanta absorbed for wavelength λ_i in colour system j, we have

$$q_{ij} = p_{ij}c_i, \tag{8.2}$$

Where c_i is the input quanta and p_{ij} the absorption spectrum. For two patches of light judged equal (with wavelengths λ_2, λ_3),

$$q_{1j} = a_{2j} + q_{3j}, \quad q_{1k} = q_{2k} + q_{3k}, \tag{8.3}$$

or, substituting (8.2) into (8.3) and collecting terms,

$$c_2 = \frac{c_1(p_{3k}p_{1i} - p_{1k}p_{3i})}{p_{3k}p_{2i} - p_{2k}p_{3i}}, \tag{8.4}$$

$$c_3 = \frac{c_1(p_{1k}p_{2i} - p_{2k}p_{1i})}{p_{3k}p_{2i} - p_{2k}p_{3i}}.$$

Here c_2 and c_3 correspond to the intensities of λ_2 and λ_3 required for the match. Similar solutions to linear equations result in the c_2^*, c_3^*, and c_4^* values for matches in the trichro-matic case. These constitute support for the relative absorption spectra shown in Fig. 8.4 for the three-colour systems.

   Wavelength mixing curves (or surfaces in the case of trichromacy) are obtained by plotting

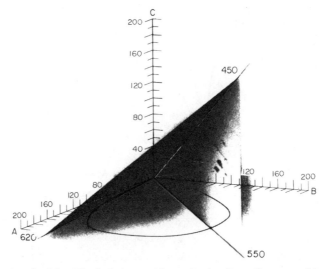

FIG. 8.5. Wavelength mixing. The shaded pyramid contains the effects of every possible combination of lights at wavelengths 450, 550, and 620 nm, and, conversely, any mixture of wavelengths whose effects lie within the pyramid may be exactly matched by the appropriate combination of 450, 550, and 620 nm. (From Cornsweet, 1970.)

the relative absorption values of the wavelengths for each colour channel, being axes in a Euclidean space. So if we take three wavelengths (say 450, 550, and 620) the effect of mixing these, with adjustable intensities, is contained in the triangular pyramid shown in Fig. 8.5.

The concept of colour space being a surface in a three-dimensional Euclidean space was developed by Helmholtz in 1896 (see Wyszecki and Stiles, 1967), where discrimination between various mixtures is seen as indexed by distance on the surface. From the colour-matching functions $(\tilde{x}_\lambda, \tilde{y}_\lambda, \tilde{z}_\lambda)$, Helmholtz argued that the characteristic spectral response functions for each colour mechanism $(\tilde{r}, \tilde{g}, \tilde{b})$ was determined by the linear equations:

$$\left.\begin{aligned}
\tilde{r} &= h_{11}\tilde{x}_\lambda + h_{12}\tilde{y}_\lambda + h_{13}\tilde{z}_\lambda, \\
\tilde{g} &= h_{21}\tilde{x}_\lambda + h_{22}\tilde{y}_\lambda + h_{23}\tilde{z}_\lambda, \\
\tilde{b} &= h_{31}\tilde{x}_\lambda + h_{32}\tilde{y}_\lambda + h_{33}\tilde{z}_\lambda.
\end{aligned}\right\} \tag{8.5}$$

The total response of the receptive mechanism was then defined as the integral over the whole response curve (p_λ being the absorption coefficient)

$$R = \int p_\lambda \tilde{r}_\lambda \, d\lambda, \quad G = \int p_\lambda \tilde{g}_\lambda \, d\lambda, \quad B = \int p_\lambda \tilde{b}_\lambda \, d\lambda. \tag{8.6}$$

Finally, by assuming Weber fractions as indexing just-noticeable (jnds) differences on each dimension, Helmholtz concluded that the line element, or distance element on the Riemann colour surface (see Chapter 5), is defined by

$$ds^2 = \left(\frac{\delta R}{R}\right)^2 + \left(\frac{\delta G}{G}\right)^2 + \left(\frac{\delta B}{B}\right)^2. \tag{8.7}$$

Although this formulation of the quadratic metric was not consistent with results (Wyszecki and Stiles, 1967), the concept of representing colour space as a Riemann surface continued. Even today no other *geometric* representation has been proposed to replace this formulation, except for simpler forms of the general model including colour spheres, etc. Two other quadratic metrics were proposed to replace the (8.7) version of Helmholtz. Schrödinger in 1920 (see Wyszecki and Stiles, 1967) proposed that two patches of light appear equally bright if any change in luminance in one of them increases the number of jnds required to pass from one colour to the other on a geodesic line in the space defined by the line element. From this added assumption he proposed

$$ds^2 = \frac{1}{a_1 R + a_2 G + a_3 B}\left(\frac{a_1}{R}dR^2 + \frac{a_2}{G}dG^2 + \frac{a_3}{B}dB^2\right). \tag{8.8}$$

However, counter evidence to this formulation was found by Bouma and Heller (Wyszecki and Stiles, 1967). Finally, Stiles (1946) suggested that the line element should be

$$ds^2 = \left(\frac{\mathscr{S}(R)}{\rho}dR\right)^2 + \left(\frac{\mathscr{S}(G)}{\gamma}dG\right)^2 + \left(\frac{\mathscr{S}(B)}{\beta}dB\right)^2 \tag{8.9}$$

for

$$\mathscr{S}(x) = \frac{9}{1+9x}; \quad \frac{1}{\rho^2}=0.610; \quad \frac{1}{\gamma^2}=0.369; \quad \frac{1}{\beta^2}=0.019.$$

For high luminances (8.9) reduces to

$$ds^2 = \left(\frac{dR}{\rho R}\right)^2 + \left(\frac{dG}{\gamma G}\right)^2 + \left(\frac{dB}{\beta B}\right)^2, \tag{8.10}$$

resembling the earlier Helmholtz formulation.

The Stiles' line element produces constant increments around a point as ellipses on the colour surface. McAdam (1942) had fortunately measured such chromasticity discrimination ellipses empirically, and the comparison is shown in Fig. 8.6a. Figure 8.6b also shows the relationship between the McAdam chromasticity scale surface and that predicted by Stiles' line element. Such numerical approximations to the Riemann surface defined by quadratic forms as (8.10) are derived by the following simple iterative scheme. Let the colour surface be defined by the two-parameter form $\{R(u,v), G(u,v), B(u,v)\}$. Then the quadratic form

$$ds^2 = g_{11}\,du^2 + 2g_{12}\,du\,dv + g_{22}\,dv^2$$

for $du/ds = \lambda^u$, $dv/ds = \lambda^v$ becomes

$$g_{11}(\lambda^u)^2 + 2g_{12}\lambda^u\lambda^v + g_{22}(\lambda^v)^2 = 1. \tag{8.11}$$

We saw in Chapter 5 (eqn. 5.27) that the geodesics on a surface are defined by

$$\frac{d^2u}{ds^2} + T_{11}'\left(\frac{du}{ds}\right)^2 + 2T_{12}'\frac{du}{ds}\frac{dv}{ds} + T_{22}'\left(\frac{dv}{ds}\right)^2 = 0,$$

$$\frac{d^2v}{ds^2} + T_{11}^2\left(\frac{du}{ds}\right)^2 + 2T_{12}^2\frac{du}{ds}\frac{dv}{ds} + T_{22}^2\left(\frac{dv}{ds}\right)^2 = 0, \tag{8.12}$$

where T_{jk}^i were the Christoffel symbols of the second kind. Substituting λ^u, λ^v into (8.12)

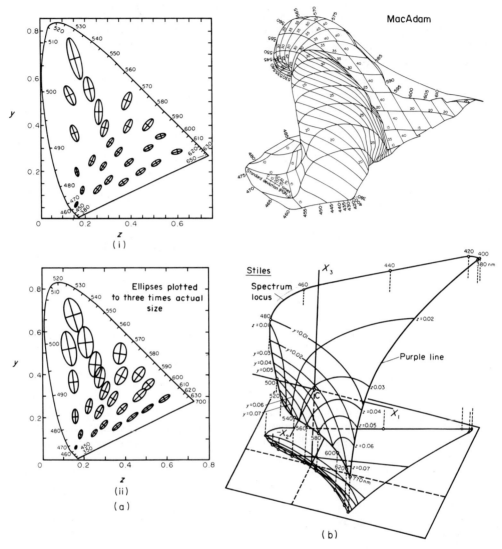

FIG. 8.6. (a) CIE chromaticity diagrams for (i) the MacAdam ellipses, and (ii) those derived from Stiles' line element. (b) The corresponding chromaticity surfaces generated by the MacAdam and Stiles quadratic metrics. (From Wyszecki and Stiles, 1967.)

gives

$$\frac{d\lambda^u}{ds} + T^1_{11}(\lambda^u)^2 + 2T^1_{12}\lambda^u\lambda^v + T^1_{22}(\lambda^v)^2 = 0,$$

$$\frac{d\lambda^v}{ds} + T^2_{11}(\lambda^u)^2 + 2T^2_{12}\lambda^u\lambda^v + T^2_{22}(\lambda^v)^2 = 0.$$

If we choose a point (u_0, v_0) and a direction $\theta_0 = \tan^{-1}(\lambda^v_0/\lambda^u_0)$ such that λ^v_0, λ^u_0 satisfy (8.11), then new points (u_1, v_1) are

$$u_1 = u_0 + \lambda^u_0 \delta s, \quad v_1 = v_0 + \lambda^v_0 \delta_s.$$

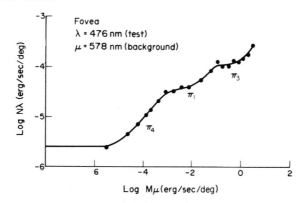

FIG. 8.7. Increment threshold curves where each segment represents the response characteristics π-mechanism. (From Stiles, 1959.)

In general new coordinates u_{i+1} and v_{i+1} are determined by

$$u_{i+1} = u_i + \lambda_i^u \delta s; \quad \lambda_{i+1}^u = \lambda_i^u + \frac{d\lambda_i^u}{ds}\delta s,$$

$$v_{i+1} = v_i + \lambda_i^v \delta s; \quad \lambda_{i+1}^v = \lambda_i^v + \frac{d\lambda_i^v}{ds}\delta s. \tag{8.13}$$

So (8.13) determines the geodesic chromatic distances on the colour surfaces shown in Fig. 8.6.

The Stiles' increment threshold experiments involved the detection of a small spot of light of one colour on the background of another. Typically the background subtended a $10°$ adapting field (wavelength μ); the foreground, a briefly exposed $1°$ source (wavelength λ). Detection thresholds are calculated for the test source ($1°$) as a function of background intensity and colour. Figure 8.7 shows the increment threshold curve for a test

TABLE 8.1. The relationship between Stiles' π" components of the adaptation curve and the four photoreceptor mechanisms[a] (From Uttal, 1973).

Mechanism	Symbol	Remarks	Wavelength of maximal sensitivity (nm)
Rod	π_0	Absent at the fovea	503
	π_1	At approx. 2.6 log units	4440
Blue cone	π_2	At approx. 1 log unit	? (between 440 and 480 mμ)
	π_3	At approx. 4.0 log units	440
Green cone	π_4		540
Red cone	π_5		575 (very flat max.)

[a] This table also indicates the peak sensitivities of the spectral absorptions of the four photoreceptors in the human eye (adapted from Stiles, 1959).

spot of 76 mμ and background of 578 mμ. Here the responses fall into three groups corresponding, in Stiles' terms, to activity of π_4, π_1, π_3 mechanisms. The "π-mechanisms" were proposed by Stiles to represent the apparently different response components of these curves and are not simply the colour receptors, as pointed out by Stiles (1959) and illustrated in Table 8.1.

Most of the current research in colour perception involves the further qualification of these π-mechanisms: how they may process colour, interact with each other, and their neurophysiological response properties. It is impossible to fully expand on these developments. Rather, we should illustrate the direction by selected work. For example, Pugh and Mollon (1979) have recently developed a model for the π_2, π_3 mechanisms (blue, Table 8.1) by using the Grassmann laws of metameric matching (Krantz, 1974) and an RC (resistor-capacitor) model for a low-pass filter that receives a feed-forward signal from the primary receptors (see Chapter 4 for characteristics of the RC network). Specifically, Pugh and Mollon define a metameric match as the inability to distinguish two sources (A, B) in photopic vision ($A \equiv B$). By defining physical superposition as point-by-point addition of components $\oplus$ and $A \oplus B$ being the resultant spectrum, these authors define the two Grassmann laws of invariance and additivity by:

Invariance: $A \equiv B$ implies for any constant $\alpha > 0$

$$\alpha * A = \alpha * B.$$

Additivity: $A \equiv B$ if and only if for any C

$$A \oplus C \equiv B \oplus C.$$

Here, $*$ is neutral attenuation, where $\alpha * A$ is the spectrum obtained by multiplying all components by α.

These authors propose that three types of models may well describe many aspects of the π_1 and π_3 mechanisms. First, the static models have (a) a pathway for detecting short-wavelength flashes, (b) a "first-site" of adaptation controlled by the "blue" cones, and (c) a "second-site" of adaptation (or attenuation) controlled by the steady-state signal of the blue–yellow input. These three factors translate into (a) each site having a "gain" similar to the $\mathscr{S}(x)$ function of Stiles (8.9), and (b) the gain of the two-stage process is the product of the gain of its two components. For spectral absorption curves $\alpha(A), \beta(A), \gamma(A)$ (α, β, γ corresponding to short ($\lambda_{max} \approx 435$ nm), middle ($\lambda_{max} \approx 535$ nm), and long ($\lambda_{max} \approx 570$ nm) wavelength sensitive cones), the output gain is

$$g(A) = \mathscr{S}_1(K_0 \alpha(A)) \, \mathscr{S}_2 \{ |(K_1 \alpha(A))^n - (K_2 \beta(A))^n - (K_3 \gamma(A))^n|^{1/2} \} \qquad (8.14)$$

for estimates of n and the (coupling) coefficients (K_0, K_1, K_2).

The dynamic models (feed-forward and feed-back)—as shown in Fig. 8.8—were proposed to represent the temporal response patterns of the π_1 and π_3 mechanisms. For $V_\alpha(t)$, $V_\beta(t)$, and $V_\gamma(t)$ being the time-dependent signals of the three cone types, (σ, ρ) constants, where $\sigma > \rho > 0$, $z(t) = V_\alpha(t) - V_\beta(t) - V_\gamma(t)$, define:

$$f(z) = \begin{cases} < 0, & z < 0, \\ = 0, & z = 0, \\ > 0, & z > 0. \end{cases}$$

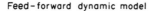

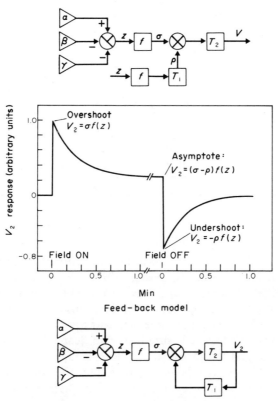

FIG. 8.8. Network models for the temporal response patterns of π_1 and π_3 mechanisms (From Pugh and Mollon, 1979.)

By letting $V_2(t)$ be the "polarized" state of site two, the authors conjectured that the equation

$$\tau_2 \frac{dV_2}{dt} + V_2 = \sigma f(z) - \frac{\rho}{\tau_1} \int_0^t f(z(t')) \exp[-(t-t')/\tau_1] dt', \qquad (8.15)$$

is representative of the dynamic (RC) system (Pugh and Mollon, 1979, p. 305–307). This system has time constants (delays) τ_1, τ_2 as shown in Fig. 8.8.

Rather than elaborate further on the Pugh and Mollon models, we should point out that this type of analysis was precursed, in a less-specific or quantitative way, by opponent processes models such as the Hurvich and Jameson (1957) one. As shown in Fig. 8.9, the neural mechanism is aimed at coding three opponent units: blue–yellow, red–green, and black–white. Here inhibitory and facilitatory effects are shown by the usual $\{-, +\}$ nomenclature.

Shevell (1979) discusses the general neural models for increment threshold detection. It is clear that all such models do assume a critical neural signal strength for threshold and that the signal due to a test flash of intensity λ is $\lambda/(\lambda + \sigma)$ without any background source (σ is saturation constant). The issue which differentiates the models is the way in which this background source is assumed to affect the signal (flash) detection. For example, the

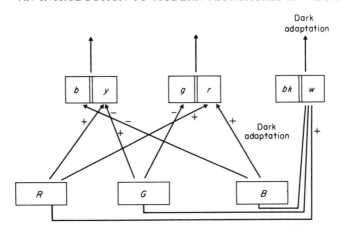

FIG. 8.9. Possible neural mechanism for relating the trichromatic photoreceptor coding to central opponent processes. (From Uttal, 1973.)

Alpern *et al.* (1970) model assumes that the test flash is attenuated by a factor $\theta/(\theta + k)$, θ being noise—and variable. Other models (subtractive) assume the test signal is reduced by a factor $\theta/(\theta + k)$ where k is a constant (Shevell, 1979).

So, all in all, recent developments in colour vision indicate an attempt to approximate colour mechanisms via network and control mechanisms such as RC circuits, filters, and gain control principles. Yet, again, the earlier geometric approaches to colour-mixing data, and the CIE standards (see Chapter 2), supply us with clear evidence for the non-Euclidean nature of colour space and the proper use of Riemannian geometry in vision research. What is not clear, to date, is how these new models for the π-mechanisms may affect our formulations of the quadratic metric, or, as we saw in Chapter 6, we are not clear on the strict relationships between such mechanisms and the phenomenal geometric structure of colour perception.

Of course, this section does little justice to the well-developed area of colour vision, and the interested reader is referred to texts as Wyszecki and Stiles (1967), Le Grand (1968), Cornsweet (1970), Uttal (1973), and Stiles (1978), for more details. It may well be the case that neurophysiologists will find clear evidence for such mechanisms in the visual pathways both in terms of the concept of primary and secondary sites and the adaptive networks suggested (see Pugh and Mollon, 1979, for some review on recent physiological findings related to these mechanisms).

Finally, it should be pointed out that colour, as like most parameters of the image, inter-acts with other spatial and temporal parameters of the image in terms of what is perceived. Both at the physiological and psychophysical levels many observations have now been made which confirm this. From the colour-coded electrophysiological responses of primate lateral gericulate and striate cells, as, say, recorded by Gouras (1974), to the many orientation, frequency, and motion specific colour effects (and after-effects) observed over recent years, one message is clear. Opponent colour responses predominate when colour contingent effects seem to be involved with other parameters of the image. So not until the opponent–processes models can be accounted for by the π-mechanism models will we be sure that these new principles are useful descriptions of the phenomena.

We should now move onto another specific topic in vision before the author makes a total fool of himself by endeavouring to review some developments in an area that is not central to his own research. We move onto binocular vision and then stereopsis.

8.1.3. Binocular space perception

As implied in Chapter 6 there are recurrent concepts and explanations in perceptual research where each reformulation adds a new quality or quantitative aspect which furthers our understanding. One such recurrent concept is that of the existence of a unified geometry of the visual fields. It was known over 2000 years ago that the simple geometry (now known to us as Euclidean geometry) of agriculture, planar, and three-dimensional solid objects, did not seem to hold in the visual system. It may well be argued that one major cause for the development of such "objective" geometries was because of the discrepancies between our perceptions and "common sense" (see Pedoe, 1976, for an excellent history of the geometries in conjunction with the liberal arts). We reviewed evidence in Chapters 6 and 7 for various non-Euclidean geometries which may capture salient aspects of contour perception, motion, illusions, and other perceptual events. In contrast to these theories, where stimulus configurations are conjectured to create different perceptual geometries, the theory of binocular vision proposed by Luneburg (1947) and Blank (1958, 1978) is a theory of the Gansfeldt or visual space itself.

With a history of observations such as the Blumenfeld alleys experiments (Blumenfeld, 1913), where perceived parallel and equidistant sets of light sources in the horizontal plane are not physically parallel, and the knowledge that a binocular geometry was not adequately represented by Euclidean coordinate systems, Luneburg (1947) reformulated the geometry of binocular vision. By using bipolar and modified bipolar coordinates, Luneburg was able to express the position of a point in three-space in a way consistent with the optical properties of binocular vision (Fig. 8.10).

Here

$$x = \frac{2\cos\theta}{\cot\alpha + \cot\beta}, \quad \cot\alpha = \frac{y+1}{\sqrt{x^2 + z^2}},$$

$$y = \frac{\cot\alpha - \cot\beta}{\cot\alpha + \cot\beta}, \quad \cot\beta = \frac{1-y}{\sqrt{x^2 + z^2}},$$

$$z = \frac{2\sin\theta}{\cot\alpha + \cot\beta}, \quad \cot\theta = x/z,$$

$$\theta = \tfrac{1}{2}(\beta - \alpha) \quad , \quad \gamma = \pi - (\alpha + \beta).$$

where θ is termed the angle of deviation, ϕ the biopolar latitude, and γ the biopolar parallax angles. The Vieth–Müller circles occur for $\gamma = $ constant, the hyperbolae of Hillebrand for $\phi = $ constant being specified by

$$x^2 + y^2 - 2x\cot\gamma = 1$$

and

$$-x^2 + y^2 + 2xy\cot 2\phi = 1$$

respectively (Fig. 8.11). γ corresponds to the angle subtended by the lines of sight at the convergence point. When the optical axes are parallel to the x-axis (Fig. 8.10) the bipolar

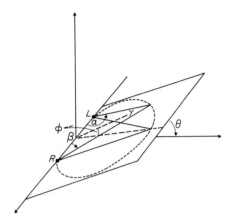

FIG. 8.10. Bipolar angles α, β, θ and modified bipolars ϕ, γ for binocular vision.

coordinates (α, β, θ) are projected onto the right and left retinae with spherical coordinates (α, θ) and (β, θ) respectively. The quantity $d\alpha + d\beta$ corresponds to horizontal disparity, while $\frac{1}{2}(d\beta - d\alpha)$ is horizontal extent. The (α, β) values determine the positions of the optical axes and so register depth information for the observer (see section 8.3). It should be noted (as Luneburg, 1947, observed) that an observer perceives himself as being at the centre of a Veith–Müller circle when judging the locus of positions which define the circle as, in fact, passing through the observer's eyes (Fig. 8.11).

Luneburg assumed that the physical bipolar coordinates (γ, ϕ, θ) determined perceived distance of a light source from the observer and that the judged distance was dependent on γ alone. That is, perceived elevation and azimuth corresponded to the physical θ and ϕ angles respectively. In this way Luneburg simply argued that convergence angle was the main source of depth information.

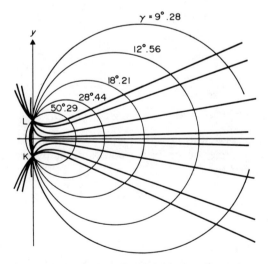

FIG. 8.11. Vieth–Müller circles and hyperbolae of Hillebrand generated from $\gamma = $ const and $\phi = $ const (in Fig. 8.10) respectively.

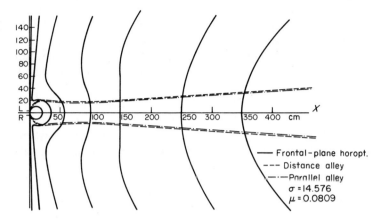

FIG. 8.12. Typical parallel and distance alley effects originally observed by Blumenfeld (1913).

From this assumption the specific iseikonic transform (see Chapter 5)

$$\gamma' = \gamma + \tau, \quad \phi' = \phi, \quad \theta' = \theta,$$

should only register motion towards or away from the observer. This is not the case with the classic Ames' room constructions, as noted by Blank (1978). As already noted, the discordance between performance and the bipolar reference system could well be due to the perceptual egocentre of the observer. That the egocentre is towards the centre of the Vieth–Müller circle is consistent with the fact that the circle is flatter, or more elliptical, than defined (Blank, 1978).

The second feature of the Luneburg theory is the issue of the psychometric function for visual binocular space and its relation to the bipolar coordinate system. From the studies of Blumenfeld (1913) it is clear that the visual space is neither Euclidean nor positive curvature Riemannian due to the hyperbolic nature of the parallel and distance alleys (Fig. 8.12). Blank (1978) shows how the bipolar coordinates may be fused with this hyperbolic metric space to produce the complete bipolar–hyperbolic metric nature of binocular vision — at least, as proposed.

For azimuth angle ϕ and radius r, the egocentric visual system assumes (Blank, 1978).

$$r = F(\gamma, \phi) = \text{const},$$

$$\phi = G(\gamma, \phi) = \text{const}.$$

With two points $(r_1, \phi_1), (r_2, \phi_2)$ being distance S apart, the hyperbolic (geometry) distance is determined by

$$\cosh s = \cosh r_1 \cosh r_2 - \sinh r_1 \sinh r_2 \cos(\phi_2 - \phi_1).$$

Using results from Hardy et al. (1951) and Foley (1964) (see Blank, 1978, p. 89), where perceived (γ', ϕ') angles are related to physical angles (γ, ϕ) by

$$\gamma = \gamma'(1 - 0.19\phi^2),$$
$$\phi' = 1.1\phi, \quad (|\phi| \le 56°),$$

Blank defines (F, G) by

$$F(\gamma, \phi) = \gamma/(1 - 0.19\phi^2),$$
$$G(\gamma, \phi) = 1.1\phi.$$

Like the issue of colour mechanisms, the bipolar coordinates and the Riemannian geometry of binocular vision are, in a most general sense, accepted as being realistic descriptors
of the binocular space. However, the details of $F(\gamma, \phi)$, $G(\gamma, \phi)$, the curvature, the role of
azimuth, and particularly the effect of egocentric vision on judged (binocular) distances,
are still open for research.

Perhaps one reason why research on this topic has switched to the study of stereopsis,
as such, is that the basis of the Luneburg model—horizontal disparity—constitutes the
mechanism for stereopsis. However, recent psychophysical and neurophysiological experiments have contributed many principles of binocular vision that, in turn, are precursors to
the above type of modelling in visual perception.

8.2. STEREOPSIS

For well over one hundred years it has been known that the fusion of the image of an
object in one eye and a small translation of the image in the other (disparity) produces the
perception of the object having a depth component, when the various depth dimensions
are a function of the disparity. Many experiments have been conducted to investigate how
such monocular cues as perspective gradients, luminance differences, and disparity values
determine this fused or stereoscopic image (Ogle, 1962). However, one important aspect
of the phenomenon was missed by these earlier experimenters—that the process by which
the disparity "pairing" between each retinal region (the association between left- and right-
eye retinal projections) was not readily defined. The basic geometry for stereopsis is illustrated in Fig. 8.13, along with the illustration of the ambiguity of disparity associations as
seen by Julesz (1971). In this section we shall restrict our attention to this problem.

Julesz, in 1961, demonstrated, via the random-dot stereogram, that shape perception
was not a prerequisite for stereopsis. Rather, from what appeared to be monocular "noise"
to both eyes, under dichoptic viewing conditions, resulted in clear stereopsis (Fig. 8.14).

The disparity value, or region, is called Panum's area, due to the early investigations of
the necessary disparities required for stereopsis by Panum (1858). Traditionally, this value

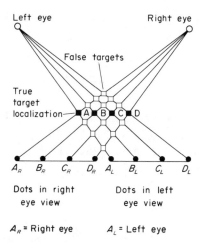

FIG. 8.13. Geometry of stereopsis. Note the inherent ambiguity (false targets) for associating left
and right disparity elements. (From Julesz, 1971).

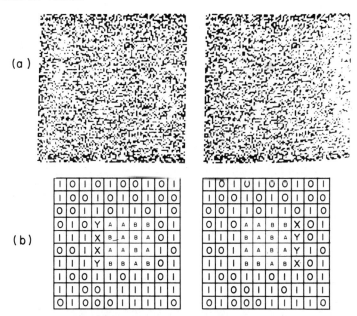

FIG. 8.14. Random-dot stereogram pair (a) which when fused produce the perception of a centre square in depth; and (b) the basic principle of generation. (From Julesz, 1971).

was between about 16′ and a few degrees of visual angle (see Julesz, 1971, for more details on this point). However, in what follows we shall see that the concept of disparity should be phrased in a different way than visual angle.

Perhaps one of the most important aspects of the Julesz random-dot stereograms was that they posed the question as to how the disparity pairing is accomplished by the visual system. Certainly it is not simply related to visual angle alone, as clearly demonstrated by Julesz and Miller (1975). Here they investigated stereopsis as a function of the fusion of random-dot stereo pairs which were filtered in their two-dimensional spatial frequency components. Specifically they found that if the stereo pair was filtered, and masking noise was added to the images that was two octaves (or more) distant from the original stereo pair components, then stereopsis could occur even while the masking noise introduced rivalry between the components. However, when the masking noise was closer in frequency components than the two-octave range, rivalry occurred without fusion of the stereo components.

The authors (1975) conclude that the results support the notion of independent spatial frequency selective channels in the visual system that operate *before* the process of stereopsis (or cyclopean vision) from an information processing perspective. The point about these results is that it is inadequate to conceive of necessary conditions for stereopsis in terms of whether (or not) two elements fall in Panum's area. The issues of signal-to-noise ratio, frequency selectivity, and the human MTF must also be considered in the delimiting of the disparity detectors in the visual cortex.

Other spatial parameters are known to inhibit the fusion mechanism in stereopsis. For example, Frisby and Julesz (1975) have demonstrated that random-line stereograms are less easily fused as the corresponding line elements differ in the orientations. In fact, we expect that most monocular spatial parameters (even some temporal, see Ross, 1976) which have known selective sensitivity in vision, would either inhibit or enhance stereopsis as a function of their similarity—as they are precursors to cyclopean vision (Julesz, 1971).

The small disparity values enables the approximation of convergence angles by a small translation component on the plane of the image pairs. But this linearity does not propagate to the perceived stereoscopic space. Recently, Breitmeyer *et al.* (1975) have demonstrated that the detection of a briefly presented stereo square, within a random-dot stereogram, was faster in the upper hemifield than in the lower, while equally easy in the left and right fields. These results indicate that the "stereo-plane" (plane of perceptually equal disparities) is inclined to the observer.

Finally, we shall return to the fundamental result of the random-dot stereogram procedure—that the disparity pairing process is not driven, apparently, by monocular cues such as shape or perspective information. Equality in luminance is desirable in order to avoid suppression or rivalry between the stereo pairs (Gregory, 1977). However, only one type of explanation has been proposed for the disparity pairing process. The original form was proposed by Julesz (1964, 1971) in terms of an analogy to spring-coupled dipoles. However, the model has been recently rephrased by Marr and Poggio (1976) in terms of a nonlinear network like those discussed in Chapters 4 and 6. The essence of this issue is that of "cooperativity". That is, the global stereopsis, which comes about by local matchings of disparities, is seen to be a product, within the random dot stereogram context, of interactions between image elements. This process was exemplified by Marr and Poggio as

$$C_{xyd}^{(n+1)} = \sigma \left\{ \sum_{x'yd' \in S(xyd)} C_{x'y'd'}^{(n)} - \varepsilon. \sum_{x'y'd' \in O(xyd)} C_{x'y'd'}^{(n)} + C_{xyd}^{(o)} \right\},$$

where $C_{xyd}^{(n)}$ corresponds to the state of the of the cell related to position (x, y) with disparity d at iteration n. S and O refer to centre and surrounding neighbourhoods of (x, y) respectively, the latter having an inhibition coefficient of ε. Here summation occurs within excitatory and inhibitory regions, weighted, and then the threshold function $\sigma\{\cdot\}$ outputs $(1, 0)$ for the net output of the interactive process at (x, y). This scheme iterates until stability occurs. This network is still under evaluation, but, again, has the same basis as described in Chapters 4 and 6—yet employs a threshold function—and so may be more representative of perceptual phenomena.

8.3. CONCLUSION

In this chapter we have briefly reviewed some of the quantitative aspects of colour, binocular, and stereoscopic vision. In all applications the relationships between mechanisms and perceptual phenomena are related to quantitative network models and their geometric spaces—usually non-Euclidean in nature. In colour vision we saw the relationships between the line element, π-mechanisms, and neural networks, which have been proposed to explain strange facets of the curved colour–space and increment threshold curves. In binocular vision we saw how attempts have been made to directly describe the geometry of binocular vision by bipolar coordinate systems and Riemann geometry. Finally, in stereopsis we have briefly seen how non-linear networks may be at the basis of the disparity detecting processes in the formation of stereoscopic images from random-dot stereograms. This theme—networks and geometry—runs through the whole of this book since, unless we can bridge the gap between the modelling of processing and the description of phenomena, our subject will still be most curious—maybe as it should be!

REFERENCES

ALPERN, M., RUSHTON, W., and TORII, S. (1970) The size of rod signals, *J. Physiol* **206**, 193–208.

BLANK, A. A. (1958) Axionaties of binocular vision, *J, Opt. Soc. Am.* **48** (5) 328–334.

BLANK, A. A. (1978) Metric geometry in human binocular perception theory and fact. In *Formal Theories of Visual Perception* (Leeuwenberg, E. and Buffart, H., eds.), Wiley, New York.

BLUMENFELD, W. (1913) Untersuchungen iiber die scheinbare Grosse in Sehraume, *Z. Psychol. Physiol Sinnesorg.* **65** (1) 241.

BREITMEYER, B., JULESZ, B., and KROPFL, W. (1975) Dynamic random-dot stereograms reveal an up–down anisotropy and left–right isotropy between cortical hemifields, *Science* **187**, 269–270.

CORNSWEET, T. (1970) *Visual Perception*, Academic Press. New York.

FOLEY, J. M. (1964) Resargnesian property in visual space, *J. Opt. Soc. Am.* **54** (5) 684–692.

FRISBY, J. and JULESZ, B. (1975) Depth reduction effects in random-line stereograms, *Perception* **4**, 151–158.

GOURAS, P. (1974) Opponent-colour cells of different layers of foveal striate cortex, *J. Physiol* **238**, 583–602.

GREGORY, R. (1977) Vision with isoluminant colour contrast: a projection technique and observations, *Perception* **6** (1) 113–120.

HARDY, RAND and RITTLER (1951) Investigation of visual space, the Blumenfeld alleys, *Arch. Ophthal.* **45**, 53.

HURVICH, L. M. and JAMESON, D. (1957) An opponent-process theory of color vision, *Psychol. Rev.* **64**, 384–404.

JULESZ, B. (1960) Binocular depth perception of computer generated patterns, *Bell Syst. Techn. J.* **39**, 1125–1162.

JULESZ, B. (1964) Binocular depth perception without familiarity cues *Science* **145**, 356–362.

JULESZ, B. (1971) *Foundations of Cyclopean Perception*, University of Chicago Press, Chicago.

JULESZ, B. MILLER, J. (1975) Independent spatial-frequency-tuned channel in binocular fusion and rivalry, *Perception* **4**, 125–143.

JULESZ, B. and TYLER, W. (1976) Neurontropy, and entropy-like measure of neural correlation, in binocular fusion and rivalry *Biol. Cybernetics* **23**, 25–32.

KRANTZ, D. (1974) Measurement theory and quantitative laws in psychophysics. In *Contemporary Developments in Mathematical Psychology* (Krantz, et al., eds.), Vol. II, Freeman, San Francisco.

LE GRAND, Y. (1968) *Light, Colour and Vision*, Chapman & Hall, London.

LUNEBURG, R. K. (1947) *Mathematical Analysis of Binocular Vision*, Princeton University Press, Princeton.

MCADAM, D. L. (1942) Visual sensitivities to color differences in daylight, *J. Opt. Soc. Am.* **32**, 247–274.

MARR, D. and POGGIO, T. (1976) Cooperative computation of stereo disparity, *Science* **194**, 283–287.

OGLE, K. N. (1962) The optical space sense. In *The Eye*. (H. Davson, ed.), Academic Press, New York, **4**, 211–432.

PANAM, P. L. (1858) *Physiologische Untersuchungen iiber das Sehen mitzwei*, Schwers, Augen Kiel.

PEDOE, D. (1976) *Geometry and the Liberal Arts*, Penguin, London.

PUGH, E. and MOLLON, J. (1979) A theory of the π_1 and π_2 color mechanisms of Stiles, *Vision Res.* **19**(3) 293–312.

ROSS, J. (1976) The resources of binocular perception, *Scient. Am.* **18**, 80–86.

RUSHTON, W. (1962) Visual pigments in man, *Scient. Am.* **207**, 120–132.

SHEVELL, S. (1979) Similar threshold functions from contrasting neural signal models, *J. Math. Psych.* **19**, (1) 1–17.

STILES, W. (1946) A modified Helmholtz line-element in brightness-colour space, *Proc. Phys. Soc. (Lond.)* **58**, 41–65.

STILES, W. (1959) Color vision: the approach through increment-threshold sensitivity, *Proc. Natn. Acad. Sci.* **45**, 100–114.

STILES, W. S. (1978) *Mechanisms of Colour Vision*, Academic Press, New York.

UTTAL, W. L. (1973) *The Psychobiology of Sensory Coding*, Harper & Row, New York.

WALD, G. (1955) Human vision and the spectrum, *Science* **101**, 653–658.

WYSZECKI, G. and STILES, W. (1967) *Color Science*, Wiley, New York.

CHAPTER 9

Conclusion

AS STATED in the introduction, the purpose of this book has been to introduce the reader to some of the current technologies employed in vision research and modelling of visual function. We have only dealt with a selection of experiments and theories in each area with the aim of illustrating how these technologies are currently employed. In this way the author has presented a rather biased view of the areas discussed.

Yet we have argued that in order to study any given perceptual phenomenon, a plurality of technologies is required. For example, with texture perception concepts from geometry, stochastic processes and Fourier analysis were employed. In contour extraction, filtering processes and network concepts were embedded in a geometrical context. In motion perception we considered the non-Euclidean nature of visual space–time in conjunction with, again, frequency and phase selective mechanisms.

Although it is quite feasible that all these technologies do reflect aspects of vision, a few principles, of the most general type, have emerged. One, possibly exemplified in the concept of "neurentropy" of Julesz and Tyler (1976), implies that the visual system can only process a fixed amount of information in the image. In order to process more spatial frequency information, it loses temporal frequency sensitivity, etc. That is, wherever an apparent duality exists in terms of information processing "channels", only a fixed *total* channel capacity is permitted. As to whether this can be expressed in terms of transmission of information to, and by, the transient and sustained cortical units discussed in Chapter 6 remains to be seen.

This principle assumes the existence of dualities (or dialectics) in visual information processing—without an exhaustive list. We have argued for phase/frequency, spatial/temporal, opponent colour mechanisms, and fusion/rivalry as examples. Yet we have not offered *a priori* conditions for establishing such processes. This cannot be done until we know just what are the appropriate codes for image processing. At present most research is concerned with the issue of coding mechanisms and not the relationship(s) between the information—as processed. For example, the issue of frequency selectivity—as a code for information processing—has to be studied as such and not in relation to phase processing (see Chapter 6).

Analogous to the ability of the human brain to create these technologies, as varied as they are, we have argued that a singular approach to explanation in visual perception is probably too simplistic. For example, visual illusions are most probably due to many components from optical to highly cortical and cognitive perspectives (Coran, 1978), each having its own technologies. So to simply contend that such illusions are due to a given low-pass filter mechanism operating in the primary projection area of the vertebrate cortex, is too restrictive. This is not to criticize model building as such, but rather to point out that we should delimit the domain of the model to its intended functional stage.

One gets the strong feeling from current research and competence, within the areas covered, that we are much within the "variations on a theme" stage of research contributions. Armed with the new technologies (and varying mainly in quantity) we have done little over the past decade to advance our deepest thoughts about visual information processing. Maybe this has more to do with the sociology of academia rather than the state of creativity within our subject. However, we are all getting rather tired of yet another "grating article".

The more fruitful approaches seem to lie within the areas that correlate the technologies (e.g. the geometric implications of specific filtering mechanisms), but maybe I am biased. It remains to be seen whether multiple microelectrode electrophysiology will reveal similar interneural activities as suggested from the various psychophysical models discussed in Chapters 6, 7, and 8. One thing is clear, however, that if even the simplest forms of linear systems apply to visual psychophysics the neural mechanisms which underly this linear process is probably highly non-linear. For example, the type of interneural activity, which would generate the response profile for a band-pass filter, the general class of sinc functions, involves network summation procedures as discussed in Chapter 6.

There are some who believe that vision research is not ready for theory as yet and so argue that the main function of perceptual inquiry should be to observe and clearly delimit the specific features of an image that determine given phenomenal effects. The problem with this position is that it is impossible to conduct such experiments without assuming a theoretical position on parametric representation of image parameters, processing assumptions, and the underlying assumptions about the importance of the response to image processing. The philosophy behind this volume has been that explicit use of technology in research is far less equivocal than the implicit theorizing which occurs in any heuristic approach to research. Perhaps it would be appropriate to finish on that famous statement of Dirac (1954):

"The moral of the story is that one should have faith in a theory that is beautiful. If a theory fails to agree with experiment, its basic principles may still be correct and the discrepancy may be due merely to some detail that will get cleared up in the future."

... the domains of psychological theory and issues should not be restricted to the lowest common denominator of thought!

REFERENCES

COREN, S. and GIRGUS, J. (1978) Visual illusions. In *Handbook of Sensory Physiology: Perception* (Held, R., Leibowitz, H., and Tember, H., eds.), Vol. VIII, Springer-Verlag, New York.

DIRAC, P. (1954) Letter, *Sci. Monthly* **79** (4)

JULESZ, B. and TYLER, W. (1976) Neurotropy, an entropy-like measure of neural correlation in binocular fusion and rivalry, *Biol. Cybernetics* **23**, 25–32.

Index

Aberrations 28–29
Absorption coefficient 176
Absorption spectra 174–5
Accommodation process 31
Adaptation, definition 1
Adaptation effects 127
Additivity 180
Adjacency principle 156
Affine geometry 71, 79–81
Affine transformations 80
Algebra 96
Algorithms 1
Aliasing 50
Ametropia 31
Amplitude spectrum 41, 43, 47, 51, 125
Analogy role 1
Analysis of variance 67
Apparent motion 163–9
　Korte's laws of 164
Astigmatism 29, 31
Autocorrelation approaches of contour perception
　130–1
Autocorrelation function 51, 131
Autocorrelation theory 130
Autocorrelogram 131

Band-pass filter 47, 107, 113, 191
Bessel function 41, 42, 46
Bieth-Müller circles 99
Binocular space, psychometric function for 185
Binocular space perception 183–6
Binocular vision 103
　geometry of 183
Biopolar latitude 99, 183
Biopolar parallax 99
Biopolar parallax angles 183
Biopolar coordinates 99, 183, 186
Blumenfeld alleys experiments 183
Bode plots 66
Break frequency 66

Capacitance 58
Cathode-ray tubes 19–21
Cauchy-Schwartz inequality 82
Channel hypothesis 113
Channel model 137

Characteristic equation 50
Christoffel symbols 92, 177
Chromatic aberration 28
Chromaticity diagram 16
'City block' metric 98
Coding mechanisms 190
Collimators 33
Collineation 79–81
Colour-matching functions 186
Colour mechanisms 174–83
Colour space concept 186
Colour vision 172–86
　retinal encoding 172–4
　spectral sensitivity 172–4
Computer pattern recognition 130
Conics 77
Constancy explanation of illusions 138–9
Constancy models 143
Constancy structures 138
Contour perception 125–37
　autocorrelation approaches 130–1
　network models 131–7
Contrast perception 103–15
　Fourier and low-pass filter approaches 129–30
Contrast sensitivity 111, 113
Contrast sensitivity function 108
Convolution theorem 44
Convolutions 35–56
Co-operativity 125
Coordinate systems 77
Cortical cells 3, 109–10, 127, 131, 140
Cortical units 111
Cross-product 82, 85
Cross-ratios 74–75, 78, 79, 82
Curvature
　Gaussian 91
　geodesic 92
　mean 91
　normal 91
　principal 91
Curvature vectors 84–86, 132
Curves
　properties of 83–87
　transformations of 93
Cylindrical function 42

Damping ratio 67

Decision problem   68
Decision theory   69
Delta functions   128–9
Derivative of vector function   83
Desargues' theorem   75
Descartes' law   22
Detection rates   70
Detection thresholds   179
Differential operator   95
Diffraction   29
Diffraction patterns   30
Diffraction waves   30
Digital image processing   48–50
Diopter   31
Dipole detection mechanisms   120
Dipole orientation statistics   5
Dirac delta function   44–5
Discrete Fourier transform   44–5
Disparity concept   186–8
Distortion prediction   134–5
Dot configurations   139
Dot (scalar) product   95
Dualities   190

Edinger-Westphal nuclei   64
Electric charge   57
Electric current   57, 59
Electromagnetic field   12
Electromagnetic waves   9, 11
Electrophysiology   57
Elliptical geometry   73
Epicyclic motion   154
Equilibrium condition   62–64
Equilibrium equation   62
Euclidean geometry   72, 73, 183
Euclidean metric   97
Euclidean space
  embedding   87
  linear transformation   93
Excitatory postsynaptic potential (EPSP)   63
Exponential decay filter   133–7
Eye   30–31

Faraday's law   58
Fast Fourier transform (FFT)   54, 56
Feature-coding strategy   126
Feature-specific tuning curves   127
Feature specificity   3
Fermet's principle   22
Figure/ground perception   120
Figure/ground relationships   115
Figure-perception process   119
Filters   35, 47, 125, 129
  band-pass   111, 113, 191
  band-pass spatial frequency   107
  concept of   147, 164
  exponential decay   133–7
  low-pass   129–30, 133–7, 180
  polarized   18
  spatio-temporal   167
First fundamental form   89
Fluorescence   12

Focal length   27, 28, 31
Focal point   25
Fourier analysis   65, 103, 114
Fourier coefficients   37
Fourier methods   35–36
Fourier series   35–44
Fourier series approximation   109
Fourier spectrum   46
Fourier theorem   36
Fourier transform   35–44, 48–51, 56, 59, 110, 129
  discrete   44–45
  inverse   48
Fourier transform (FFT) algorithm   45
Fourier transform pair   38–39, 46, 115
Fourier transform routines   55–56
Fraunhofer diffraction   30
Frequency of seeing curves   104
Frequency analysis   65
Frequency selectivity   110, 111
Frequency sensitivity   190
Fresnel diffraction   29
Fresnel equations   24
Fronto-parallel motion   156, 158

GABA antagonists   110
Gain control   61, 105
Gauss-Weingarten equations   91
Gaussian curvature   91
Geodesic curvature   92
Geometry   71–100
  affine   71, 79–81
  elliptical   73
  Euclidean   72, 73, 183
  introduction   71
  non-Euclidean   72, 183
  perspective (or projective)   71, 73, 98
  relationships between common structures   72
  Riemannian   89, 182, 186
Global stereopsis   188
Global transformation group   96
Grassmann laws   180

Haar function   51
Haar transform   54
Hadamard matrix   53
Harmonic set   76–77
Harmonic waves   35
Helmholtz, H. von   147, 176, 177
Holograms   19
Homogeneous system   78
Homothetic transformation   81
Huygens' principle   22, 23
Hyperbolae of Hillerbrand   99, 183
Hyperopia   31

Illuminance values   14, 15
Illusion perception   125–37
  autocorrelation approaches   130–1
  Fourier and low-pass filter approaches   129–30
  network models   131–7
Illusions   190

constancy explanation of 138–9
Image processing   50, 51, 139
Image transforms   43
Impulse function   41
Impulse response   46
Incandescence   13
Increment threshold curve   179
Increment threshold detection   181
Individual cells   4–5
Inductance   58
Information processing channels   190
Information processing units   64
Information transmission   150
Inhibitory coefficient   105
Inhibitory postsynaptic potential   63, 136
Inhibitory threshold   105
Integrator model   70
Intensity distributions   107
Intensity perception   103–15
Interference   30, 35
Interpolation functions   48
Invariance   141, 180
Invariant vector fields   143
Inverse Fourier transform   48
Inverse metre   31
Inverse-square law   12
Involutions   76
Iso-dipole textures   119

Jacobi identity   97
Julesz, B.   115

Kinetic depth effect   138, 157
Kirchhoff's current and voltage law   59
Klein model   98
Korte's laws of apparent motion   164

Language problems   1, 3
Laplace domain   60
Laplace transform   50, 59, 60, 65
Lasers   18–19
'Least square' problem   68
Lenses   26–28, 31
Lens-makers' equation   27
Lie algebra   96
Lie transformation groups (LTG)   96, 97, 139, 140,
     142
Light   9
   measurement of   13–19
   nature of   9–16
   polarized   17
Light sources   17–21
Limulus   2, 61, 107, 131
Line elements   174–83
Linear regression equation   68
Linear systems   46, 47
Local metric   89, 92
Lorentz factor   150
Lorentz transformations   150, 151
Low pass filters   129–30, 133–7, 180
LTG. See Lie transformation groups
Luminance profile relationships   107
Luminance values   14, 15
Luminescence   12

Luneburg theory   100, 184–6

Mach bands   105
Mauls' law   18
Maxwell equations   9, 22–23
Maxwellian viewing system   32
Mean curvature   91
Mechanisms approach   126, 127
Meta-contrast   107
Metalanguage   1, 139, 143
Metrics   81–83, 97–98
Mexican hat function   42, 46
Microelectrode recordings   1, 60
Minkowski r metric   97
Mirrors   24–26
Modulation transfer function (MTF)   46–48, 65,
     107–8
Motion, definition   147
Motion perception   147–71
   apparent motion   163–9
   depth effects   157–63
   past treatments   150
   properties of   154
   psychophysics of   148
   relativistic perspective   148–57
   3D motion   158–63
   transformations and analysis in   157–63
   vector analysis of   154–5
Motion thresholds   154
Motion vector   10
Müller-Lyer illusion   135
Multiple microelectrode electrophysiology   191
Multiple regression   68
Myopia   31

Natural frequency, parameters   67
n-disc (n-point) configurations   117
Neon tube   12
Network analyses   59
Network models   57
   contour perception   131–7
   illusion perception   131–7
   π-mechanisms   180
Networks   57–70
   definition   57
   electrical   57
   in vision   60–67
   introduction   57–60
   RLC   59, 60
   theory   57–70
Neural activity, measures of   3
Neurentropy concept   190
n-gram analyses   120
Non-homogeneous coordinate   78
Non-linear transforms   51
Normal curvature   91
Normal plane   89
Nyquist diagrams   66
Nyquist rate   50

Ohm's law   58
Optics   9

Orientation   112, 113
Orientation interactions   134
Orientation selectivity   126
Orientation sensitivity   110, 126

Panum's area   186, 187
Pappus' theorem   75–76
Parametric equation   83
Parseval's formula   51
Pattern perception   125, 126, 130–2
Perceptrons language   1
Perceptual frames of reference   149
Perceptual invariants   137–44
Perspective geometry   71, 73, 98
p-graph analyses   120
Phase spectrum   41, 43, 51
Phosphors   20
Photodiode   16
Photometers   15–16
Photon emissions   103, 104
Photon flux   12
Photon flux density   12
Photons   12–13, 19
Photopic luminosity   13
Photoreceptor mechanisms   179
π-mechanisms   180, 182
Planck's constant   12
Poggendorff illusion   135
Point display image   44
Point-spread function   46
Poisson distribution   33, 63
Poisson law   103
Polarization   17–18, 35
Polarized light   17
Power   58
Poynting vector   12
Presbyopia   31
Principal curvature   91
Principal normal   85
Probability analysis   67–70
Probability summation   5, 69, 113
Product functions   35
Product term   96
Projective coordinates   78
Projective transformation   78–80
Psychometric function for binocular space   185
Psychophysical data   113
Psychophysical functions   112, 123
Psychophysical studies   134
Psychophysics   4–5, 191
   of motion perception   148
Purkinje shift   174

Radamacher function   51
Radiant energy   13, 16
Radiant flux   12
Radius of curvature   85
Ray-tracing   27
RC (resistor-capacitor) model   180
Receiver-operating-characteristic (Roc curve)   69
Reflectance   24
Reflection   9, 21–24

Refraction   9, 21–24, 26
Refractive index   22, 26, 28
Regression analysis   68
Resistance   58
Retinal cells   61
Retinal encoding   172–4
Retinal ganglion cells   147, 148
Retinal physiology   105
Rhodopsin molecule   172
Riemann metric   98
Riemann space-time surface   151
Riemann surface   92
Riemann colour surface   176
Riemannian geometry   89, 182, 186
Rigid planar motion   93
Rod and cone receptor distributions   30–31
Rotation group   94
R-values   122
R-variance differences   123

Saturation constant   181
Scalar functions   83
Scalar products   83
Schrödinger   177
Scotopic luminosity   13
Second fundamental form   90
Sensitivity function   108
Sequency   51
Serret-Frenet equations   86, 91
S-functions   48
Shannon's sampling theorem   49
Shape perception   143
Signal-noise ratio   69
Simultaneous contrast   105
Sine function   41, 42, 46
Sine-wave gratings   19
Single cells   2
Slope   83
Snell's law   22
Spatial equivalences   137–44
Spatial frequency   109, 112, 148, 190
Spatial frequency tuning curves   127
Spatial vision   103–46
Spectral decomposition   9
Spectral response   12
Spectral sensitivity   172–4
Spectrophotometer   16
Spherical aberrations   29
Spherical surfaces   24–30
Spherical waves   24–30
Square wave   37, 40
Statistical analysis   67–70
Statistical decision models   67
Steradian   13
Stereographic projection   98
Stereographic transform   98
Stereo-plane   188
Stereopsis   186–8
Stiles-Crawford effect   15
Stimulus parameters   67
Surfaces
   properties of   87–93
   transformations of   93

Tachistoscope   21
Tangent plane   88, 90
Tangent vector   84, 85, 132
Taylor expansion   94, 96, 142
Temporal frequencies   112, 148
Texture autocorrelation   116
Texture dipoles   116
Texture discrimination   4, 117, 121–2, 124–5
Texture distributions   123
Texture gradients   124
Texture pairs   122
Texture perception   115–25
Texture symmetry   125
3D motion   158–63
Threshold function   188
Time constants   181
Torsion of a curve   86
Torsion vector   86
Transformation group   94, 96, 142
Transmittance   24
Tristimulus values   16
Troland   14

Unit normal vector   88

Vector analysis   81–83
  of motion perception   154–5
Vector function   83

Vector pairs   85
Vectors   81–83
  binormal   85
  orthogonal   85
  unit normal   88
Vieth-Müller circles   183–5
Visible spectrum   9
Visual perception   103
Voltage   57
Volterra expansions   64

Walsh function   53
Walsh-Hadamard transforms   54
Walsh transform   54
Walsh transform domain   54
Wave motion   9, 10
Wavelength mixing curves   175
W-cells   110
Weak coupling   63
Weber-Fechner law   65
Weber fractions   176
Weighting function   125, 129, 130, 131, 133
Whittaker-Kotelnikov-Shannon theorem   49, 51

X-cells   109

Y-cells   110